# Encyclopaedia of Scheduled Tribes in India

# Encyclopaedia of Scheduled Tribes in India

## In Five Volume

## Vol. 4 – East

P.K. Mohanty

ISHA BOOKS
DELHI-110 033

Encyclopaedia of Scheduled Tribe In India

ISBN: 9788182050525(Set)
ISBN: 9788182053588(Vol-4)



Published in 2006 in India by
Isha Books, D-43, Prithviraj Road,
Adarsh Nagar, Delhi-110 033

*Laser Typesetting at* : Tact Computer Graphic's, Delhi
*Printed at* : Salasar Imaging System, Delhi

# Contents

# Preface

Traditionally, the term 'tribe' has been used for those groups of human beings, whose place of residence is situated in remote areas like hills, forest, sea coasts and islands; and whose style of life is quite different from the present day civilized men. Local indigenous people residing in these places of the world are termed a tribe or tribal, to distinguish them from other people of the world. Like other societies, tribal society is also not static, rather is quite dynamic. The rate of change in tribal society is very slow. That is why they have been backward and poor in comparison to other people.

India is one of the countries having a large concentration of tribal population. In this, it ranks second in the world and comes next only to Africa. There are 537 different tribal communities spread all over India. According to the 2001 census, tribal peoples constitute roughly 8 per cent of the nation's total population, i.e., over 84 million people. Tribal peoples are particularly numerous in the Indian states of Orissa, Bihar, Jharkhand, and in extreme northeastern states such as Mizoram. Officially recognized by the Indian government as "Scheduled Tribes" in the Fifth Schedule of the Constitution of India, they are often grouped together with scheduled castes in the category "Scheduled Castes and Tribes", which is eligible for certain affirmative action measures.

The Scheduled Tribes (ST) differs considerably from another race, language, culture and beliefs in their myths and customs. The groups are speaking about 105 languages and 225 subsidiary languages. The areas inhabited by the tribals constitute a significant part of the under-developed areas of the country. The tribals live mostly in isolated villages or hamlets. A smaller portion of their population has now settled in permanent villages as well as in towns and cities.

In India, one concentration tribes lives in a belt along the Himalayas stretching through Jammu and Kashmir, Himachal Pradesh, and Uttaranchal in the west, to Assam, Meghalaya, Tripura, Arunachal Pradesh, Mizoram, Manipur, and Nagaland in the northeast. In the northeastern states of Arunachal Pradesh, Meghalaya, Mizoram, and Nagaland, upward of 90 per cent of the population is tribal. However, in the remaining northeast states of Assam, Manipur, Sikkim, and Tripura, tribal peoples form between 20 and 30 per cent of the population. Another concentration lives in the hilly areas of central India (Chhattisgarh, Madhya Pradesh, Orissa, and, to a lesser extent, Andhra Pradesh); in this belt, which is bounded by the Narmada River to the north and the Godavari River to the southeast, tribal peoples occupy the slopes of the region's mountains. Other tribals, including the Santals, live in Jharkhand and West Bengal. Central Indian states have the country's largest tribes, and, taken as a whole, roughly 75 per cent of the total tribal population live there, although the tribal population there accounts for only around 10 per cent of the region's total population. There are smaller numbers of tribal people in Karnataka, Tamil Nadu, and Kerala in south India; in western India in Gujarat and Rajasthan, and in the union territories of Lakshadweep and the Andaman Islands and Nicobar Islands. About one percent of the populations of Kerala and Tamil Nadu are tribal, whereas about six percent in Andhra Pradesh and Karnataka are members of tribes.

In India, different tribal groups are living in various degrees of socio-economic backwardness. They live generally in inhospitable terrain where productivity of the soil is low and their hamlets are found in the interior forest areas along with the hill streams. There are no communication facilities between the various isolated tribal groups, as well as between the tribal and the world at large. Normally they are below the poverty line, because their average daily income has been estimated about Rs. 2. Their lands are dry, alienated and there are not irrigation facilities. They do not utilize chemical fertilizers, improved seeds, pesticides etc., in their lands. Tribal area agriculture is therefore somewhat different from other areas mainly on account of the difference in natural topography. And also the typical topography of undulating and hilly areas has made tribal area agriculture less profitable. Like all other sectors of socio-economic life, educationally the tribal people are at different levels of development but on the whole formal education has made very little impact on tribal groups.

The extreme economic and educational backwardness of the tribals in the country has drawn the attention of the state and Central Governments. The anthropologists have studied the socio-cultural system and taboos of the tribals and have produced volumes of literature. Many socioeconomic measures to uplift the tribals were initiated by India under the Colonial British rule. The efforts of various commissions and legislative measures have proved futile. A number of developmental activities intended for protecting the tribals from exploitation and meant for helping them to further their socio-economic development have not yielded fruitful results as expected.

The post-independence era witnessed a large number of developmental measures, policies and programmes that focussed on the overall development of the tribal areas. Ever since the planning process was initiated in the country through five-year plans, the tribal uplift in the country has gained importance. The Constitutional provisions and legislative measures both during the British rule and during the Post-independent period to protect the tribal rights, property, culture, had a significant bearing on the overall tribal economy and socio-cultural system but they failed to have any impact on the improvement of the economic conditions of the tribal population. To relieve the tribals from the burning issues of poverty and exploitation, a greater emphasis should be given by the union government and the state governments to the implementation of various developmental programmes for their upliftment.

This encyclopaedic work in five volumes covers almost all related and relevant information about the Scheduled Tribes of India. The vast and detailed information contained in the this work makes it an ideal and invaluable reference tool for the confirmation of sociological, anthropological, ethnological, historical, and cultural facts about the scheduled tribes spread all over the Indian subcontinent. This comprehensive, exclusive and exhaustive work will be an invaluable refernce tool for scholars, researchers, planners, administrators, policy makers, government officials and others concerned with Scheduled Tribes and their development.

***Editor***

# 1

# Tribes of Andaman and Nicobars

The Andaman and Nicobar are a group of picturesque Islands, big and small, inhabited and uninhabited, a total of 572 islands, islets and rocks lying in the South Eastern Part of the Bay of Bengal.They lie along an arc in long and narrow broken chain, approximately North-South over a distance nearly 800 kms. It is logical to presume a former land connection form Cape Negris at South part of Burma to Achin Head (Cape Pedro) in Andalas (Sumatra). The flora and fauna of these islands, however, indicate that this land connection if it existed, should have been prior to the development of their present life form.

The original inhabitants of the islands lived in the forests on hunting and fishing. There are four Negrito tribes, viz., the Great Andamanese, Onge, Jarawa and Sentinalese in the Andaman group of islands and two Mongoloid Sentinalese are still hostile. They are still keeping a separate entity and have not yet learnt the concept of covering their bodies.

## Tribal Communities

The original tribal people who lived here are the great Andamanese, Jarawas, Sentinelese and Onges in the Andaman group and the Nicobarese and Shompens in the Nicobar group. Along with them, the present-day Andaman and Nicobar Islands are the homes of descendants of hundreds of prisoners from all part of India who constituted the penal settlement during the British Raj. They are the offspring's of the Moplas of Malabar deported during the Mopla Rebellion, the Kilafat movement and of refugees from the rest while east Pakistan who settled over thirty years ago with hope for a new life; or ex-servicemen of the Indian Army; of jobseekers and adventurers from every corner of India.

In Andaman and Nicobar Islands more than 50 percent of the population is made up of settlers from the mainland India. That is why many describe Andamans as a Little India or a mini-India. Everyone speaks Hindi no matter which part of the mainland he comes from. The settlers or ancestors of these settlers came either prior to 1947 or after 1947.

In the course of seven or eight decades, till about the thirties, thousands of prisoners form north, south, east and west and central Indian regions were brought in. Many women came there as prisoners or as relations to liberated prisoners. Majority of prisoners after serving their term chose to stay on. There was a lot of social mixing without any inhabitation of traditional social restraints. There were inter-caste and inter-creed marriages. Thus a new social order and culture evolved, discarding the values of traditional society and culture of the mainland.

In the early twenties several hundred Moplas or Mappillas were deported following the Malabar revolt. Many of them later brought their families and relatives to settle down in the Andamans. Many villages in South Andamans are inhabited by them forming a big chunk of Malayalam speaking population there. In the case of Moplas their traditional life style has not changed much. They still maintain their separate identity.

Karens migrated in 1925 to work as forest Labourers. Later they settled down on agricultural land in Middle Andamans. At present some of them live in separate settlements doing fisherman's job and hunting in Maimyo and Herbertabad. Many Burmans in Maimyo and Burma after 1966. They too had come as convicts. The few who remain have preserved their distinct identity. The Karens are concentrated in webi, Base and Letaw.

Bhantus are a tribe which robbed people in North and Central India in the early 20th century. In 1926 a gang of them were sent to Andaman's from Indian Jails. They had volunteered for the migration. These people and their descendants now inhabit some villages in South Andaman's and are now leading a peaceful life as respectable citizens. Growth of such homogeneous communities in respective pockets were encouraged by the British administration. Special schools were run for their sake. These helped in their healthy rehabilitation and survival as such homogeneous group

After the partition of the country and Independence i.e. after 1947, the influx has been mainly of Bengalese-refugees from the East Pakistan (now Bangladesh). Such Bengalese now form the largest single linguistic group in the territory. These Bengalese refugees are settled in villages in South, Middle, North and Little Andaman's .Most of them were landless Labourers and of low caste status. Now as landowners they are doing well.

Each family has been given five acres of cleared land on plains for paddy cultivation and five acres more of un-cleared land for homestead and horticultural purposes together with ex-gratia grant of Rs.1050 to each family. The money was for house building, animals and the rest for seeds. They have brought the customs and folk culture of their original habitat. Other Moplas and Malayalis both Hindus and Christians also came after 1947 in search of office jobs. They are working in offices.

Some tribal people from Chota Nagpur Region have also migrated here in search of jobs. They are working in Forest, Public works Department, etc. In the past, during British regime people from Chota Nagpur Tribal belt were brought to work as forest Labourers. They are hardly and good workers and are in great demand. Their main settlement is at Baratang in Middle Andamans.

They originally had belonged to various places and groups like Oraon, Kharia, Munda, Mahli Turi Ghasi, Cheek and Dom etc. But in Andamans they are labeled as Ranchis as Ranchi was their recruiting centre. They are a heterogeneous group but the common factor of tribal life than strings them is their addiction to traditional Tribal drink called Handia.

The second largest linguistic group are the people settled from Tamil Nadu. They are elites from the mainland manning senior positions in Government offices, enterprises and tourist organizations etc. Various social, cultural and economic factors are at work to create co-existence of various ethnic groups in a composite culture.

The tribal people of the Andaman and Nicobar Islands belong to distinctive racial groups and have different forms of cultural and social behaviour. The tribal groups in the two respective regions have very little in common in the ethnic, linguistic or cultural sense. Their life styles are also very different.

The tribal element in the Andaman group of Islands is relatively very small. The Andaman Tribes belong to the Negrito stock and they are relatively short-statured highly dark complexioned and have woolly hair. Their facial structure is easily distinguished from that of the Negroid people of Africa. They are some of the surviving representatives of a once flourishing Negrito race that once dominated the entire south-east Asian region including the Islands.

They speak distinctive dialects not mutually understood. The few surviving Great Andamanese were scattered in various parts of south and Middle Andamans but the Andaman and Nicobar Administration has settled them all on the strait Island, a small island off the eastern coast of Middle Andaman. The Jarawas is on the western coast of south and Middle Andaman.

The Sentinelese are the sole inhabitants in the North Sentinel Island situated south-west of Port Blair. The Onge live in Little Andaman which is the southern-most island in the Andamans. The Andamanese never discovered any technique of fire making. They have only kept it alive over thousands of years. They do not eat salt. They cannot count beyond three. But these handicaps did not affect their survival. Their contact with modern society of threatening their ethnicity.

Majority of the inhabitants of the Nicobar region are the original tribes. The Nicobarese live in twelve island communities in the Islands of Car Nicobar, Chowra, Teressa, Bompoka, Katchal, Camorta, Trinkat, Nancoury, Pulo Milo, Little Nicobar, Kondul and Great Nicobar. There is also an interior tribe called the Shompen.

They live in the river valleys of Great Nicobar on both the eastern and the western coasts along with the coastal Nicobarese community. A majority of the Nicobarese have been converted to Christianity. As a result some of their traditional beliefs and customs have lost their force.

The Andamanese skin is smooth, greasy, satiny and black. The hair is sooty black to yellowish brown. It grows in small rings and distributed evenly over the head, appears to take the form of tuffs. The mouth is large, the palate hard and slightly arched and the lips well formed. The hands and feet are small and well made. The ears are small and well shaped. The eyes are dark to very dark brown, bright, liquid and clear but prominent. The teeth are white, good and free from disease.

The muscular strength is great but the vitality is low and individuals apparently robust die quickly. Recovery from sickness is usually rapid. Idiocy, insanity and natural deformities are rare but epilepsy and homicidal mania occur. No parts of the body are intentionally pierced, injured or deformed. The flattening of the skull in parts is accidental and due to the use of straps in carrying weights.

The figures of the men are muscular and well formed and generally pleasing. A young man is often distinctly good-looking. The women are liable to early stoutness and ungainliness of figure. Variation from type is much common among the men than the women.

### Great Andamanese

Great Andamanese is a collective term used to refer to related groups or tribes of indigenous peoples who lived throughout most of the Great Andaman archipelago, the main and closely-situated group of islands in the Andaman Islands. Their collective identity is put forward mainly on the basis of linguistic analysis; the languages spoken by the different groups were (from what is known) clearly related, and formed one of the two identified families of indigenous Andamanese languages (the Great Andamanese family).

By the time the British established a permanent settlement and penal colony in the Andaman Islands (the 1860s), there were 10 distinct linguistic / territorial groups of Great Andamanese, who had persisted on these islands for thousands of years largely unmolested by external influences. However as migration of settlers to the islands increased over the succeeding decades, the numbers and societies of the Great Andamanese peoples progressively deteriorated. Today, there are only at most a few dozen individuals left of Great Andamanese descent, and the cultural and linguistic identities of the individual groups has been lost.

The Great Andamanese peoples are collectively distinguished from other indigenous Andamanese groups, by culture, geography and language. The peoples of the southern part of Great Andaman - South Andaman Island and Rutland Island - as well as Little Andaman Island and North Sentinel Island speak languages which are classified in a separate family of the Andamanese languages, South Andamanese.

The 10 distinct Great Andamanese groups were generally distributed in territories which "partitioned off" segments ranging along the narrow archipelago of Great

Andaman, which runs essentially in a north-south line for approximately 350 km, but is only some 50 km at its widest extent. This peculiar geography meant that groups typically only had two sets of neighbouring tribes. Roughly arranged from north to south, the different Great Andamanese peoples were:

— Aka-Cari

— Aka-Kora

— Aka-Bo

— Aka-Jeru

— Aka-Kede

— Aka-Kol

— Oko-Juwoi

— A-Pucikwar

— Aka-Bale

— Aka-Bea

### *Jarawa*

The Jarawa are one of the indigenous peoples of the Andaman Islands, located in the Bay of Bengal approximately 200 km south of the nearest continental mainland, Cape Negrais in Myanmar. Their present numbers are estimated at between 250-350 individuals. Since they have shunned most interactions with outsiders, many particulars of their society, culture and traditions are little understood. Indeed, the word jarawa is an exonym and not their own name; it means "enemy" or "hostile people" in Aka-Bea.

Along with other indigenous Andamanese peoples they have inhabited the islands for at least several thousand years, and most likely a great deal longer. The Andaman Islands have been known to outsiders since antiquity; however, until quite recent times they were infrequently visited, and such contacts were predominantly sporadic and temporary. For the greater portion of their history their only significant contact has been with other Andamanese groups; the experience of such a lengthy period of isolation almost completely lacking in external cultural influences can at most be equalled by only very few other peoples in the world, if at all.

Before the 1800s their homelands most probably ranged over most of South Andaman Island and nearby islets; with the subsequent arrival of Indian and Karen (Burmese) settlers their territory has altered, and they are now concentrated along the western side of South Andaman and Middle Andaman Islands. They are noted for vigorously maintaining their independence and distance from external groups, actively discouraging most incursions and attempts at contact. Of the remaining Andamanese peoples, only the Sentinelese have been able to maintain a more isolate situation, and their society and traditions persist with little variance from their practices they observed before the first significant contacts were made.

The Jarawa are a largely uncontacted people, living on the Andaman Islands in the Indian ocean. Both British and Indian settlers have moved onto their islands over the last 150 years, but the Jarawa have chosen to maintain an almost complete isolation. They are very different in appearance to their Indian neighbours, and DNA tests suggest that their closest relatives are African.

Because of the Jarawa's voluntary isolation, and the fact that no one outside the tribe really speaks their language, very little is known about them. We do know that the they live a hunter-gatherer lifestyle, hunting pig and monitor lizard, fishing with bows and arrows, and gathering seeds, berries and honey. They are nomadic, living in bands of 40-50 people. They resisted all contact with the outside world until 1998, when some Jarawa started coming out of their forest to visit nearby towns and settlements. From what can now be understood of their language, it seems that pressure from poachers on the coast had driven them inland. Although a few Jarawa, particularly women and children, still come out onto the road or into settlements to visit they continue to live a self-sufficient life in the forest.

The main threats to the Jarawa are encroachment on their land – sparked by the building of a road through their forest in 1970 – and the risk of being settled forcibly – as planned by the authorities in 1991 and urged by a local lawyer in a court case brought in 1999. The road has increasingly brought settlers, poachers and loggers into Jarawa land, who steal the tribe's game and expose them to disease. Forced resettlement was fatal for other tribes in the Andaman Islands, and has always been so for newly contacted tribal peoples worldwide: it introduces diseases; destroys the sense of identity and society; robs tribes of their self-sufficiency; and leaves them vulnerable to alcoholism and despair.

### *Sentinelese*

The Sentinelese are one of the Andamanese indigenous peoples of the Andaman Islands, located in the Bay of Bengal. They exclusively inhabit North Sentinel Island which lies westwards off the southern tip of the Great Andaman archipelago. They are noted for vigorously maintaining their independence and sovereignty over the island, and resisting attempts of contact by outsiders. By their long-standing separation from any other human society they are among the most isolated and unassimilated peoples on Earth, their social practices being almost entirely free of any recorded external influence.

The present population of the Sentinelese is not known with any great degree of accuracy, and estimates have been produced ranging from a low of fewer than 40, through to a median of around 250, and up to a maximum of 500. In the 2001 Census of India, officials recorded 39 individuals (21 males and 18 females); however, out of necessity this survey was conducted from a distance and almost certainly does not represent an accurate figure for the population who range over the 72-km2 island. Any medium– or long–term impact on the Sentinelese population arising from the 2004 Indian Ocean earthquake and resulting tsunami remains unknown, other than the confirmation obtained that they had survived the immediate aftermath.

The Sentinelese and other indigenous Andamanese peoples are frequently described as negritos, a somewhat indistinct anthropological term, which has been applied to variously widely-separated peoples in Southeast Asia, such as the Semang of the Malay archipelago and the Aeta of the Philippines, as well as sometimes to other peoples as far afield as South America and Australia. The defining characteristics of these 'negrito' peoples include a comparatively short stature, dark skin and "peppercorn" hair. The Sentinelese themselves appear however to be somewhat taller on average than other Andamanese peoples.

The Sentinelese maintain an essentially hunter-gatherer society, obtaining their subsistence through hunting, fishing, and collecting wild plants; there is no evidence of any agricultural practices among them. It is frequently asserted that they rely upon natural events such as lightning strikes to obtain fire, but it is not known whether they also manufacture it; certainly, since the earliest reports of these people it has been observed that they maintain campfires on a nightly basis. Metalwork among them is unknown, as indeed is any likely source of the raw materials on the island. However, it has been observed that they have made adroit use of metal materials which have washed up or been left behind on their shores, and incorporated these into weapons and other items. For example, in the late 1980s two international container ships ran aground on the island's external coral reefs, from which the Sentinelese retrieved several items of iron.

Virtually nothing is known of the Sentinelese language, and no word lists or language samples have been collected by researchers. It is presumably an Andamanese language, but how closely it may be related to other languages of that family is unknown.

Their island is nominally part of and administered by the Indian Union Territory of Andaman and Nicobar Islands; however, in practice the Sentinelese exercise complete autonomy over their affairs and the involvement of the Indian authorities is restricted to occasional monitoring, even more infrequent and brief visits, and generally discouraging any access or approaches to the island.

From the early 1990s the Indian authorities in Port Blair embarked on a programme of official but limited attempts at contacting the Sentinelese, under the auspices of the Director of Tribal Welfare. These "Contact Expeditions" consisted of a series of planned visits which would progressively leave "gifts", such as coconuts, on the shores, in an attempt to coax the Sentinelese from their customary hostile reception of outsiders. For a while these seemed to have some limited success; however the programme was discontinued in the late 1990s following a series of hostile encounters resulting in several deaths in a similar programme practiced with the Jarawa people of South and Middle Andaman Islands. The Sentinelese remain skeptical and generally hostile to any approaches from outsiders.

### Onges

Onges are one of the most primitive tribes in India. The Onges are inhabiting the Little Andaman Island. This Hunting and Gathering tribe has also been settled by the Andaman & Nicobar Administration at Dugong Creek and South Bay on Little Andaman Island at present. Coconut plantation has been raised for the benefit of Onges Medical care, free ration etc. are being provided at these two Settlement by the Administration. Onges go for hunting and fishing occasionally. The present population of Onges is 105.

The Onges are one of four Negrito tribal communities still surviving on the Andaman islands. Nomadic hunter-gatherers, Onges are thought to have inhabited the island for thousands of years. In 1957 the entire island was declared the Onge Tribal Reserve under the Andaman and Nicobar Protection of Aboriginal Tribes Regulation (ANPATR), 1956.

But a 'colonisation' plan put together in the 1960s resulted in about 30 per cent of the island being freed up for the creation of settlements of migrants from mainland India, for agriculture, horticulture, and timber extraction activities. This started the process of marginalisation of the original inhabitants. According to the 2001 Census, the total population of Little Andaman is 17,528.

The Andaman archipelago is a unique ecosystem that has been internationally recognised as an immensely significant bio-diversity hotspot. The indigenous communities of the Andamans are a remarkable people who have an amazing understanding of the forests and oceans of their island home. Logging, clearing of forests for oil palm plantations and other developmental activities in Little Andaman clearly violate the Andaman and Nicobar Protection of Aboriginal Tribes Regulation (ANPATR). In 1957, this Regulation accorded the status of a Tribal Reserve to Little Andaman. But in 1972 and 1977 around 20,000 hectares were removed from the reserve to accommodate settlers from outside. However, a substantial part of the island—52,000 hectares—continues to be a tribal reserve even today.

For the last 20 years, since logging operations commenced, the Andaman and Nicobar Forest Plantation and Development Corporation has been logging more timber from a larger area than permissible. Shockingly, the forestry operations have even spread to areas directly within the tribal reserve. Such logging, which continues even today, is being undertaken without a Working Plan. This is in violation of the Supreme Court order of 1996 which clearly stated that '....the felling of trees in all areas is to remain suspended except in accordance with the Working Plans of the state governments, as approved by the Central Government.'

Apart from the attack on the Onges' forests, their cultural and social systems are also being eroded. The Onges face exploitation at the hands of the settlers, who have taken over their lands and resources. They are being forced to give up their nomadic hunter-gatherer life styles and their food habits have been altered to the point where they are becoming dependent on State and welfare agencies.

The logging operations have opened up the forests, encouraging encroachments into the tribal reserve and poachers who fear no authority. This crossfire has resulted in a drastic decline of many Schedule I species like the monitor lizard, the dugong and the endemic Andaman wild pig. These species are important food sources for the Onges, who exploited them sustainably. They are also an integral part of their culture and society. Little Andaman is a treasure trove of rare and threatened flora and fauna. Deforestation destroys this and in the process also ruins other ecosystems such as the coral reefs around the island that are being smothered by soil erosion.

With the destruction of the Onges and their ecosystem will be lost, their traditional knowledge bank, which scientists recently discovered, might hold the key to the battle against diseases such as malaria. In fact, recently, an attempt was made to patent a probable cure for cerebral malaria, using a plant source taken from the Onges. The fate of the Onges and that of the forests that support them is interlinked. It is imperative that the present development and tribal policies in the islands be reviewed and sensitively changed.

The Andaman Trunk Road (ATR) connecting Port Blair in South Andaman to Diglipur in the North has been responsible for the destruction of large tracts of virgin evergreen forests and has had severe adverse impact on the original inhabitants of these forests, the Jarawa tribe. There are now plans to double-lane the road, which has facilitated the movement of settlers from mainland India into these forests and surrounding areas, increasing manifold the interaction and conflict with the Jarawas. It is also one of the main causes for a devastating measles epidemic that recently affected the Jarawa community, resulting in several deaths.

When the Great Sumatran Earthquake and tsunami disaster of December 26, 2004 struck, the majority of the Onge population was based in the Dugong Creek, in the northern end of the island. The community did not suffer any casualty. But the moment the water receded, the Onges started moving into the forest, away from the coastline.

### *Nicobarese*

The Nicobarese are from the Nicobar Islands which are a chain of 19 islands in the Bay of Bengal. Only 12 of the 19 islands are inhabited, the largest and main island is Great Nicobar. The term Nicobarese refers to the dominant tribes of the Nicobar Islands. On each island, the people have specific names, but together they are the Nicobarese. They call themselves Holchu, which means friend.

The Nicobarese may not have been the first people to live in the islands, they appear to have shared the islands with those of Malay descent and then as years passed the Shompen came to the islands. The islands have been under the power of Asia, in the 1500's, Great Britain, from 1869-1947, and then in 1947 they were under power of India. Today they are administered by India as part of the UnionTerritory of the Andaman and Nicobar Islands.

The Nicobarese are part of the Austro-Asiatic language family. All of the different islands speak different dialects of the Nicobarese language. The separate islands are categorized into four groups, although most of the people understand the Car dialect.

On the Nicobar Islands, men and women have approximate equal status. The women have a lot to do with their own choice of husbands, and after marriage they are free to live with either of the couples parents. The Nicobarese men value the women economically because they not only take care of household duties, but also tend to the plantations and gardens. The villages on the islands consist of sporadically placed huts strewn about in designated. The huts are normally round with dome shaped roofs. They are typically lifted up from the ground and they have ladders that they climb up to get into the huts that they bring in at night.

Most of the people of the islands are of the Christian religion, which was taught to them by a man named John Richardson who translated the New Testament into Nicobarese. Besides Christianity, other Nicobarese follow the traditional religion of the islands, which is animistic in nature. They believe in spirits, ghosts, and the existence of the soul. A person becomes a ghost after their death when their soul leaves their body and the ghosts of all the Nicobarese are all around the islands. They believe that the spirits are responsible for all of the occurrences on the island, Shaman are called upon to handle to bad spirits.

The Nicobarese have a traditionally horticultural economy, they base their monetary existence on the growing of coconuts, pandanus, areca palms, bananas, mangoes, and other fruits. They also hunt, fish, raise pigs, make pottery, and make canoes. Many of the older Nicobarese are illiterate, however today the younger Nicobarese receive free education through the government. As more Nicobarese become educated they receive jobs as teachers and clerks, among other occupations.

### *Shompen*

The Shompen are one of the indigenous peoples of the Nicobar Islands, part of the Indian union territory of Andaman and Nicobar Islands. Current population is estimated at approximately 400 members and located on Great Nicobar island. They practice a hunter-gatherer subsistence economy. Six members were reported to have died in the Great Sumatran Earthquake and tsunami disaster of December 26, 2004.

The Shompens are semi-nomadic, hunting, gathering and fishing tribes who practise simple horticulture and rear pigs. Like the Nicobarese, they belong to the Mongoloid race. The Shompens are scattered over the whole of Great Nicobar Islands. The east coast Shompens remain close to the sea-shore or in the valleys while the west coast Shompens prefer the interior and the slopes of hills. The Shompens huts are of a primitive type and are invariably built with wood, cane and leaves.

The habitation of Shompens is the Great Nicobar which is the largest among the Nicobar group of Islands. The Shompens have two divisions, the smaller division being known as Mawa Shompens. They inhabit areas very close to the coastal region along the river valleys. They are very shy. They are quite intimate with the Nicobarese and of the major group of Shompens, the hostile Shompens are living in Alexendra and Galathia river areas and also on the east coast of the area in the interior of the Island. In the past, frequent attacks are believed to have been made on the Mawa Shompens by the hostile Shompens. But now, such hostility has been stopped. It is probably because they have been largely reduced in number due to various diseases. The Mawa Shompens are the victims of diseases and physically very weak. With the establishment of the settlement at Campbell Bay in Great Nicobar, Shompens have been visiting the settlers and they are gradually shaking off their shyness and indifferent attitude towards the civilised people.

## Customs and Practices

The Andaman Islands, consisting of four main and some 200 small islands, are located in the eastern part of the Bay of Bengal. Formerly under British administration, these islands, together with the Nicobar Islands, now form one of the states of India. The four main islands are generally divided into two groups called Great Andaman and Little Andaman. Great Andaman consists of three large islands named North Andaman, Middle Andaman, and South Andaman. Little Andaman is a smaller island located some distance to the south of the main group.

The Andaman Islanders speak a variety of dialects and/or languages which are classified by Greenberg within his Indo-Pacific phylum. After the establishment of continuous British administration in 1858, such government officials as Edward Man began to provide the first substantial information on these people. They were found to be divided into 12 or 13 "tribes" or tribal units, most of whom differed mainly in dialect.

On the basis of more pronounced linguistic and cultural differences, these tribes are usually clustered into two major groups correlating roughly with the main geographical division notes above, namely a Great Andaman Group and a Little Andaman Group. The latter group consists of only 2 or 3 tribes, while the former consists of 10 tribes, who in turn may be divided into 2 subgroups varying somewhat in cultural and linguistic features.

The ecological setting is basically tropical rain forest. The daily temperature varies little throughout the year, averaging about 30 degrees C. There are two seasons--the wet, or monsoon season, from mid-May to mid-November, and the dry season, from mid-November to mid-May. Rainfall is heavy and, depending on the location, averages 264 to 437 cm. annually. The land is covered with dense tropical foliage. Although the environment is not rich in land mammal species, the reefs and harbors abound in marine fauna. Any discussion of the Andaman Islanders' economic and social organization must be prefaced by a qualifier concerning the data. Western contact brought about rapid cultural disintegration and decimation of the population.

From an estimated precontact population of about 5,000, there were perhaps 2,000 Andaman Islanders left by 1901, when Temple led a British census team. By the 1950s, there remained less than 700 inhabitants in both the Great and Little Andaman groups. Thus, discrepancies in information between various authors may be due to a number of factors, including inter-island variability, sociocultural change, and differing methodological and theoretical orientations among the investigators.

The Andaman Islanders were foragers, subsisting on whatever they could hunt, fish, or collect. Some authors divide them into two adaptive types: those depending largely on coastal resources and those utilizing mainly inland resources. Bows and arrows are used for both hunting and fishing. Harpoon fishing and hunting with dogs appear to have been later introductions. Reef collection was done with nets.

Males were primarily hunters and fishers, but also engaged in secondary collection activities. Females were primarily collectors of vegetable products, reef fauna, and small animals. The Andaman Islanders' animal foods included pig, civet cat, lizards, rats, snakes, insects, birds, turtles, fish, mollusks, and crustaceans. The bulk of their diet, however, came from fruits, roots, seeds, and other plant products. Seasonal feasts of wild honey are also noted in the literature.

The Andaman Islanders were organized into local groups, or bands, consisting of about 20-50 members. Each group was associated with a traditional resource territory, throughout which it moved during the year. Members of the local group had equal rights to the resources within the territory, and local groups could usually obtain permission to forage in neighboring territories. The settlement pattern included three kinds of encampments:

(1) permanent camps in which the same dwellings were occupied from year to year;

(2) temporary camps which were occupied for one season; and

(3) hunting camps, consisting of little more than a few lean-tos thrown up by small hunting parties.

The local group comprised a number of nuclear families plus a few unattached adults. Investigators differ on the matter of local group leadership and on whether the local groups were organized politically, or merely linguistically, into tribes. Man states that there were tribal as well as local group "chiefs".

Radcliffe-Brown, on the other hand, argues that there were no tribal chiefs and that leadership on the local level was informal, based on respect for the advice of older and more talented members of the community. Social control was informal, with disputes settled by the interested parties. Integroup contacts were generally peaceful. People moved between neighboring groups either to visit or to change residence.

Neighboring groups sometimes joined together for festivities at times of abundance. Such intergroup feuds as arose were quickly terminated with peace agreements. The typical household seems to have been the monogamous nuclear family. Marriage restrictions prohibited near kin, including cousins, but otherwise choice of partners was not restricted. Partners were frequently found in other groups or tribes, and postmarital residence patterns were flexible.

Divorce was rare, especially after the birth of the first child. Infanticide is not reported for these people. Adoption was a common feature of Andaman society. Most children by the time they reached ages 6-10 were given by their parents to another family. Both males and females underwent puberty rites. The role of shaman was achievable by either males or females, but such achievement depended on the acceptance by the group of the individual's claim to special powers. Shamans were thought to have special powers for curing, sorcery, and dream interpretation.

The cosmology of the Andaman Islanders contained a variety of animistic spirits and spirits of the dead. Some sources concerning the islands in general include Guha, an anthropological survey focusing on settlement patterns and the population composition of local groups; and Sen, a survey of physical geography incorporating a cultural summary of each of the main tribal divisions and a sketch of the culture history of the islands.

The Andamanese are in the food gathering stage and subsist on whatever nature provides them near their environment. All their skills and culture are for optimum exploitation of the naturally available food resources. Most of their time is spent in search of food.They have their own preferences about eating. There is a semi-nomadic life and they move in bands within their respective territories. Their food is of wild pig, honey, various roots, tubers, turtle fish, molluses, seeds, roots, honey etc.

The eating habits of the Great Andamanese have of late changed as a result of close contact with the settlers. The Onge have now got used to tea and tobacco, rice, flour etc. The people never starve, though they are habitually heavy eaters. Food is always cooked and commonly eaten very hot. The Andamanese are expert cooks and adepts at preparing delicacies from parts of animals and fish.

All occupations and all industries arise out of the personal necessities of the people. They make their own bows and arrow, harpoons and spears, string and nets of string, baskets and mats, unglazed circular cooking pots, bamboo baskets and canoes hollowed out of tree-trunks. The ornamentation is crude but customary and conventional. Their implements are quartz flakes chipped off and natural stones never Celts. They are unadventurous seamen, poling and paddling canoes at considerable speed but they never go out of slight of land.

The social emotions are not generally expressed. The Andamanese have no words for ordinary salutations, greetings or for expressing thanks. On meeting they stare at each other for a long period in silence, which the younger breaks with a common place remark and then follows an eager telling of news which an Andamanese always delights in hearing. Relatives sit in each other's laps at meetings, huddled together, weeping loudly and demonstratively and this may last for hours. The Onges are less demonstrative and caress each other with their hands. At parting they take each other by the hand and blow on it exchanging sentences of conventional farewell.

An Andamanese will often part readily with ornaments to any one who asks for them. A very rude barter exists between tribes of the same group in regard to articles not locally obtained made of a special clay found only in certain parts of the islands. The barter is really a gift of one article, in exchange of another of corresponding value in return and disputes occur if it is not forth coming.

The Andaman Islanders were foragers, subsisting on whatever they could hunt, fish, or collect. The origin of the indigenous population of the Andaman and Nicobar Islands is shrouded in mystery. It is believed that Negrito communities may have migrated here from the east and north when the islands were connected to Burma, or the sea was sufficiently shallow to allow transport by canoe. Their survival has been under constant threat ever since Western traders and colonizers introduced disease, indulged in widespread deforestation and brought about rapid cultural disintegration of the population.

It is estimated that of the 5000 aborigines in 1858 less than 700 inhabitants remained by 1950 in both the Great and Little Andaman groups. Divided into 12 or 13 'tribes' or tribal units on the basis of linguistic and cultural differences, the Andaman Islanders are clustered into two major groups; a 10-tribe group in the Great Andamnas and 2 or 3 tribes in the Little Andamans.

On the Nicobar Islands, the Mongoloid Nicobarese claiming descent from a Burmese prince have integrated with recent settlers and while they continue to live in small communities of grass huts raised on stilts, have adopted modern agricultural methods, raising pigs rather than hunting. Less than 200 of the still unaccustomed Shompen of Great Nicobar live on the coast and barter in honey, cane and nuts with the Nicobarese in isolated pockets further inland. The Shompen of Great Nicobar live on the coast and barter in honey, cane and nuts with the Nicobarese in isolated pockets further inland.

Most of Great Andamanese died of diseases contracted from western settlers and the trickle who remain are settled today on Strait Island, north of South Andaman. The Jarawas who were originally located on the present site of Port Blair, now live on the western coasts of Middle and South Andaman, hemmed in by the Andaman Trunk Road, which since the 1970s has cut them off from hunting grounds and fresh water supplies. Nevertheless, possessive about their land, they remain unwilling to mix and contact with settlers is limited to gift-exchange at each full moon, a time of celebration.

The Onges were once used by the Chinese and Japanese to dive for valuable shells in exchange for alcohol and opium. Today the largest tribe on the Andaman Islands they live on Little Andaman and Rutland Island in communal shelters (bera) and construct temporary thatched huts (korale). Unlike other tribes, the Onges do not practice tattooing, but they paint their bodies with white clay and ochre, and the women smear themselves with yellow dye from orchids.

The most evasive tribe of all, the Sentinelese, live on North Sentinel Island west of South Andaman. In 1991, the local administration established some contact with them by way of gifts left on the beaches every month. on Strait Island, north of South Andaman. The amazing racial and cultural mix of the present day settlers correctly describes the Andamans as mini India.

The Andaman Islanders were foragers, subsisting on whatever they could hunt, fish, or collect. The Andaman communities, divided into eramtaga (jungle-dwellers), and ar-yuato (coast dwellers) subsist on fish, turtles, turtle eggs, pigs, fruits, honey and roots. Bows and arrows were used for both hunting and fishing.

Harpoon fishing and hunting with dogs appear to have been later introductions. Reef collection was done with nets. Males were primarily hunters and fishers but also engaged in secondary collection activities. Females were primarily collectors of vegetable products, reef fauna and small animals.

The Andaman Islanders' animal foods included pig, civet cat, lizards, rats, snakes, insects, birds, turtles, fish, mollusks and crustaceans. The bulk of their diet, however, came from fruits, roots, seeds and other plant products. Seasonal feasts of wild honey are also noted in literature.

Local groups, or bands, consisted of about 20-50 members; each group associated with a traditional resource territory, throughout which it moved during the year. Local groups could usually obtain permission to forage in neighboring territories. There were no tribal chiefs and leadership on the local level was based on respect for the advice of older and more talented members of the community. Disputes were amicably settled by interested parties.

The typical household seems to have been the monogamous nuclear family. Partners were frequently found in other groups or tribes and post marital residence patterns were flexible. Divorce was rare, especially after the birth of the first child. Adoption was a common feature of Andaman society. Both males and females underwent puberty rites.

Shamans were thought to have special powers for curing, sorcery and dream interpretation and was achievable by either males or females, but such achievement depended on the acceptance by the group of the individual's claim to special powers. The cosmology of the Andaman Islanders contained a variety of animistic spirits and spirits of the dead.

Daily ritual dances central to communal life were held on land enclosed by huts. Intergroup contacts were generally peaceful; their dwellers getting together at times of abundance. The present day settlers comprise people of all faiths - Hindus, Muslims, Christians, Sikhs who speak languages like Hindi, Bengali, Malayalam, Tamil, Telugu, Punjabi. They live together in complete harmony. Inter-religion and inter-regional marriages are common. The amazing racial and cultural mix correctly describes the Andamans as mini India.

The religion is Animism and consists in fear of the evil spirits of the wood, the sea, disease and ancestors and in avoidance of acts traditionally displeasing to them. There is neither ceremonial worship nor propitiation. An anthropomorphic deity, Paluga, is the cause of all things though acts displeasing to him are avoided for fear of damage to the products of the jungle. Paluga dwells now in the sky but used to live on the top of Saddle Peak, their highest mountain. The Andamanese have no idea of heaven or hell or any idea of a corporeal resurrection in the religious sense. They have much active faith in dreams which sometimes control subsequent conduct and in the utterances of wise men, dreamers of prophetic dreams. These practice an embryonic magic and witchcraft. There is no oaths, covenants or ordeals nor any forms of appeal to supernatural powers.

Puluga who is fundamentally to be identified with some definiteness with the storm (Wuluga) mixed up with ancestral chiefs has many attributes of the deity that it is fair to translate the term by God. He has a wife and a family of one son and many daughters. He transmits his orders through his son to his daughters who are his messengers. The two great harmful spirits are Eremchauga of the forest and Juruwin of the sea. Like Puluga, both have wives and families. The sun is the wife of the moon and the stars are their children, dwelling near Puluga. But there is no trace of sun-worship. The people twang their bows and make fun of the moon during an eclipse while a solar eclipse keeps them silent through fear customs - naming, marriage, death, beliefs and superstitions.

### *Family*

An Andamanese belongs to a family, which belongs to a sept, which belongs a tribe, which belongs to a group of tribes or divisions of the race. The first two of these are recognized by the people. They are twelve tribes in three groups. They are Northern or Yerewa group, Southern or Bojnji group and outer group or the Onge Jaraa tribes. All the tribes inhabit in the Great Andaman, except the Balwaa of the Archipelago, the Onge of the Little Andaman, and the Jarawa of the North Sentinel and parts of the south Andaman and Rutland Islands. Each group has certain salient characteristics like the form of the huts, bows and arrows, and canoes, of ornamentation, female's clothing, hair dressing and utensils, of tattooing and of language being common generally to the group.

The Nicobarese can be treated as one people whose affinities are towards the Far Eastern and not towards the mainland races. Their own idea of themselves is that they came from the Tenasserim coast, an idea borne out by Physical structure, social habits, trend of civilization and language. They are of the highest ethnological interest. The tribal feeling is friendly within the tribe and hostile to every stranger. The once custom that has served to make the various septs of a tribe hang together is that of a very free adoption of each others children, only those under six or seven usually living with their parents. Hunting and honey collection are men's job and the women and children collect roots and tubers. There is a high degree of individual freedom among the sexes and monogamy is the rule. Husband-wife and parent-children relationships are based on mutual respect and deep affection.

Small local groups are constituted by a number of primary families with a close sense of mutual social obligations. During heavy rains they share a common beehive-shaped communal hut but in the warmer days a series of small huts provide shelter. Leadership is acquired and maintained by qualities like generosity, skill at hunting and other work and wisdom based on age and experience. They have a rich collection of myths and songs sung when dancing or at work.

The Andamanese are a standing puzzle to ethnologists. The various tribes form one race of Negritos, speaking varieties of a single fundamental language. The central space in their habitat is the dancing ground. A hut is merely a thatch about 1 metre (4 feet) long by slightly less than a metre (3 feet) wide sloping from 20cm(8 inches) behind to 103cms (41/2 feet ) in front, placed on four uprights and some crosspieces without walls. In unsheltered spots and at the headquarters of septs large circular huts are built with a good deal of ingenuity, having caves nearly touching the ground. These may be as much as 4.5m (15 feet) high and 9.14m (30 feet) in diameter. For hunting purposes mere thatched shelters are erected for protection from the wind close to every hut is a very small platform for scruples food, about 18 inches from the ground and within it at least one fire is carefully preserved. This is the only thing that the Andamanese are really careful about for they do not know how to produce fire though they show much skill in carrying smouldering logs by land or sea so that they are not extinguished. Both men and women join hands in making huts.

In the Little Andaman and among the Jarawas of the South Andaman, large permanent huts for use in the wet season are built up of a solid materials to 9.14m (30 feet) in height and 18.28m (60 feet) in breadth, to hold the fires of seven to eight hunting parties, with about eight persons to each breadth. The Jarawa hunting camp is much the same as that of any other Andamanese and his great communal hut is built on the same principle as the larger huts of the other tribes. For hunting and fishing they use simple bows and arrows, spears, harpoons and nets. They use dugout canoes for hunting and for transportation. They Jarawas use rafts.

Andamanese are childishly fond of games and have an indigenous blind-man's-buff, leapfrog and hide-and-seek. Mock pig and turtle hunts, mock burials and ghost-hunts are favourite sports-Matches in swinging, swimming, throwing, skimming (ducks and drakes), shooting (archery) and wrestling are practised. The great amusement of the Andamanese is the formal evening or night dance which is a curious monotonous performance accompanied by drumming the feet rhythmically on a special rounding-board. The dance takes place every evening whenever there are enough people for it and lasts for hours and even all night at special meetings of the tribes or septs. Both sexes take allotted parts in it. This and turtle hunting are the only things which will keep the Andamanese awake all night long. There are five varieties of the dance among the tribes.

### *Naming*

Every child is named for life by the mother after one of about twenty conventional names without reference to sex, immediately upon pregnancy becoming evident. To this is subsequently added a nickname varying occasionally from personal peculiarities or sometimes from flattery or reverence. Girls also receive 'flower names' after one of sixteen selected trees which happen to be in flower at the time they reach puberty. The honorifics maia and mam are prefixed out of respect to the names of elderly males and chana to all names of married women. Girls are addressed by the 'flower name' and the elders by the honorific.

### ***Marriage***

The Andamanese are monogamous. Divorce is rare and unknown after the birth of a child. Unfaithfulness after marriage is not common and polyandry, polygamy, bigamy and incest are unknown. Marriage after the death of one party or divorce is usual. Before marriage free intercourse between the sexes within the exogamous limits is the rule, though some conventional precautions are taken to prevent it. Marriages are not religious but are attended with ceremonies.

Marriages are the business of parents or guardians who have a right to betrothal which is regarded as a marriage. There is no caste feeling and tribes will in circumstances favoring it, inter-marriage and adopt each other's children. Within the tribe there is so general a custom of adoption that children above six or seven rarely live with their own parents.

Only husband and wife can eat together. Widows and widowers, bachelors and maidens eat with their own sex only. A man may not address directly a married woman younger than himself nor touch his wife's sister. All this creates a tendency towards the herding together of the women.

### *Beliefs and Superstitions*

The Andamanese idea of the soul arises out of his reflection in water and not out of his shadow. His reflection is his spirit which goes after death to another jungle world, Chaitan, under the earth which is flat and supported on an immense palm-tree. There the spirit repeats its former life, visits the earth occasionally and has a distinct tendency to transmigrate into other creatures. Every child conceived has had a prior existence and in naming a second child after a previous dead one, because the spirit of the latter has been transferred to the living one.

The superstitions and mythology of the Andamanese are the direct outcome of their beliefs in relation to spirits. Thus fire frightens Eremchanga. They avoid offending the sun and the moon by silence at their rise. Puluga shows himself in storm and so they appease him by throwing explosive leaves on the fire and deter him by burning bees wax because he does not like the smell. Earthquakes are sport of the ancestors.

There are lucky and unlucky actions and a few omens and charms. Animals and birds credited with human capacities. Convicts murdered by Jarawas at the beginning of the century have been found with heavy stones placed on them and stones are placed along their pathways. Every Andamanese knows that this is a warning to the birds not to tell the English that the men had been murdered and that the murders had passed along the path in front.

The greater part of the mythology turns on Puluga and his doings with Tomo, the first ancestor, to whom and his wife be brought firi and taught all the arts and for whom he created everything. This belief is still alive and every natural phenomenon is attributed to Puluga. Other stories relate in a fanciful way the origin of customs. For example tattooing and dancing, of the arts, articles of food, harmful spirits and so on. An important ethnological item in these stories is the constant presence of the ideas of metempsychosis and metamorphosis into animals, fish, birds, stone and other objects in nature. The fauna chiefly known to the Andamanese are considered to be ancestors changed supernaturally into animals.

The Anadamanese believe in the spirits of the forest, the sky and the sea and in the existence of the souls of their dead ancestors. But the ceremonies and rituals characterising their social and religious life are marked by extreme simplicity.

### *Deaths*

Deaths occasion loud lamentation from all connected with the deceased. Babies are buried under the floor of their parent's hut. Adults are either buried in a shallow grave or tied up in a bundle and placed on a platform in a tree. Wreaths of cane leaves are then fastened conspicuously round the encampment and it is deserted for about three months. Burial spots are also sufficiently well marked. Mourning is observed by smearing the head with grey clay and refraining from dancing for the same period.

After some months of the bones of the deceased are washed, broken up and made into ornaments to which great importance is attached as mementoes of the deceased and because they are believed to stop pain and cure diseases by simple application to the diseased part. The skull is worn down the back suspended from the neck, usually but not always by the widow, widower or nearest relative. Mourning closes with a ceremonial dance and removal of the clay. The ceremonies connected with the disposal of the dead are conventional, reverential and with some elaboration in detail.

## Festivals

When the immigrants from the mainland settled in these islands, they brought with them their own rituals and festivities. Now the people of Andaman & Nicobar Islands celebrate several festivals.

### *Island tourism festival*

A 15 days long festival organised by the Andaman and Nicobar Administration every year gives a festive look to the islands. The exhibition, on the occasion, highlights the developments and the other aspects of these islands. Cultural troups and the artistes of the National and International fame from the mainland are invited to perform during the festival. Water sports competitions and Nicobari "HODI" race are organised. The festival projects the image of the islands as on eco-friendly tourist destination.

### *Local religious festivals*

The special festive celebrations of particular groups include Durgapuja for the Bengalis, Panguni Uthiram for the

Tamils, Pongal for the Telugus and Onam for the Malayalis. The Local Born of the Andamans, who are divided into Hindus, Muslims and Christians, celebrate the festivals of all the three religions. Some of their main festivals are Shivratri, Janmastami, Holi, Diwali, Ramanavami, Idd, Christmas, Good Friday etc. All three religious groups among the locals participate in one another's festivals.

Thus the people of the Andaman and Nicobar Islands, irrespective of the regions that they originally come from or the religion they practice or the language or dialect they speak have many common cultural traits. A remarkable feature of Andaman and Nicobar society is the amicable co-existence of the people belonging to the different religions. Communal violence is unheard of here. There is amicable participation of all in religious festivals and the incidence of inter-religious marriages is increasing. Also part of these festivities are local performers. Water sports competitions & Nicobari Hodi race are a treat to watch. An exhibition depicting the progress made by these islands is woarth a visit. Other not to be missed attractions are the Floating restaurant, Bay show, Puppet show, Magic show, Dog show, Scuba Diving, Canoe race etc.

## Arts and Crafts

The Andaman & Nicobar Islands are characterised by two distinct native cultures. One is of the Negrito population in the Andmans and other is of the Autochthones, i.e. the Mongoloid Nicobarese and Shompen. Both during pre- and post-British periods and even after Independence, these two cultures have maintained their distinct identities.With the British occupation of these islands and the establishment of the penal settlement, the cultural scenario started changing. As a large number of aliens were brought and settled in the Andamans, the cultural pattern of the islands began to change.

The tribals became the minority and the immigrants emerged as the dominant group. People from different states, with varied linguistic and cultural affiliations, began to live in the same settlement side by side. Under these circumstances, their cultural life began to assume some common features.The situation was different in Nicobar. With the coming of the British, the missionaries started arriving and converting a large number of Nicobarese to Christianity. The Christian Nicobarese now mostly live in north and central Nicobar.

Practitioners of the traditional tribal religion, however, still live in some remote islands. Moreover, Christianity, modern education, formal legislations, etc., have brought modernisation and westernisation only to people of Car Niocbar and a few other islands.

## Tribals and Ecological Issues

The Andaman and Nicobar islands, a chain of 300-odd islands in the Bay of Bengal, are geographically one of the most scenic and beautiful and historically and sociologically one of the most interesting areas of the Indian Republic. They are situated between 60 and 140 North latitude and 920 and 940 East longitude. The evergreen tropical islands are washed by two heavy monsoons a year and the equatorial sun keeps them hot and dry from January to early May. Their total area is 8293 sq km and their total population according to the 1981 census was about 189,000. Of these 84 per cent live in the Andaman islands and the other 16 per cent in the Nicobar islands.

The total population has since risen to about 2,81,000 (1991 census) — an increase of about 92,000 in a ten-year period — mostly through immigration from the mainland. Only 34 islands are inhabited, the rest lacking any permanent human habitation. As per official records, 87 per cent of the land area is still under forest cover. The island's forests are rich in tropical fauna and flora but the only mammals are wild boar, civet cat and spotted deer (introduced by the British administration in the nineteenth century). The dark blue waters of the sea abound in marine life. Very few islands have perennial streams, as most of the rainwater washes down to the sea.

The entire Andaman and Nicobar islands provide a broadly similar natural setting and environmental conditions, though micro-level variation exist, with the islands being spread over 600 nautical miles of sea. But as has been very well established by a wealth of data provided by anthropologists and human geographers, very different cultures can flourish in terms of their adaptation to similar ecologies. That is inevitable because each human group, in its collective wisdom and inclinations, makes its set of choices from among the numerous possibilities that exist, to evolve and develop cultural traditions to adapt their life-styles to the conditions in which they live.

There are five small traditional hunting-gathering tribes, the Great Andamanese, the Onge, the Jarawa and the Sentinelese on the Andaman islands and the Shompen on the Nicobar islands. The Nicobarese of the Nicobar islands are spread across twelve islands of the archipelago.

By far the predominant population of the islands consists of migrants from the mainland who have settled here from 1858 onwards. The vast majority live in the Andamans and only a few thousand are in the Nicobars. The rural population is attached to land, practising agriculture and animal husbandry. Subsumed under this category are also people living in urban and semi-urban areas working as unskilled, semi-skilled and skilled workers and in white-collar jobs.

The hunter-gatherers are today very small tribes in terms of their populations, which range from 28 to 200 or so. The four tribes who occupy a few pockets of land or forest area in the Andaman islands are of negrito stock, while the Shompen, living in the forests of Great Nicobar, are of Mongoloid stock (like the other Nicobarese). In popular parlance and even in official correspondence they are referred to as 'primitive tribes'. Along with the Nicobarese they are listed as scheduled tribes by the Andaman and Nicobar administration.

The Nicobarese live in large, well-organised permanent coastal villages. Their relatively large population of 21,172 (1981 census) is spread out in twelve Nicobar islands, and a small number have in recent years settled in the Little Andaman island. The Nicobarese are herders of pigs and horticulturists, with plantations of coconut, areca nut, yams, bananas, pandanus, etc. A majority of them are converts to Christianity, major conversions having taken place from 1945 onwards. While all the hunting-gathering tribes are pre-literate and hence illiterate in census terms, the Nicobarese show a literacy rate of about 31 per cent (1981 census). They have been attending church and government schools with great interest. This percentage is quite high when compared with the situation among tribes elsewhere in India. The Nicobarese, for obvious reasons, are not considered or referred to as 'primitive', but all the same are looked upon as 'backward' by the settlers.

Besides, the six scheduled tribes mentioned above, there is a huge migrant population from India (189,000 according to the 1981 census) that has settled here since 1858 when the penal settlement was established at Port Blair by the British. The bulk of them (158,000) are concentrated in the Andaman islands. In the Nicobars there are only about 6,000 settlers, and most of them are on the Great Nicobar island, the largest and the southern-most island in the Nicobars. Prior to 1947 most of the people were brought here as individual prisoners or as groups (e.g. Mopla, Bhatu and Karen, etc.) by way of punishment or otherwise and some came here as government officials, traders, workers, etc. Many of them settled here for good. These are the 'old settlers'.

After 1947 the first people brought here by the Government of India as free settlers were Bengali-speaking Bangladeshi (erstwhile East Pakistan) refugees. They kept on coming here, even on their own, through the 1970s. Besides, large groups kept coming here from Kerala, Tamil Nadu and Andhra Pradesh in search of white-collar jobs or to work as labourers, artisans, and fishermen and small traders.

Since 15 August 1947 (when India achieved independence from British rule) the Bay Islands have constituted a Union Territory that is directly administered by the through an administrator designated as the Lieutenant-Governor (earlier called the Chief Commissioner). There is an indirectly elected Pradesh Council whose role is advisory. The Lieutenant-Governor nominates a tribal leader from among the five small tribes to represent their interests, while the Nicobarese are able to elect their own on the basis of their numerical strength. The Andamans and Nicobars are districts of the territory each administered by a Deputy Commissioner. The islands elect one member to the Lok Sabha (lower house of Indian Parliament).

The existence of the Bay Islands has been known to travellers, explorers and geographers during the last 2000 years, as references in various reports show. But in place of authentic accounts there have been many myths, weird tales and lots of mystery about them. The more reliable information has come only after European missionaries and explorers started visiting the islands from the fifteenth century onwards. Colonisation efforts started from the eighteenth century onwards on behalf of the European powers. By all accounts, the Negrito hunter-gatherers and the Mongoloid Nicobarese are the oldest known inhabitants of these islands. The probability is that the Negrito people held sway in large areas of the South-East Asian mainland and migrated to these islands several millennia ago, perhaps under pressure from migrant Mongoloid hordes from mainland China. At a later stage Mongoloid people also migrated to these islands and they confined themselves to the Nicobar islands. This story remains yet in the realm of speculation.

However, the hunter-gatherers apparently found these islands very suitable and seemed to flourish here except for the occasional visits of Malaysian pirates who would try to collect birds' nests (a great delicacy) and also try to capture the Andamanese negritos to be sold as slaves in South-East Asian markets. But in return the Andamanese would try to kill foreigners and destroy their vessels whenever they could. The islands thus acquired a fearsome reputation. In any case, the Andamanese and the Nicobarese were not seriously disturbed by any outside elements.

***Settlement***

The situation changed drastically and decisively when the European colonial powers started exploring these areas with a view to establishing permanent settlements. In 1788 the islands were surveyed by Lt. Archibald Blair and Lt. Colebrook of the British navy, and a year later the first penal settlement was established by the British East India Company on South Andaman. The settlement was shifted to North Andaman in 1794 and abandoned in 1796 due to heavy casualties.

In 1858 the British came back, following the great Indian Mutiny of 1857, and established a second and more permanent settlement. In the mean time the Nicobar islands had passed under the control of the Danish East Indian Company, but Denmark ceded the area to Britain in 1869 through a treaty.

The Andamanese, who were the sole inhabitants, thus came into direct conflict with the British administration over the occupation of their lands and forests and coastal areas (their resource areas). The conflict and skirmishes lasted several years in various areas, but the Andamanese had to give in eventually to superior technology and might at the cost of hundreds of lives. Subsequently, when peace and friendship were established on most of the islands, the Andamanese came into closer and more intimate contact with the local administration, the British soldiery and the convict supervisors. This close contact led to the spread of new diseases in epidemic form that caused a sharp demographic decline among the negritos. An estimated population of 5,000 in 1858 was reduced to less than 2,000 by 1900, and by 1931 to a mere few hundred.

Today the total population of these tribes has stabilised around a few hundred, though estimates for individual tribes vary (Table 1). In the case of the Shompen the 1981 census figure is 214, but Rizvi in 1984 reported a population of only 134 (1990).

*Table 1. Estimated/actual population of Andaman tribes from 1901 to 1990*

| Year | 1901 | 1911 | 1921 | 1931 | 1951 | 1961 | 1978 | 1980 | 1990 |
|---|---|---|---|---|---|---|---|---|---|
| Tribe | | | | | | | | | |
| Gerat Andamanese | 625 | 455 | 209 | 90 | 23 | 19 | 24 | 25 | 29 |
| Oonge | 672 | 631 | 346 | 250 | 150 | 129 | 106 | 97 | 98 |
| Jarawa | 585 | 114 | 114 | 70 | 50 | 300 | 250 | 250 | 200 |
| Sentinelese | | 117 | 117 | 50 | 50 | 100 | 100 | 100 | 80 |

*Table 2. Populations of Shompen and Nicobarese*

| Year | 1901 | 1911 | 1921 | 1931 | 1951 | 1961 | 1971 | 1981 |
|---|---|---|---|---|---|---|---|---|
| Tribe | | | | | | | | |
| Shompen | 342 | 375 | 375 | 200 | 20 | 71 | 92 | 214 |
| Nicobarese | 6501 | 8818 | 9272 | 10240 | 12009 | 14563 | 17874 | 21172 |

The stark fact that emerges from the above two tables is that the most serious problem being faced by the five small tribes of the A&N islands has been their sharp demographic decline following their close contact with outsiders. The worst sufferers have been the ten original Great Andamanese tribes. From an estimated 3,000 to 3,500 in 1858 they have come down to a group of a mere 28 souls today. The fate of the Onge-Jarawa-Sentinelese group has been relatively less calamitous, as an estimated 400 survive against an estimated 1,500-2,000 population in 1858. The reason is not far to seek. The former have been in the longest and most intimate contact with the settlement and bore the brunt of the ill effects of long drawn out conflicts and skirmishes and new diseases. In the case of the latter, less contact must have helped.

### *Tribals and Interaction with Environment*

*Hunting and nomadic trines*

*The Great Andamanese:* Their total population is only 28 souls. They have been settled on a small island called Strait island (off the eastern coast of South and Middle Andaman islands) since 1970. The settlement was built by the A&N administration and is being maintained at government cost. Each small family has a wooden house and they get monthly their requirements of food, a cash allowance plus other periodical needs. Those members who work in specific jobs (like those of teacher, medical assistant, plantation worker) are paid for their work. The leader of the group gets an extra cash allowance. The government also meets the entire expenditure on their medical care, including special treatment in mainland hospitals. A plantation has also been established in Strait island. Efforts at having a piggery have not been very successful. The social worker who stays there permanently is required to take general care of the people and the settlement. Also the idea was to encourage the Great Andamanese to do useful work for their own benefit instead of idling away their time.

Besides, the habits of opium addiction and drunkenness are discouraged and medically treated wherever necessary. It was also hoped that over a period the members of the community would develop a sense of belonging and greater social cohesion. This has happened, but to a partial degree. One has to remember, of course, that the present community has come into being by bringing together the surviving members of the disorganised original ten Great Andamanese tribes. These tribes had ceased to be viable communities due to the trauma of demographic destruction caused mainly by new diseases and the upheavals resulting from their uprooting by the British administration.

In the last two decades opium addiction has been controlled to a large extent but drunkenness remains a problem not yet solved. Attention is also being paid to the serious question of outside people trying to exploit the tribals. Their young women have been physically exploited or have willingly developed liaisons with outside people, which has even led to the birth of children. There is also a case of a non-tribal woman marrying an Andamanese man and bearing him a child. The couple are now separated. But this woman's sister is in love with another young Andamanese man and wants to marry him.

All told, the 28 members of the Great Andamanese community have been pulled out of an abyss into which they had been driven due to total neglect by all concerned and their own loss of nerve and social will due to overwhelming destructive factors beyond their control. But for the intervention of anthropologists and the A&N administration since 1968, there would have been only a small fraction of this population living today, or they might have disappeared altogether.

*The Onge*: Friendly contact with the Onge was made in 1885 (110 years ago). But prior to that there had been several violent and hostile encounters with British ships and their crews. Sometimes the latter got killed and on other occasions the Onge had to retreat, leaving heavy casualties. The population on the island of Little Andaman and the nearby smaller islands could have been around 1,000 in the mid-nineteenth century. But by 1931 the estimates had come down to 250, in 1951 it was 150 and in 1961 the census head count was 129. In the 1971 census they were 112, in 1980 they were 97, and today they are 98. The Onge were left more or less alone by the British administration except for occasional visits by the administrators and occasional visits by Onge groups to Port Blair (quite often in their own canoes). This situation continued till the late 1960s. In 1953 a coconut plantation was built by the Agricultural Department at the Dugang Creek Onge settlement, though coconut is not a traditional food item of the Onge or other Andaman tribes.

In 1967 a big change occurred when the island of Little Andaman was opened for resettlement of outside people and with the starting of a red oil palm plantation by the Forest Development Corporation. Today the Onge share the island with several thousand settlers in several big villages. These include the Nicobarese (near the South Bay Onge settlement) and Bengali and South Indian migrants. A big jetty and breakwater have been built near Hut Bay (once an Onge settlement area). This has been a major new development, as for the first time the Onge have had to live face to face in their once exclusive habitat with an alien population (3000 or so) which is 30 times their own number and likely to increase.

During the 1970s and 1980s the two major Onge settlements were redesigned with new huts of an altogether new design being built, with consequences which have not been too happy. This has gone on with parallel efforts to sedentarise them to enable the official agencies to take welfare aid to them more easily. A social worker, a doctor and a nurse, a plantation worker, etc., have been posted there. A teacher was also there for several years, but this did not lead to any literacy among them. Among the Great Andamanese only some adults and children can read and write a little Hindi. Several health surveys were done among the Onge, starting with an ICMR team which visited them in March 1969. Health records are brought to Port Blair whenever required or possible. But this kind of help during the last 20 years has not helped check the decline in their population, though it has remained steady at the level of about 97 to 49.

The closer contact with the settlers and the supply of rice, flour, etc., has led to a change in food habits. Tea and tobacco they had taken to since British days, but now they eat and cook like other Indians, using salt, sugar, oil and condiments and similar cooking techniques (as against the traditional boiling and roasting methods). Some Onge speak Hindi quite well. They have access to money paid as wages for work done in various welfare projects in their own community, some of which seem hardly relevant to their urgent daily or long-term needs (e.g. collecting resin for the contractor, working in their gardens under supervision, working on the electric generator, etc.) as per their own perceptions.

The Onge life-style has undergone certain important changes but these have not necessarily or always improved the quality of their life. It has actually led to a certain confusion in their minds regarding the direction of their own life, as they are unable to take their own decisions about what and how to do whatever they may like to do. Most of the time decisions, however good they may be (but that is not the case always), are imposed on them. Because of demographic problems some boys and men are unable to have marriage mates. Further, the ill effects of the inbreeding of a small population of less than 100 are not yet visible, but sooner or later they will appear. However, socially the Onge society is still viable and well-knit in spite of the changes that have taken place during the twentieth century. There is hope yet that it will be able to cope with the unwise and presumptuous interference with its functioning.

*The Jarawa*: During the nineteenth century, while the British succeeded in bringing around the ten Great Andamanese after several years' efforts (involving the use of force and blandishment), the eleventh tribe in the Great Andaman area (South Andaman to be precise) continued to remain highly suspicious of the settlement and the settlers. They were what are known as the Jarawa. There were numerous hostile contacts and encounters with them during the late nineteenth and the first half of the twentieth century. In fact during the 1920s and 1930s the British were obliged to send many armed punitive expeditions to the Jarawa areas in the deep forests on the western coast of South Andaman. The Jarawa themselves found it expedient to spread out to the western coast of Middle Andaman under these pressures.

A special Bush police force was also created to deal with the Jarawa. After 1947 this policy underwent a basic change as the new Indian government, influenced by Nehru's philosophy, did not subscribe to the principle of punitive expeditions against tribes except under conditions of overt and conscious violent political rebellions against the legally established government. The situation here is altogether different, as the Jarawa are still not consciously aware of being citizens of the Indian Republic. However various 'Jarawa incidents' continued from the 1950s to the 1970s, and they occur even today though to a much lesser extent. These incidents are mostly caused by the fact that the Jarawa feel disturbed by movements and certain activities of outside people in their territory and wish to discourage these by attacking the 'culprits' if very much provoked. Since 1968 much thought has been given to this matter by anthropologists and the A&N administration and certain useful measures have been taken to remove prejudice on either side.

Being under considerable pressure from politically vocal sections of the people, the A&N administration appointed an Expert Committee under Dr S.C. Sinha (anthropologist) to make recommendations regarding the extension of the Andaman Trunk Road alongside Jarawa territory in the South and Middle Andaman. The committee gave conditional approval for constructing the road. But while the road has been made the conditions important for safeguarding Jarawa interests remain mostly unfulfilled due to difficulties faced by the administration and lack of will. This road remains a big hazard for the survival of the Jarawa. Their population of about 200 has an area of 600 sq km of reserved forest and tribal area. But they are surrounded by more than 105,000 settlers. Their territory could be overrun in the coming decades unless very sensible and effective measures are taken to avoid such an eventuality.

*The Sentinelese*: They are estimated to be about 80 to 100 and are the sole inhabitants of North Sentinel island (area about 50 sq km). They are the most isolated of all the tribal communities in India and perhaps in the world. Except for occasional visits by official parties since the British days (and perhaps poachers) nobody goes there nobody else lives there. Because of the sea, where they can get turtles and a whole variety of fish and molluscs as food, they can live comfortably even as hunter-gatherers.

However, their suspicion of outsiders did not encourage them till January 1991 to have any face-to-face or handshaking contacts with us. But they do not mind gifts of coconuts, bananas, some simple iron implements or iron pieces. They let us put these things ashore while they watch from a distance. What they do not like they throw into the sea. They also come out in their dugout canoes to pick up coconuts thrown into the sea close to the beach.

Since January-February 1991 the Sentinelese have relented and have had closer and more friendly contacts with us. It was then that they accepted gifts of coconuts, bananas, etc., from the hands of the members of the gift party. A number of visits have been paid since and lots of gifts have been passed on to them. The Sentinelese population appears to have reduced since 1974, when many more people were encountered on the shore and even photographed.

*The Shompen:* Contact of the Shompen with the outside world, directly and through the coastal Nicobarese of Great Nicobar, has existed since the early nineteenth century. It has become closer since the first half of the twentieth century. One saving grace for the Shompen has been the vast forest area that has been at their disposal. In the late 1960s and 1970s it was decided to open the Great Nicobar island for development and rehabilitation of ex-servicemen. Circular and diagonal roads were built to join the east and west coasts in the southern part of the island (403 sq miles in area). This causes very serious disturbances for the Shompen.

It also seems that probably disease and intra-group hostilities among the Shompen had earlier caused the dwindling of their population. Their camps are very small and scattered over vast areas. Hence any welfare measures are difficult to take to them. In 1983-84 a Shompen complex was built to attract them so that medical aid, food supplies and some elementary educational facilities could be extended to them through a social worker and medical staff. Besides, on many occasions clothes, utensils, rice, etc., have been distributed among them. But the Shompen complex has not proved as efficacious as was expected in the absence of truly dedicated social workers and proper supervision. The welfare programme remains mostly on paper.

### *Welfare and Development*

Work on the measures described is governed on these islands by popular notions of their meaning. The ultimate objective is understood to be to bring such communities into the 'mainstream' as they can find meaning only in merging with it. In the popular mind this means the broad merging of cultural and social identities of the smaller or weaker communities with that of the dominant culture, society or people. Quite often it starts with copying the use of externals, material objects such as clothes, domestic articles, food materials and the visible life-style. Learning of the dominant language helps greatly in achieving the goal set by the dominant people. They are satisfied if this process is effected, but neither they nor the official agencies show any sensitivity to the thought processes, the mental tensions, the humiliations and the deprivations that a relatively small 'primitive' community might undergo in the process.

There are also the popular but very subjective and unscientific notions of what is 'civilised'. Joining the mainstream also means that the smaller community is hopeful of getting the benefits of modern science and civilisation. In actual practice this may not happen. By these ideas the down-and-out Great Andamanese could qualify as a more civilised mainstream community, but the Jarawa would not. Left to themselves, the Jarawa life-style is qualitatively far superior to that of the Great Andamanese and the Onge. What a travesty of perceptions!

Anthropologists (like some environmentalists) have often been blamed for advocating 'protectionist', 'human zoo' concepts for tribals. There is no doubt that the five small tribes of the A&N islands are among the beleaguered human communities. They need to be protected and looked after by responsible official agencies under proper scientific supervision and guidance so that they not only survive but live as self-respecting communities. Also, they must not be hustled into getting hopelessly embroiled in the 'mainstream' conceptual monstrosity. They have to change, but the change must not be forced and thoughtlessly harsh in its implications or its speed nor entirely imposed by half-baked social workers or ignorant and unsympathetic administrators or politicians voicing the concerns and extreme selfishness of the dominant groups.

In 1986 the Government of India appointed a high-powered committee of experts to recommend special measures for these small tribes. The committee, headed by Dr S.C. Sinha, met several times, visited these tribes and made several recommendations to prepare them for change while giving them sufficient time. The idea was to appoint a team of well-chosen specialists which would actually involve itself in researching, planning and monitoring all new measures involving the people at all stages and treating their values, views and opinion with respect so that highly sensitive programmes could be evolved and implemented over a period of 10 or 15 years. But these recommendation are now in cold storage both at Port Blair and in New Delhi.

### *Herders and Horticulturists*

The Nicobarese have followed their traditional occupations of keeping large herds of pigs and cultivating large plantations of coconut, areca nut, yams, bananas, pandanus, etc. The pigs are reared with loving care and piglets are paid special attention till they grow strong enough to take care of themselves. And adult pig, besides its normal food, may be given 5 or 6 fresh coconuts a day. The Nicobarese live in settled villages, mostly near the coast. The plantations are grown not far from their homesteads. In fact the impression one gets in Nicobar is that houses are built amidst coconut groves. Coconut trees and fruit are of great economic importance. The nut is eaten, its water drunk, its oil used for cooking, etc. The tree is used for the construction of houses, its branches as fuel and leaves for sundry purposes. The pandanus fruit and yams are important sources of food. Fishing is a most enjoyable activity and is carried out by day and by night using various techniques. The daily catch is an important source of protein. These days the Nicobarese keep some poultry also.

While the coastal areas are used for settlement and plantations, the core areas of the islands are maintained as forest land. Here pigs are taken for pasturing and to provide shady areas for rest. The forest area also provides privacy and for romantic interludes to young boys and girls. The forest serves many other needs also in day-to-day life.

The Nicobarese are seafaring people and have been travelling from one island to another in their dugout canoes for barter, trade and social visits. The Nicobarese keep their own calendar by reading the movements of the moon, the stars and the sun. They also have deep faith in various kinds of benign and evil spirits and the souls of dead ancestors. All these have to be propitiated periodically according to customary rites, rituals and sacrifices.

Pigs are eaten mainly on festive occasions. Their herds are not looked upon primarily as a source of food but as wealth bringing prestige, as precious items of barter, as symbols of general well-being and celebration of life. The blood of a pig is also a medicine and is rubbed on the body to relieve pain.

The Nicobarese enjoy sports like canoe racing and man-pig wrestling, and are very fond of dancing and singing. The coconut tree also provides them with freshly brewed toddy, which is a very popular drink among them. Grated coconut provides coconut milk in which rice is cooked. It is a delicacy.

There is no provision for individual and private ownership of land among them. All land belongs to the kin group and the produce is shared among the members. Each kin group has a head and the village has a council and head (also called captain). There is also an island council and chief captain on each island.

Until 1945 the Nicobarese followed their own traditional religion and customs. But from then onwards there have been large-scale conversions to Christianity mainly through the efforts of their own Bishop Richardson, a resident and early convert to this faith in Car Nicobar.

The entry of traders and the growth of the cooperative movement under government patronage has helped the Nicobarese to sell their surplus produce of coconut and arecanut. The traders also introduced new consumer items of all kinds. This has led to some degree of consumerism. Over the decades this has also helped develop, in the midst of a traditional egalitarian economic system, an incipient class system. Some Nicobarese have acquired a lot of wealth in money terms, which has given them access to new goods and services. These have become the new symbols of status and social prestige. There are others who can only watch and envy. However, even today no member of Nicobarese society can die of starvation. The community takes care of all those who are unable to take care of themselves for reasons of health, physical disability or lack of work.

As per the 1981 census the literacy rate among the Nicobarese was about 31 per cent. In 1992 it was reported to have risen to 39 per cent (informal sources). The people are making fair use of the facilities provided by the government. Quite a few boys and girls have passed out from secondary and senior secondary schools or acquired university degrees in arts, sciences, medicine and engineering. Nicobarese youth have thus been able to occupy white-collar and technical posts, including the administrative services, to some extent. This trend will continue and more and more Nicobarese are likely to move away from their traditional moorings in terms of occupation. But as yet there are no signs of any serious conflict within their society between ordinary people and 'modernists'. The church and the adaptive processes within their cultural tradition are helping to mediate the situation of potential conflict!

***Agriculturists***

Agriculture, animal husbandry and fishing and a whole lot of sundry urban-oriented trades and occupations are followed by the settlers from mainland India who were brought here by the British (1858-1945) and later under various schemes of the Government of India. But hundreds and thousands have been coming here on their own, especially from Tamil Nadu, Andhra Pradesh, Kerala, Bengal, Bihar, etc. This composite group goes in for jobs of all kinds both in the public and private sectors. These include thousands of jobs provided by various state and central government departments and related institutions. In 1961 their population was about 45,000 but in 1991 they numbered about 250,000, which is an almost sixfold increase in three decades. The bulk of this population lives in the Andaman islands and some in the Nicobars.

The ecological conditions of the Bay islands are rather fragile. The topography is uneven and hilly and the soil rocky and porous with a very thin topsoil. The heavy rains that two monsoons bring simply flow down to the sea. The soil has little capacity for retaining water. In cleared spaces thousands of tons of topsoil are washed down to the sea every year. Only in two islands, North Andaman and Great Nicobar, are there perennial sources of sweet water in the shape of big streams.

All over the settlement areas there is a terrible shortage of drinking water and water for daily needs and agricultural purposes. The only saving grace is that large areas are still covered by forest and vegetation. But it is not so in the large settlement areas, where there are constant demands on forest resources. With the influx of increasing numbers of people from the mainland there are heavy encroachments on forest land and a demand for other natural resources. Because of this, and in absence of effective regulatory and corrective measures, even the vast mangrove forests and coral reefs are getting damaged.

This demographically, socially, politically and economically dominant population is all-pervasive in its hunger for resources, without a thought for the immediate or distant future. The people who have come here to settle either as individuals or as fragmentary groups are culturally uprooted entities. Hence their minds, their psyches and their cultural visions and world-views remain mutilated and blind. Their experience and wisdom made sense in their native environment. Here they do not recognise even by name most of the fauna and flora. There is no idea nor any anxiety on their part to relate in any significant way to the local environment. There is, therefore, no sense of restraint or doubt in their interaction with it. The outlook is: take what you need or want and do not worry unduly about anything that comes in the way, including human beings such as the indigenous tribal populations.

There is vast ignorance all around and a lack of effort to build informed opinion to counter it. A serious environmental and human problem is gaining momentum in the Andaman and Nicobar islands which has to be dealt with in a scientific and human way. The situation in the islands in ecological terms has not yet reached a stage of desperation and can be amenable to a well-thought-out constructive, corrective and preventive policy. Much of the responsibility lies with the Government of India and the Andaman & Nicobar Administration.

# 2

# Tribes of Bihar

Bihar is situated in the eastern part of India with the Himalayan Kingdom of Nepal to its north and the states of Orissa, West Bengal, Uttar Pradesh and Madhya Pradesh flanking its sides. It is today home of more than 90 million Indians. The state is endowed with an enviable mineral resources base, has some of the finest industries, is country's one of the largest producers of fruit and the second largest producer of vegetables. However, this rich state in terms of natural and human resources and the second most populous in the country has been slow to harness its natural and human resources for the development of the state and its people.

The social fabric of Bihar reflects the Indian social macrocosm. A majority of the people are Hindus; a minority practises Islam and there is a substantial number of Christians, area specific to the tribal belt. Bihar has gained notoriety for the internecine caste wars between the upper and lower caste Hindus particularly in the backward interior regions. For the most part, Bihar is a feudal society that still perseveres with traditional social biases that lead to class and caste conflicts. A degree of anarchy prevails in the state despite its respect for education and its tolerance for religious diversity. The majority of the people in the state are Hindus while there are sizeable minorities of Muslims and Christians. Also found in certain pockets are large numbers of Sikhs and Buddhists.

## Tribal Communities

The Constitution Order of 1950 has classified thirty different tribes in Bihar. They are:

1. Asur
2. Baiga
3. Banjara
4. Bathudi
5. Bedia
6. Bhumij
7. Binjhia
8. Birhor
9. Birjia
10. Chero
11. Chik Baraik
12. Gond
13. Gorait
14. Ho
15. Karmali
16. Kharia
17. Kharwar
18. Khond
19. Kisan
20. Kora
21. Korwa
22. Lohara, Lohra
23. Mahli
24. Mal Paharia
25. Munda

26. Oraon
27. Parhaiya
28. Santal
29. Sauria Paharia
30. Savar

The tribal population of Bihar not only differs considerably from its non-tribal counterpart, but even from one another. The Cheros possibly migrated from the sub-Himalayan tract, and differ in features from most of the other tribes that are dark-skinned, short-statured, curly-haired and broad nosed.

Representatives of Negrito, Proto-Australoid, Mongoloid, Mediterranean and Nordic races are found in the population of Bihar. Certain Negrito features were noticed by anthropologists among the aborigines of the Rajmahal hills. The Proto-Australoid features are found in the Kharwar Munda, Bhumij and Mal Pahariyas. Some admixture of Mongoloid blood may be found among the Tharus of Champaran. No clear picture of the origin and composition of these tribals of Bihar has emerged.

Austric speaking groups include Munda, Santhal, Ho, Birhor, Kharia and others. There is a considerable difference between the Mundas and Oraons. The differences between the Santhals and the Sauria Pahariyas are significant as they are indicative of the differences between the Austric-speaking and the Dravidian-speaking people.

The chief representatives of the Dravidian races inhabiting the tribal region are the Hos, the Santhals, the Oraons and the Mundas and they together constitute almost four-fifths of the total tribal population of the state. More than one half of the Santhals are found in Santhal Parganas division and about a quarter in Hazaribagh and Singhbhum districts. They are not negligible in Dhanbad, Purnia, Munger and Bhagalpur. Over three-fourths of the Oraons are confined to Ranchi and Palamu. The Oraons are also found in a few blocks in Rohtas and Champaran districts.

Nearly three fourths of the Mundas are found in Ranchi district and the bulk of the balance in Singhbhum district. The Hos are virtually confined to Singbhum. These four tribes have taken to settled cultivation as their mode of life and are gradually getting the benefits of the employment available in the mineral and industrial undertaking scattered over the plateau region. A few tribals have yet to take to settled cultivation or are still dependent largely on food gathered from the forest to sustain themselves. Asur and Korwa communities are still very backward and deserve assistance through special programmes. Birjhia is a community akin to Asur. The Chick Baraik community engages itself in weaving cloth, the Lohara and Karmali are both blacksmiths who make agricultural implements, the Mahlis are mostly bamboo workers and blacksmiths, the Kisans are settled cultivators noted for their industrious agricultural activities and the Birjhias are settled cultivators and keep cattle. The largest chunk of the tribal population still lives in the rural areas.

### *The Santhals*

The Santhals still preserve two features inherited from an earlier stage of civilization. They excel in clearing forests and show considerable skill in converting jungle and waste lands into fertile rice fields. Their harmonious flutes sound sweeter, their drums find deeper echoes and their bows and arrows utilized effectively. They are excellent hunters. Their happiest day in the year is the one, on which they have a common hunt, when armed with spears, axes, bows and arrows, clubs, sticks and stones, they beat through the jungle in thousands, killing every beast and birds they come across. There was a time when in their ordinary dealings they displayed a cheerful straight forwardness, open bluntness and simple honesty which were refreshing to those accustomed to the gloomy and secretive inhabitants of the plains.

The Santhals are noted for their highly organised social structure. This is evident from Bitlaha - a unique form of punishment meted out to sexual offenders. The Santhals inform each other of a sexual offense by means of a dharwak (signal) conveyed from village to village, consisting of a twig with its leaves stripped to indicate the countdown to the Bitlaha. The result is an enormous crowd that expresses collective resentment against the culprit's misdeeds. The Bitlaha commences with the village headman calling for a joint meeting of the five manjhis (village headmen) who review the crime. Once ratified, amidst the beating of drums and the singing of obscene folk songs, the adivasis, or tribal people gather around the offender's house to urinate along the walls and defecate in his courtyard.

### *Asurs*

The Asurs and Lohras are traditionally blacksmiths and iron smelters. The Asurs are believed to be the subcontinent's first iron smelters who were driven from the Gangetic Plains to the plateau of Chotanagpur. Goraits are traditional drummers who support themselves through agriculture and the sale of forest produce. A number of Dravidian tribes like the Gonds, Khonds, Korwas and Koras seem to have migrated from the neighbouring states.

### *Hos*

The Hos have a lot of good qualities and are firm with their manly independent bearing. They are physically and morally superior to the Mundas, Bhumij and Santhals. The Hos waste their stores of rice in making rice-beer for their various festivals and parts with their land for most inadequate price. The Hos are remarkable for their exclusiveness and insensitiveness to outside influence.

### *Mundas*

The Mundas, found in the south of Ranchi district and the Khunti sub division, are divided into a number of exogamous clans known as Kilis. Though they were gleaners and hunters not long ago, they have entered the maze of industrial economy now. They live in urban surroundings, eat food available from the markets, spend money on jewellery and trinkets, join in demonstrations, shout slogans, strike work and have produced leaders from among themselves. The Mundas worship 'Sing Bonga' - the sun god and also their ancestors, whose spirits are known as the Ora-bongako or the house hold gods.

The Mundas (in Mundari, the word refers to a man of prestige and wealth) are the oldest of the tribes of Bihar, and love to live in harmony with other tribes. The best known icon of this tribe is Birsa Munda, the man behind the Ulgulan Movement of 1900 that expressed tribal anguish and resentment against the British rule, and fuelled the agrarian crisis. Contemporaries of the Buddha, the Mundas are believed to have rejected the Buddha's doctrine. However, the Cheros accepted the Buddhist dharma, and much later became the rulers of Palamau. They are quite industrious and proud of their descent, and still indulge in extravagant shows. The rich among them marry the local Rajputs. The Cheros, along with Bhumijs (children of the soil), were active participants in the 1832 and 1857 rebellions.

### *Oraons*

The Oraons are Dravidian-speaking, short-stature, narrow headed and broad-nosed people living mostly in the Ranchi and Palamu districts. They are divided into several clans or gotras. There are many resemblances between the Oraons and Mundas. The Oraons are much less conservative and exclusive than Mundas. Oraon youths have their hair tied in a knot behind and a small mirror stuck in it and ornaments in their ears. The headman of their village is called the Mahto and the official who presides over their spiritual affairs is the Pahan.

The Oraons employ methods of cultivation which are much advanced compared with those of other tribes in Bihar. Their most important social institution is the

Dhumkuria or the boy's youth dormitory, an institution which has put them on the ethnographic map of the world.

An important institution associated with the Oraons is the Dhumkuria that has put them on the ethnographic map of the world. The dhumkuria is a dormitory that segregates boys and girls, while simultaneously training them to share the responsibilities of the community. It is here that traditions are handed down by more experienced youths to the younger ones. Oraon parents find it undesirable to have their children see them sleep together. Therefore children above the age of ten are housed separately. The Jonkh-erpa takes care of the boys while girls sleep under the care of an elderly widow in the Pello-erpa.

### *Bhumijs*

The Bhumijs are believed to be the earliest settlers of the Manbhum region in southern Bihar. They are ethnically related to the Mundas, whom they closely resemble. This tribe worships Hindu gods, besides their tribal deities. While some of the tribes practise the Hindu custom of cremating their dead, others have retained their tribal practice of burying the bodies in burial grounds called Sasan or Harshali. However, the Paharias (the hillmen dwelling in the Rajmahal area, who take pride in their tradition of shifting agriculture, known as Kurwa) are free of totemic influence, while almost all tribes have their individual village priests, Naikaor Pahans. The Pahans take care of the Sarna, or the sacred grove where the village deities reside amidst some old trees.

### *Bhumij Kols*

The Bhumij Kols who occupy parts of the two Singhbhum districts west and south of the Kasari river, are ethnically related to the Mundas and resemble them in physical appearance. Dark brown in complexion, they have thick noses and lips, broad chests, well developed hands and are short in stature. Since they claim to be Hindus and employ Brahman priests they are accepted as such, but their exact position in the Hindu caste hierarchy is not well defined. They do not appear to have fully assimilated the essential elements of Hinduism and completely jettisoned their tribal religion. Many among them still worship their own village deities. Their totemic exogamous clans are fast being forgotten and they have adopted the surname of 'Singh'. Their agricultural technique is not so advanced.

### *Cheros*

The Cheros who have Dravidian physiognomy and vary in colour, at one time ruled over the Gangetic provinces and claim to be Rajputs. They are divided into two sections; Barahazar and Tarahazar. The former rank as the higher and include most descendants to the former ruling families in Palamu. The social status of the Cheros was very high even in the Mughal period and they were given the rank of Mansabdars in Akbar's court. Their children were invested with the sacred thread by a Brahman priest at the time of marriage.

Agriculture is their original occupation. Nowadays they keep shop, do carting, work on roads or in coal mines and collect tasar, lac and catechu. They are on the whole, a proud race and have never forgotten that they were once a great people and that their descents are honourable ones. They are also found in the villages of Rohtas and in the Morang region.

### *Kharias*

The vast majority of the Kharias are found in the Ranchi and Singhbhum districts. The hill Kharias practice a crude type of shifting cultivation and hunt with bows and arrows, sticks and with spears. The Birhors are mostly found in the districts of Hazaribagh and usually live in huts made of twigs and leaves but during the rains in semi-permanent settlements. They sustain themselves by gathering wild forest produce, including honey and beewax, by hunting deer and other animals and by catching birds and monkeys.

### *Pahariyas*

The Sauria Pahariyas live in the inaccessible hilly region and are confined to Godda, Rajmahal and Pakur sub divisions. They do not posses any totemic clans. The Mal Pahariyas, a Hinduized section of Pahariya tribe, employ advanced methods of cultivation, invariably using plough and bullocks to till the small tablelands of the plateau on which they raise quite substantial dry crops.

### *Sarhul*

The most important festival for the tribals of Chotanagpur is Sarhul, which translates as the Sal tree blossom, held at the beginning of spring. Sal trees are worshipped in the sacred grove. Different tribes have different ways of celebrating this festival, but each one worships the spirit of the Sal tree to seek its blessings for a good harvest.

## Tribal Life and Culture

Each of the tribes in Bihar comprises a number of clans. Member of a particular clan are said to have descended from a common ancestor and bear the same surname. Hence sexual relations between two persons of the same clan are strictly prohibited. Almost all tribal villages in the state are inhabited by two or more clans. Seldom does one come across a one clan village.

### *Tribal Dwellings*

The villages of most of the tribes are usually situated near the forest, except for the Paharias who prefer the hills. The Birjias opt for the spurs of the highest hills, while the nomadic Birhors' semi-permanent dwellings are made of twigs and leaves. The Mundas and Oraons prefer the highest level ground, and the layout is not confined to any pattern, while the Santhals construct their houses on both sides of well-planned streets. The Ho villages are often situated on riverbanks.

### *Tribal Houses*

Most of the tribes live in mud thatched houses with baked tiles for roofs. often they have kitchen gardens that supply them vegetables, and a space for cattle. Unlike the haphazard dwellings of the Oraons, or the leaf houses of the Birhors, the housesof the Santhal (most predominant and prosperous among the tribes of Bihar, accounting for 37% of the tribal population) are the best planned, with separate apartments for the elderly.

### *Occupation*

Usually members of a tribal family work together in their plots, at times, accompanied by other villagers. Hunting is now rare as forests are fast disappearing. However Birhors can still be seen chasing monkeys with their nets. They consume its flesh while its skin, used as drumheads, is bartered. Other products sold or bartered by the tribals include rope, baskets, honey, cocoons, etc. Another interesting and no less popular product sold by the tribal people is the Hanaria, or the home-brewed rice beer also associated with tribal worship. During festive occasions, Hanaria flows like water. While it lends energy to the dancers, spectators consume it for its relaxing effects. Nowadays, tribal women come to the weekly haats (markets) with the Hanaria in big pots. Others sell Mahua, or can be seen stitching cups and plates of sal/pala leaves with tiny bits of sticks, to sell in the market. They can easily be identified by their dark complexion, elaborate tattoos, brass and silver ornaments. A good number of tribal men in Chotanagpur work in coal mines and other industries, while others are involved in agriculture.

### *Food*

The most important crop of tribal Bihar is paddy. The daily tribal fare consists of boiled cereals, millets, a curry of boiled vegetables or meat or edible roots, and tubers seasoned with salt and chillies. Surprisingly milk and milk products are completely absent from the tribal menu. As soon as a child is born, it is first given a sip of goat's milk and then the mother's milk. Once this is done, goat's milk is a taboo for the child, as it is believed to make it quarrelsome.

The staple food of the Aboriginals is boiled rice, which they eat with cooked pulse popularly known as dal. They uses pulses of different kinds which they produce in the kitchen-garden attached to their houses. They all eat goats, sheep, fowls and pigs, but very rarely do they drink milk. They are immensely fond of liquor and they brew a sort of rice-beer commonly known as Handia which is said to be highly refreshing and invigorating and has great importance in their religious rites.

### *Dress and Ornaments*

Simplicity and plainness are the twin characteristics of the dress of the tribal people. Most of them use a narrow piece of cloth tied round the waist. They keep two sets of dresses one for home and the other for outside wear. They wear dhotis and saris while going out. Tribal ,women are excessively found of ornaments. They have a craze for hansli (a kind of necklace made of silver) brass bracelets and silver earrings. They are famed for keeping their hair tidy by applying mustard or mouha oil and combing it regularly. Tattooing the forehead arms and legs is a common practice with them. This custom is originated from their age old belief in magic.

### *Marriage*

All the tribals attach a great deal of importance to marriage. Without marriage, nobody is regarded as a full member of the tribe. Manifold are the systems of marriage prevalent among the tribals of Bihar. The most notable of them all is Diku-Andi, which is arranged by go-betweens. Another important form is Raji-Khushi, in which boys and girls take the initiative. Marriage by capture is rare. Sometimes a young woman may intrude into the house of her beloved and refuse to leave it and thus force him to accept her as his bride. This form of marriage be called 'Marriage by intrusion'. There is a marriage by service in which poor youths who have no money to pay bride price serve the beloved's father for a certain period and thus obtain her consent to their marriage. In most of the tribal areas of the state, adult marriage prevails. In some parts of the state, the age of marriage has gone down under the impact of Hindu culture. Monogamy is the general rule, polygamy is not prohibited.

The primary unit of social organization among the tribes is the family which is made up of their unmarried children. Descent is reckoned in the male line, daughters being deprived of the right to patrimony. The women in tribal culture do not possess the right to landed property. They are entitled to the possession of all kinds of moveable property which they can dispose of whenever they like. They also have the right to participate in the proceedings of tribal councils. Divorce and widow re-marriage are permissible according to the tribal law. They will call for the approval of the panchayats.

## Tribal Religion

Religion plays an important part in the life of tribals. Their belief in gods and goddesses, in bhuts and spirits is engrained in them from their childhood. The worship of these supernatural beings is supposed to protect them from all evils and calamities, both natural and supernatural enhance the fertility of their community, domestic animals and agricultural fields. Religion also serves to engender and strengthen group consciousness and solidarity among them.

Every tribal village has in one of its corners a sacred grove called Jaher or sarma. The village has a priest, he is known variously as the pathan, the deuri, the naik, the kelo and so on. It is he who performs all worship on behalf of the whole village. He is chosen from among the most ancient families of the village for a term which varied from tribe to tribe and place to place. He is held in high esteem by the villagers and enjoys manifold privileges.

People living in tribal villages have a deep-rooted faith in evil spirits, demons and witches. This accounts for the prestigious position held by spirit doctors in tribal villages. They are popularly known as Mati or Ohja. These spirit doctors are believed to cure people of the diseases and miseries caused by malevolent spirits. They are also regarded as physicians possessing knowledge of medicinal herbs and capable of curing the diseased by means of herbs as well as magical incantations.

### The Holy Deities

The deities vary in number and strength. While the Hos have to appease only two village deities, Desauli and Jahira Buru, the Oraons have as many as ten deities and spirits. However, most of the tribes worship the Singh Bonga, or the Supreme Being. Besides the Sarna, most of the tribes have an ading, or sacred space reserved in the house for the family spirits. After a death in the family, the living call back 'the shade of the dead man' to reside in the ading together with the spirits of its other ancestors. The fear of displeasing dead ancestors haunts the tribal people. Most tribal societies believe that hostile spirits, the ghosts of the dead, or the breach of some taboo causes disease and malady. Appeasing ancestral spirits is vital to the tribal people who do not let up a chance to offer sacrifices to propitiate their ancestors.

### Religion of Santhal

Religion is in extricably woven into the social life of the

Santhals. It has strengthened the social unity of these tribal people, inspired in them a sense of social responsibility and endowed them with a strong consciousness of the righteousness. They have no temples or idols for purposes of worship. They look up on natural objects like hills and dales, trees and groves with great reverential awe. The Santhal Pantheon is essentially hierarchical in character. Singbonga is the Supreme Being and the omnipotent deity who ranks highest in this hierarchy. He is believed to be the creator and destroyer of all creatures inhabiting both the visible and invisible world. There is no idol to represent him nor any temple or shrine for his worship.

Inferior in status to Singbonga is the deity called Marang-Baru, the guardian of the Santhal village who is invoked on all ceremonial occasions. Other deities are Jaher-Buri and deities known as 'five and six'. All the deities are worshipped by the Naik, village priest. He is held in high esteem by the villagers and enjoys a number of privileges denied to common folk. The Santhals have an extra priest called Kadam Naik who performs such functions as are entrusted to him by the chief priest. The mati or Ojha is a spirit doctor possessing knowledge of the herbs as well as other malevolent spirits.

### *Religion of Oraons*

The Oraons believe in hosts of Gods, goddesses and the spirits of their ancestors. Dharmes is the omnipotent deity to them who creates and destroys the world whenever he likes, he is not worshipped in any shrine or temple. The Oraons have a sacred grove for the worship of numerous other deities who are said to belong to ten different grades. They are worshipped offerings and sacrifices by the village priest popularly known as the Pahan on behalf of the entire village.

In olden days the Pahan used to be the sacerdotal as well as the secular headman of the village. Later the office of the secular headman grew very important and was entrusted to another member of the same class to which the Pahan belonged. Sometimes the Pahan has to perform so many varied functions that he is given an assistant called the Pujar. A large number of the Oraons believe in witchcraft and worship Hindu gods. The worship of the Devi Mai seems to be greatly in vogue in most of the Oraon settlement. The Oraons have borrowed this practice from Hindus. They have assimilated it so fully in their religion that one is apt to mistake it for an indigenous custom. They worship goddess collectively on behalf of the entire village. In many Oraon villages a small mud-built house roofed with tiles for the worship of this Hindu deity.

### *Religion of Mundas*

The Mundas are polytheists and worship numerous deities and spirits. Singbonga is their Supreme Being, he is not merely a spectator of their deeds but possess the authority to punish evil-doers, he ranks highest in their Pantheon. The spirits of their ancestors are called Orabongako-the house hold gods. Hatubongako or the village gods occupy the most significant place, they are regarded as the guardians of the village and their help is invoked in agricultural and other economic operations. All the deities are worshipped by the village priest known as the Pahan on behalf of the entire community.

The presence of the spirits of the ancestors is very real to the Mundas. The Mundas really feel that they are constantly with them in the house. A few days after a man dies, his spirits is brought from the grave by an elaborate ceremony to live in the house which was his during his life time. To the Mundas, there are gods or spirits in many natural objects such as mountain-peaks, waterfalls and trees.

### *Religion of Hos*

The Ho religion resembles that of the other tribes in Bihar. The village priest of the Hos known as Deuri performs all religious rituals, on behalf of the entire community. He is held in high esteem by the villagers and enjoys numerous privileges. He is not required to propitiate malevolent spirits or deities, this task is assigned to the spirit doctor known as the Deona among the Hos.

## Tribal Festivals

In tribal life, there is a succession of festivals throughout the year which are connected with agricultural operations. Most of the important festivals among them are *Sarhul, Karma* and *Soharai.* Sarhul is the most popular of all tribal festivals. It is celebrated on the last day of *Baisakh* which corresponds to the month of April. It is observed at a time when sal trees are laden with flowers. It resembles the *Vasant-mahotsava* of the Hindus and may therefore be described as the spring festival of tribals. It is an occasion of great festivity and enjoyment for people of all ages. All night maidens and youths sing and dance to the accompaniment of the drum, while the old sit and enjoy the enchanting dance.

Another festival among the aboriginals is *Soharai or Banda parab,* which occurs in the month of Pous, celebrated shortly after the harvest of the rice-crop of the year. It may be called the harvest festival of tribals. On this occasion domestic animals are worshipped after being washed, anointed with oil and smeared with vermilion. The *Karma festival* is one which observed by the tribals as well as the non-tribals. There are sufficient grounds to believe that it is an imitation of the Hindu festival. On this occasion the tribal youths spend the whole night in singing and dancing. The song sung on this occasion narrate the legends of Karma and Dharma. The typically Hindu festivals of Holi and Durga puja are also celebrated with great enthusiasm by the Hindu tribals.

A unique tribal festival celebrated by the Oraon women once every twelve years is the Mukka Sendra. The women of this tribe dress up as males, wear turbans, and equip themselves with arrows, sticks, spears, axes or any convenient tool that may prove handy during a day long hunt when they are entitled to kill any animal, anywhere and carry it back home. No one is concerned about the ownership nor can one complain about his pet being killed or carried away. Armed women hunters move from village to village in search of prey. The origin of, or the purpose behind the festival is a mystery. Anthropologists suggest different views. According to some, the woman enact the tribal defense of the Rohtasgarh Fort that was attacked by the Afghans around the time of Sarhul, when the male members of the tribe were dead drunk. The women of the tribe took charge of the situation, donned male uniforms and rushed out to fight. Others believe that the festival is celebrated to drive away disease.

Most of the tribes have a huge expanse in the village set aside for festive dances, and the same ground is used for village meetings, or the Kulidrup (an assembly of tribal adults). The council of headmen is known as Manjhis, while Parcha is the collective chief of the various villages of the entire region. The Manjhis together with their subordinates, or Paramanikas,and the village priests keep an eye on the public morals of the village.

## Tribal Arts

Handaxes and blades hailing from the pre-historic era have been discovered in the region of Pathalgarwa. Some archaeologists have found cave paintings in the Isko village. Chotanagpur has drawn the attention of researchers as being an ancient site of continuous human habitation.

### *Dances*

The tribal people of Bihar posses a very rich and distinct dance form. Their dances in the forest, specially at dusk, performed under colorful flowering trees, such as the palaas, are captivatingly romantic. Indeed, it has been rightly said that dance and music are the very fabric of adivasi life without which life will not exist for them! A well-known folk-dancer in the north was Shri Bhikhari Thakur. His dances to the tune of Bhojpuri folk-songs was extremely popular.

There are three distinct types of folk dances in Bihar - the first—the religious dances prevalent in Mithila which are based of the songs of poets, the second, the 'Adivasi' tribal dances of South Bihar and third—the most important 'Chow' dances of 'Seraikala' and other regions in the South of Bihar.The religious dances of Mithila invoke the gods and goddesses with the help of the folk songs and musical instruments such as Dhol, Pipahi or a Shehanai-like wind-instruments, Sarangi, Mridang, Manjira, Dhak, Pakhwaj and Danka etc. The dancer performs the dance with little help of the instruments. The dances are Ramlila Nach, Keerthaniya Nach, Kunjavasi Nach, Naradi Nach, Bhagata Nach, Vidapat Nach, Puja Arti Nach.In the second type of dances done by Adivasi tribes are dances generally performed separately by men and women or sometimes by both men and women.

The dances by men are performed to the accompaniment of songs and musical instruments and they strictly adhere to the rhythm of the music. But, the women tuck their hands, sing and dance in their courtyards in circles. The folk dances of women are 'Jata', 'Jaten-Nach' Sama "Urakua Nach", Jhighiya nach. However, the only mixed group dance by men and women is the 'Saturi nach' of Mithila. Another curious dance is the 'Bacho nach' performed by a married couple, on the occasion of the birth of a child. These apart, there are many more religious folk dances in Bihar. And now, we come to the important dance form of Bihar - the Chau dance of Seraikala and Kharswan district which is a popular folk dance full of vitality and spontaneity. 'Chau' means 'mask' and all the dancers wear appropriate masks. As such the Chau dancers use songs by which they express their moods and themes by bodily gestures and poses. The usual instruments are Vina, flute and drum or Nagara. As the dancers wear masks, their individuality, sex and appearance are covered by the masks. The Chau dancer has to rely on his or her skill to evoke any sentiment feeling. Hence it is objective and universal in appeal. The movement begins with foot work, then the body movement and finally the whole body is used to express the story or the situation. The mask plays a vital role in this because each mask depicts a definite character as in Kathakali make-up. There are masks depicting human beings, animals, birds etc. Long ago these masks were made of wood; but now they are made of bamboo, pumkin, cloth, paper and clay and they are coated profusely with pleasing paints.

The Dasara festival is during Durga Pooja or 'Dasara'. The dances are mainly by men visit the villages and dance to the accompaniment of Kasa - 'that' or disc, 'jalthumbi' and Mandar drum in circles. Often they show their prowess by skilful solo dances. This dance is called 'Dasai Nritya'. There are other dance such as 'Jhika Nritya' and ,Danga Nritya' performed during 'Baparva' (during holidays) and also on festive occasions such as birth and marriage celebrations.

### *Chhau dance*

The Chhau dance form of Bihar is a popular folk dance full of vitality and spontaneity. The Chhau dance is so called because the chhau or mask is an essential feature of this art. The word 'chhau' is generally traced to the Sanskrit root, chhaya, meaning shade. The techniques of Chhau dance incorporated certain basic steps and garts which seems to have stemmed from the pharikhanda system of exercise, which has always been an important part of the training of the Sipahis, or Pharikhanda. The performers all hold swords and shields in their hands while doing the exercises.

Fine stages and lighted by brilliant display of torches, lanterns and many flickering oil lamps, these dances are done in solo, duet and dance drama form .The musical accompaniment for Chhau is provided by the Nagra, a huge little drum, Dhol, a cylindrical drum, and Shehnais or reed pipes. The tunes are based mainly on the ragas of Hindustani music. Usually two distinct airs are used in a dance item and when the melody changes, so does the rhythm of the dance. The steps of the dance are governed by patterns of rhythmic syllables played on the drums, and any change of tempo is prefaced with a katan, a rhythmic flourish played three times in succession. Performed by men and boys, the item never lasts more than 7 to 10 mts each, for it is difficult to dance longer wearing a mask.

Chhau dance follows certain fundamental traditions of the classical modes as detailed in the ancient treatises. In this, therefore three main elements of the classical dance, namely Raga or melody, Bhava or mood, tala or rhythmic timing are found. In Chhau dances, there are many dance forms depicting nature and animal world such as Mayura Nritya or Peacock dance, Sagara nritya or Ocean dance, Sarpa Nritya or serpent dance etc. The Harvest dances and also stories from Ramayana, Mahabharatha are depicted quite often. The themes of the dance are taken from mythology, everyday life, aspects of nature and at times the dance is simply the delineation of a mood, state or condition.

All three traditions of Chhau dance carry what may be called an elemental pulse. In no other classical dance of India is the pounding of the rhythm so intense, so full-bodied. Here the dancer employs his entire body and his entire being, as a single unit, as his language. And this language is at once poetic and powerful. The legs in particular offer a wide range of studied extensions and sweeps, and the torso emphatic turns and thrusts. Even though the face is hidden behind the mask, the mask uncannily expresses what the body feels or wishes to communicate.

The principle occasion for the performance of Chhau in Mayurbhanj, as in Seraikella is the Chaitra Parva, which comes about the middle of April every year. Chaitra is the month for dancing and on the 25th of Chitra month, the dances start after invocation of Lord Shiva. The leading exponents of the Chhau in Saraikella have been the royal princes in Mayurbhanj, the lower classes, the rabble and Purulia farmer, tillers and the like. Though in recent years women have taken to the Saraikella and the Mayurbhanj version, mostly as a professional accomplishment, the Chhau remains by virtue of its very character, a conspicuously male-dominated art.

*Folk-music*

Folk-music is an integral part of daily life all over rural Bihar. The songs of shepherds grazing their herd, riders hauling produce or goods on their bullock-carts, or men-folk gathered under the shade of a banyan or peepal tree during summer or around a fire in winter, fill the air with their sweet and haunting sounds. Meanwhile, women also, milling wheat or maize on a hand-mill- "the chakki" or "jaanta" entertain themselves by singing while doing the chore.

Many songs are associated with the seasons, festivala or rituals. During the monsoon season as the much need gentle rains come down, young women on their swings sing songs called, "kajari", "jhoomar", and "barahmasa" (roughly translated, the Four Seasons!) "Chaiti" and "baisakhi" are songs of the hot summer season. Folk-songs are an integral part of the chhath festival. Also, during the spring season, the festival of Holi, (the rites of spring) is associated with its own raucous songs, the "phag" or "phagua" with the accompaniment of a huge drum, "the dhaal".

A wedding is enveloped with folk songs, each distinct for the many parts of the ceremony, and climaxed by the heart-rending songs accompanying the bride's departure from her old home where she had spent her entire life till that time, leaving all her kith and kin behind for her new and unknown home, the home of the bride-groom. These are the songs of "bidai". It is indeed a rare soul who is not moved at the lyrics and sounds of these songs. Another kind of folk-song, and a joyful one, is"the sohar", which celebrates the birth of a baby. Some recently written songs, particularly in Bhojpuri (the language of Champaran, Saran, Bhojpur and also of eastern UP), have acquired the status of folk songs.

They are "firangia" written by Manoranjan Prasad Sinha (late Principal of Rajendra College, Chhapra); and "batohia" written by Babu Raghubir Narayan. The enormous success of the first Bhojpuri film, "Ganga Maiya Tohe Piyari Chhadaibo", has contributed much to popularize folk-songs of Bihar. Indeed, there are many recording studies at present in Patna which record these songs for commercial purposes. One of the leading exponent of Bihari folk-songs is Shrimati Bindhyavasani Devi of Patna.

### *Folk-drama*

Folk-drama always had a place in the Bihari culture. Examples of this can be found in the ram-lilas enacted at various times in the year and also episodes from the epic Mahabharta. Also, particularly in the north, during the marraige season, light hearted performances of "netuas" can be seen. "Bahurupiyas", prevalent more extensively in West Bengal, can also be found performing in villages and on city streets, particularly in the south.

## Crafts of Tribals

Bihar is a mind boggling repository of handicrafts. A cornucopia of traditional crafts that enjoy universal appeal. A rich treasure trove of native culture as seen by the craftsmen—through his colors, shapes figures and patterns. An ageless heritage. A time bond tradition. The handicrafts heritage of Bihar is fulsome and vast. It covers a variety of material's—from stone, wood, leather, metal to textiles, lacquer and glass. Today even as the onslaught of modernisation hits the artisan and patronage of traditional crafts dwindles, the crafts have survived, miraculously.

The artisans of Bihar have been very skilful in creatings articles from local materials. Baskets, cups and saucers made from bamboo-strips or cane reed are painted in vivid colors are common articles found in Bihari homes. A special container woven out of sikki grass in the north, the "pauti", is a sentimental gift that accompanies a bride when she leaves her home after her wedding. Indeed, for the bride, next to the wooden container for "sindoor" (vermillion), namely, the "sinhora", this is a precious gift that she treasures for her entire life. The weavers of Bihar have been practising their trade for centuries. Among their products in common use are the cotton dhurries and curtains. They are produced by artisans in central Bihar, particularly in the Patna and Bihar-Sharif areas. These colourful sheets, with motifs of Buddhist artifacts, pictures of birds, animals, and/or flowers, gently wafting in the air through doors and windows, blown by a cool summer breeze, used to be one of the most soothing sights as one approached a home or an office!

Woolen carpets are woven in the Obra area of Aurangabad district. The weavers of the north, particularly in the Madhubani and Darbhanga area, under the influence of Gandhiji, beginning around 1917, after the succesful Champaran satyagraha, started spinning cotton on their charkha and producing Khadi cloth by the "miles"! This practice continues. After independence the weavers were organized into Weavers Co-Operatives. Their product is sold through outlets of the Khadi Gramodyog Bhavan.

Bhagalpur is well known for its seri-culture, manufacture of silk yarn and weaving them into lovely products. This silk is of a distinct and special type. It is known as the tussah or tusser silk. Besides Bhagalpur, other areas in India well-known as centers of silk weaving are - Kashmir in the north; and in the south, Bangalore and Tanjore.

Biharis, not well-known for self-promotion and entrepreneurship, did not exploit the commercial potential of these products for a long time. After independence, Shri Upendra Maharathi, originally from Orissa and himself a gifted artist, made a great deal of effort to revive and popularise Bihari arts and crafts and bring it commercial success. With support from the first Chief-minister of Bihar, Shri Shri Krishna Sinha, he was very successful. The result was the formation of the Bihar State Cottage Industries and Handicrafts Board. This organization supported the artisans and sold their products through their own outlets, The Bihar State Cottage Industries Emporium, located thoroughout Bihar and also at New Delhi, close to Connaught Place on the Baba Khadak Singh Marg among the emporia of various states.

### ***Paintings***

Popular art is the expression of people's sensitivity. Importance of popular art reside in the fact that it simultaneously creates a form of artistic expression while revealing the psychology of the society from which it emerges, reflecting its moral values and customs.

#### *Mithila arts*

The people of Mithila in northern Bihar stick to their centuries old custom and orthodox belief that the land of Mithila or Mithilanchal is holier when compared to other parts of Bihar. The belief possibly stems from the historic fact that Mithila was first to be brought under the influence of Aryan culture. and to this day the Mithilis take pride in their continuity of language, custom and culture. They are known to adhere to the minutest details in rituals from birth to death according to the dictates of the Shastras.

#### *Tradition wall painting*

The tradition of painting walls for beautification of dwellings in Mithila is believed to have survived from the epic period. Tulsidas gives a vivid account of Mithila decorated for the marriage of Sita with Ram. These decorations are mythological murals, added with deities of Hindu pantheon, besides regional flora and fauna. The earthquake of 1988 devastated parts of Darbhanga and Madhubani. Perhaps, the greatest damage caused was in the palace complex, replete with paintings done two centuries ago, as per the Mithila traditions.

The land of Mithila is covered by the present districts of Champaran, Saharsa, Muzaffarpur, Vaishali, Darbhanga, Madhubani, Samastipur, parts of Monghyr, Beguserai, Bhagalpur and Purnea. Madhubani is the heartland where the paintings are more profuse than elsewhere.

The ceremonial folk paintings - popularly identified as famous Madhubani paintings - are the exclusive monopoly of women artists, passing down for generations from mother to daughter. The girl learns to play with the brush and colours at an early age which finally culminates in the Kohbar (nupital room), which acquires great sanctity in the social life of Mithila. All religious ceremonies relating to the marriage are performed in the Kohbar.The deep (earthen lamp - a symbol of happy conjugal life) is kept burning in all through for four days.

The Kohbar is replete with paintings based on mythological, folk themes, and tantric symbolism, The paintings in this chamber are designed to bless the couple. The central theme of all paintings are love and fertility, though the approach may vary. It can commence with the story of Sita's marriage or Krishna - Radha episode with the ecstatic circle in which he leads the gopis. Maithilis are Sakti worshippers with the influence of Tantric rituals and so Siva-Sakti, Kali, Durga, Ravana and Hanuman also appear in their murals. Symbols of fertility and prosperity like fish, parrot, elephant, turtle, sun, moon, bamboo tree, lotus, etc are more prominent. The divine beings are positioned centrally in the frame while their consorts or mounts or simply their symbols and floral motifs forms the background. The human figures are mostly abstract and linear in form, the animals are usually naturalistic and are invariably depicted in profile. It beings with the flow of the brush without any preliminary sketching. Though natural colours and twings have given way to brushes and artificial paints, the subject of Madhubani paintings remain unchanged.

*Madhuani paintings*

Madhuani paintings have emerged as a commercial activity where children can be seen engaged in arranging the hand crafted paper or fetching the colours. The commercialisation of Maithili art took place in 1962 when an artist touring this village was attracted by the murals. He persuaded the women to paint in their traditional way on paper. This was a great success and a ticket to trade. Since then the painting medium has diversified. Wall paintings were transferred to hand made paper (which was of poster size) and gradually it preyed for other mediums and motifs like greeting cards, dress materials, sunmica etc.

In the beginning, home made natural colours were obtained from plant extracts like henna leaves, flower, bougainvillea, neem, etc. These natural juices were mixed with resin from banana leaves and ordinary gum in order to make the paint stick to the painting medium. Home made paints, though cheap, was time consuming and produced less than the requirement. The solution was to switch to the synthetic colours avaibale aplenty in the market. Now colours come in powdered form, which are then mixed with goat's milk. However, black continues to be obtained from the soot deposits by the flame of diya, dissolved in gum.

The colours are usually deep red, green, blue, black, light yellow, pink and lemon. They created mood and hence played an important role. For instance, energy and passion find expression through the use of red and yellow, as monochrome crashed over large surfaces of the painting. Concentration of energy and the binding force is best reflected in red while green governs the natural leaves and vegetation. The Brahmins prefer the very bright hues while the Kayasthas opt for mutted ones. In another class called the Harijan style of painting, hand made paper is washed in cowdung. Once the paints are ready, two kinds of brushes are used - one for the tiny details made out of bamboo twigs and the other for filling in the space which is prepared from a small piece of cloth attached to a twig.

### *Sujuni*

The first mention of a crafts similar to " Sujuni" comes in the description of bed spreads and wall hanging of uzbeks, they were popular as 'SUJUNI' (from persion and Tadjik ward for needle). Sujuni is a labour intensive but simple embroidery. Tiny running stitches cover the entire fabric, which is traditionally white or red, with the main outlines of the motive high lighted in a thick chainstitch. Filling stitches inside the motive are done in coloured thread, those outside are done in white or the colour of the base fabrics. The fabric is generally lined with a finer muslin backing before embroidery , giving a quilted effect to the design . Motibs generally cover the gamut of figures, flower and founa, done in naif pictorial style, often illustrating folk look and religious iconography.

### *Sikki Works*

The sikki grass articles made by the women of North Bihar are entirely different from anything else you see in any other part of the country. Sikki seems to grow almost anywhere in this region, even by the road side , tall and rush with a lovely golden shade, it is most attractive. It is out only once after the rain and the cut pieces are stored for use throughout the year. As it is intimatily connected with important ceremonies and rituals, it has evidently come down from very ancient times.

The coiling technique, which is the oldest, used in sikki. The common long grass is wired and stitched together with the pasikki, dyes in several different shades, using a thick needle called takua. Espacially in constructing the sclespturelque a forms, the whole build up is made by the coils. There are human figures, animals, birds.

Tasels are used for extra embellishment and brilliantly hoed wings of the betle or coloured buttons to emphasise eyes and ears. Every functional item such as a box for keeping cloths,spices toilet articles are all wrought out of sikki in multitude of shapes in dazzling colours.

### Bamboo Work

Bihar is greatly noted for its bamboo work. Bamboo sends itself to multifarious uses. The use of cut bamboo as a containers to drink water is an ancient practsice; as also simple scoops for kitchen use. Large containers far storing grain are a comman sight. In fact the rural people in remote, bamboo graving are as still keep their precious possessions in bamboo basket with side.

Against this tradition, commendable experimentes work has been done in Patna to adopt these very objecte to modern use, In fact a whole house can very neatly be filled up through bamboo articles. Finely shaped lamps and lanterns, elegant furniture, complete tableware, travel kit, almost anything seems possible to get from the bamboo.

### Wood Inlay

Woodinlay is one of Bihar's ancient industries. The inlay continues to be done with different materials, metal, ivory and, stage horn chips of woods in other grains or tints are used to get varied effects to great advantage. Apart from decorative pieces like wall hanging , tabletops, trays, a number of utility articles are also ornamented with inlay work. Patna also manufactures articles in deaper work utilising waste pieces of wood. The old skill, the experienced eye, the innate taste of the vetran craftsman is seen here in the marvellous objects that are turned out in the way of trays, boxes and other articles far the household. The designs are mostly geometrical but very fine and colourful.

### *Clay Toys*

Bihar has a wealth of clay toys, all in abstract folk style. Some of these are astonishingly reminiscent of the ancient excavated Mauryan pieces. There is a whole away of various kinds of elephant. They are delightfully simple, yet so alive some have even vivacious expressions. In Bihar, the making of clay toys as of images is closely connected with seasonal and religious festivals, and special toys are made for each occassion. Darbhanga has special clay toys. There is a special highly decorated elephant with clay ornaments on the head and over the ears and a big bowl on its back. This is kept on the roof of the house when a marriage is taking place.

### *Tikuli Art*

This art originated from the gold foiled Tikuli, bindis with a glass base, adoring the forehead of the Queens and Aristocrats ladies of yore. Today hard board, enamel paints and Madhubani motils are used to create produce for interior decorations and utility items like tablemats and coaster. Making of the hard board plates follows a Japanese technique.

### *Tapper Mats*

Tapper mats are made on a large scale in Palamau district, Bihar. Tapper is rather like jute, taken out of the sun hemp plant. The usual method of soaking and using pressure is used to extract the fibre which is then spun into yarn and used for making tapper. This is said do be more durable than jute fibre. The yarn is dyed generally in indigenous colours which used to transport grain on any heavy stuff. Today a number of article, of modern use are made like travel kit and hand bags, some of them quite, stylish looking. Hazaribagh and Purnea also produce tapper.

### *Metalware*

The metalware in India may be roughly divided into the religious images, ritualistic items and objects of utility. The metal used are brass, copper and bell metal. The raw material is obtained either through smelting minerals or more often by melting old scrap and how more often through sheet metal. The shopping of an object is done either by beating with a hammer the ingot or sheet metal to the approximate shape while heating, or by pouring the malted metal into a mould made of eleey for ordinary ware, wox for more delicate objects. Polishing is done by vigorous rubbing either by hard or if it is a plate by feet, using a rag or by machine where power is used.

### *Mask*

Mask making is an exciting craft, for it calls for something more than more workmanship. The dance in Bihar is highly sophisticated and uses masks. The mask one may say mirrors the essence of the dance, for the totality of the emotions is crystallized in it. Among the paper mask of Bihar, apart from the figures, there are others of quite distinctive variety. As mask is an essential item in certain presentations, mask making has been a heredity vocation. But the various thing is that traditionally only those who were dancers were permitted to make their masks. Originally, they were made of wood, later of bamboo, then pumpkin shells and now of papier mask.

# 3

# Tribes of Chhattisgarh

The state of Chhattisgarh is spread over an area of 135194 square kilometers and comprises of sixteen districts of Koriya, Surguja and Jashpurnagar to the north, Korba, Bilaspur, Janjgir Chhampa and Raigarh in the North central, Kawardah, Rajnandgaon, Durg, Raipur, Dhamtari and Mahasamnd in the centre and Kanker, Bastar and Dantewara in the South. According to the 1991 Census, the total population residing in the Chhattisgarh was 1.761 crores, which was 2.1 percent of the population of India. The state of Chhattisgarh is carved out of 30.49 percent of the land area and 26.6 percent of the population of the undivided Madhya Pradesh.

The state of Chhattisgarh has 20378 village of which 19,720 are inhabited villages. The state have a total of 96 tehsils and 146 janpad panchayats or blocks. Out of the total 465 cities and towns of the undivided Madhya Pradesh, 95 cities & towns is in Chhattisgarh, including 6 Class 12 towns. The Population of Chhattisgarh was 1.761 crores in 1991 and has a population density of 130 persons per square kilometer. The new state had an urbanisation rate of 17.4 percent in 1991, much lower than that of Madhya Pradesh, which was 25.3 percent. Of the five main rajbhogi towns of undivided Madhya Pradesh, Chhattisgarh has one, Raipur.

As per the 1991 census, the state of Chhattisgarh has 28.6 percent of the total rural population of the undivided

Madhya Pradesh. The population of Chhattisgarh is notable for the high proportion of Scheduled Tribes and for specific Sects primarily constituted of Schedule Castes. Of the total population of Chhattisgarh, tribals constitute at least 37.1%, which is a significantly high percentage. In the last few decades, the demographic profile of tribal dominated areas has undergone a change. This is a cause for concern as it represents large-scale intrusion of non tribals in tribal areas. This changing demographic profile is strongly evident in Bastar, where the proportion of tribals has decreased in the last few decades.

The tribal areas of Chhattisgarh have witnessed several rebellions starting from 1774 onwards against the intrusion by outsiders, primarily the British, in the domain of traditional rights and the tribal way of life. Interestingly, since the 17th century, the social history of the non-tribal areas of Chhattisgarh has been marked by reform movements such as the Satnam sect. Kabir Panthis and the Movements of share croppers and agricultural labour. Despite presence of a high tribal population and religious reform movements, the region is also the domain of classic Hindu culture (although in some rituals the impact of tribal rituals can be identified), in which the cult of Ram assumes an essential and central role. Impact of this domination in evident and has its manifestations in the growth of sectarian formations is contemporary politics.

In India, the combined population of the Scheduled Castes and Tribes is 23.6% of the total population and for Madhya Pradesh; this figure rises to 37.1%. The combined population of Scheduled Castes and Tribes in Chhattisgarh is significantly higher at 44.7% and this is largely due to a high proportion of tribal population, Although the Scheduled Castes do not constitute a very high proportion of the total population they are critical for understanding the social history of Chhattisgarh, which has been deeply influenced and effected by the religious reform movements.

## Tribal Population

The scheduled tribes, with a population of over fifty seven lakhs constitute 32.5 percent of the State's population as per the 1991 Census. Almost 98.1% of this population lives in the rural areas and only 1.9% lives in urban Chhattisgarh. Amongst the larger states in India, Chhattisgarh has the highest percentage of population of people from the Scheduled Tribes. However, Madhya Pradesh is still the home to the largest population of Scheduled Tribes in India.

The Scheduled Tribes are concentrated in the southern, the northern and the north-eastern districts. The highest concentration is in the erstwhile Bastar district. The new district of Dantewara has 79 percent tribals followed by Bastar (67 percent) Jashpur (65 percent), Surguja (57 percent) and Kanker (56 percent).

The Gonds at 55.1 % form the largest proportion within the tribal population. They are distributed almost equally, in urban and rural areas. The Oraons the Kawars, the Halbis, the Bharias or Bhumiars, the Bhattras and the Napesias also form a substantial portion of the tribal population. Thirty other Scheduled Tribes have small population residing in various pockets across Chhattisgarh. The Gonds are concentrated in the hilly parts of Southern Chhattisgarh but are also spread across most districts, whereas the Baigas, Bharias, Korwas and Napesias occupy only specific pockets. The Bhattras, Kolams and Rasjas largely live in Bastar and the Kamars in Raipur. The Halba tribe inhabit parts of Bastar, Raipur and Rajnandgaon and the Oraons live in Surguja and Raigarh districts.

There are 9500 villages, or 48 percent of all inhabited villages, which have more than half their population belonging to the tribal groups. Thirty percent of all inhabited villages have more than three fourths population from the scheduled tribes. Tribals constitute 100 percent of the population in 1262, or 6.4 percent villages. The districts of Raipur, Durg and Janjgir Chhampa have less than twenty percent tribals.

## Tribal Communities

There are a total of 42 tribes in Chhattisgarh, principal among then being the Gond tribe. Besides, a large population of Kanwar, Brinjhwar, Bhaina, Bhatra, Uraon, Munda, Kamar, Halba, Baiga, Sanwra, Korwa, Bharia, Nageshia, Manghwar, Kharia and Dhanwar tribe are also found in the State.

### *Bastar Tribes*

Bastar, the land of tribes and natural resources, is the largest tribal district of the newly formed Indian state of Chhattisgarh. About 70% of the total population of Bastar comprises of tribals, which is 26.76% of the total tribal population of Chhattisgarh. The major tribes of the Bastar region are the Gond, Abhuj Maria, Bhatra, Halbaa, Dhurvaa, Muria and BisonHorn Maria. The Gonds of Bastar are one of the most famous tribes in India, known for their unique Ghotul system of marriages. Gonds are also the largest tribal group of central India in terms of population.

The Bastar tribes of Chhattisgarh are the following:

— Gonds

— Bison Horn Maria

— Muria

— Abhuj Maria

— Halbaa

— Bhatra

— Dhurvaa

The tribes of Bastar region are known for their unique and distinctive tribal culture and heritage in all over the world. Each tribal group in Bastar has their own distinct culture and enjoy their own unique traditional living styles. Each tribe has developed its own dialects and differ from each other in their costume, eating habits, customs, traditions and even worship different form of god and goddess. A large number of Bastar tribals are still living in deep forests and avoid mixing with outsiders in order to protect their own unique culture. The tribes of Bastar are also known for their colorful festivals and arts and crafts. The Bastar Dussehra is the most famous festival of the region. The tribals of Bastar were also amongst the earliest to work with metal and have expertise in making beautiful figurines of tribal gods, votive animals, oil lamps, carts and animals. Bastar is also blessed with exceptional natural beauty and promises to be a favorite destination for researchers, anthropologists, wildlife enthusiasts and nature lovers.

### *Gonds*

Gonds who call themselves 'Koytoria' ,the largest tribal group in the state in terms of population. Though Gonds can be found almost in all the districts of the state , there are two important concentration regions. The first is the central Madhya Pradesh and the other region is the southern part of the Chhattisgarh state — i.e., Bastar Division.

More than 20 % of the Gonds in Chhattisgarh state are in Bastar district. In Bastar the three main subcastes of Gonds are Maria, Muria, and Dorla. The name Gond is extracted from the Telugu word 'Konda' which means hill. Agriculture, collecting minor forest produce, forging metal goods in cottage industries, fishing, hunting, other primary sector activities are the main activities of Gonds. Marriages are preferred within the blood relations mostly according to Hindu rites and customs. Sometimes mock elopements are also arranged.

Gonds have pro-fertility mentality. Divorces, remarriages, widow marriages, marriages with the wives of the brothers and between brothers and sisters are common. In the event of the death of the husband the widow can marry the younger brother and in all cases he need not be unmarried.She also can marry the elder brother of the deceased husband or any one else. Dowary system is also existing among them- But the groom has to pay bridal price to the father of the girl and this system gives respect to women and held their position on top.

*Halbaas*

The Halbaas are spread over Madhya Pradesh, Chhattisgarh, Maharashtra and Orissa. In Chhattisgarh even though they are found in the districts of Raipur and Durg, they are mostly found in Bastar district. Mainly there are three types of Halbas—Chhatisgarhia, Maratia and Bastaria. The Halbaas of Bastar district have affinities with the tribals of the Warangal district of Andhra Pradesh. They are probably known as Halbaas because they used to use 'Hal'. e.g., the plough—which means they are primarily agriculturists. Now the Halbaas can be found to be enguaged in many other activities also.

Halbaas are one of the developed and rich tribal groups mainly due to the fact that they are land owners and some are land lords also. Halbaas enjoy high 'local caste status' amongst the tribals in the state. Because of their costume,dilect and social activities makes them different from Gonds tribes. Their dilect is a raw mixing of the languages Marati, Oriya and Chhattisgarhi.

*Abhuj Maria*

The Abhuj Maria tribals are one of the main Gonds tribes. They live in interior forest of Narayanpur Tehsil of Bastar districts. The area in which they inhabited is known as Abhuj Maria region which has been spread over 1500 sq miles which is a dense forest area.

The Abhuj Marias are hill Marias who are virtually living in isolation. They used to dreaded by the out siders since the Abhuj Marias could shoot down the strangers with their arrows. Since they are living in isolation, keeping themselves away from the touch of the outerworld and leading a savage life, their traditional culture, moral living values and social security has not yet been disturbed. They are one of the rare tribal groups of India living in this traditional way.

In the matter of dress their needs are very small and money they do not covet at all. Both men and women wear only a piece of cloth round the waist , and for ornament several iron rings , some times as many as 20 round their necks. Small brass rings are sometimes strung on the large iron rings. Ear rings are commonly worn , when women being found with 14 holes bored in her ear and two rings in each of some the holes. These people are not cleanly in their habits , and even when a Maria does bathe he does not wash his solitary garments but leaves it on the bank. When drinking from a stream they do not take up water in their hands but put their mouth down to it like cattle.

### *Bison Horn Marias*

The Bison Horn Maria tribals is another type of Gonds tribes. Their culture and living ways is almost similar to Abhuj Marias. They reside in the south of Indravati river , Jagdalpur Tehsil. The Bison Horn Marias adorn the bison horns during their dancing rituals. They collect minor forest produce. The Bison Horn Marias do not plough the earth as it would mean inflicting pain on her body.Pointed wood pieces are used for piercing earth crust for cultivation. Stone implements are used for harvesting produce. They perform the marriages through Ghotul System. Divorces and remarriages are common but adultery is not allowed. Marriages amongst the offsprings of blood relations are common.

### *Murias*

Murias are another sub caste of Gonds tribes found in Bastar district. They live in the Narayanpur and Kondagaon Tehsils of Bastar district. Unlike Abhuj Marias who live in dense forests, the Murias live in Plains and are a lot more developed in comparison to the primitive Abhuj Marias. The economy of the Murias is based on agriculture and collection of the forest produce.Rice growing is common.Minor Forest Produce is consumed as well as sold also.

There are several totems and several gods of villages and tribal sub-groups. Murias have their own superstitious and sorcery practises. There is no functional division of castes ie Barbers, Cobblers, Weavers or Washermen. The tribals of this area have their own socio-legal hierarchy of tribal administration. Murias have started practising sedantary cultivation also. The Murias prefer ' Mahua' drinks rather than medicines for their ailments. The tribals of this area is famous for their 'Ghotuls' where the prospective couples do the 'dating' and have free sex also.

### *Bhatras*

The Bhatras are one of the major tribal groups of the Chhattisgarh found mostly in Bastar and Raipur divisions of the state. Bhatras are known for their unique costumes and traditions but their origin is still a mystery. Bhatras have three sub-groups - Pit, Amnet and Sebhatra. Women folks enjoy high status in the society and the Bhatra girls have full freedom to choose their husbands or live as wife with the person they like with or without marriage. As far as their eating habits are concerned, like other tribals they too prefer liquor consumption, fruits and animal food.

The Bhatras practice shifting cultivation type of agriculture and don't have private lands. Other major activity of the Bhatras is collecting minor forest produces and selling that to the traders of Bastar. Most of them work as farm or household workers for their survival. They love intoxicating Mahua drinks and the Mahua tree is so much revered by them that the marriage ceremonies can't be completed without taking rounds of this tree. Like other tribes, Bhatras too are superstitious and believe in magic and sorcery.

*Dhurvaa*

The Dhurvaas are one of the most important tribal groups in Bastar district. Also known as Parjaas (the public), they rank only second in the hierarchy of the Bastar tribals after Bhatras. To prove their high status among the tribals of the region, they preferred to be called as Dhurvaas that connotes the status of some type of Mukhia (the Village Chief). They are very caste conscious people and do not mix with tribes of lower status. The practice of polygamy, having more than one wife, is quite common among them. Like other tribal societies, the women of Dhurvaas too enjoy high status and are liable for most of family maintenance. Normally, men are lethargic and work less except hunting, agriculture and protection of the family.

The primary activities of Dhurvaas mainly include agriculture, hunting, crafts with cane and gathering minor forest products which they sell to traders at a throw away price. Dhurvaa tribes are very brave and can do anything to protect their prestige and dignity. Also, they are very religious and worship many village goddesses. Feasts and animal sacrifices are very much part of their social life and sacrifices of goats, pigs, ducks, chicken and coconuts are made to appease the village goddess. Marriage system is quite similar to other tribes and their women folks enjoy better status in the society. The tobacco and liquor consumption (Mahuva drinks) is a must for celebrations and evening activities of Dhurvaas and are used by men and women, young and old, alike.

## Social Change among Tribals

Chhattisgarh primarily due to its large tribal population has historically not been a part of the mainstream and has therefore remained underdeveloped. Critical indicators for education and health have remained low. However, as stated above, the region was influenced by mainstream traditional Hindu culture as the overaching organising principle despite the presence of a large percentage of Scheduled Castes and Tribes. This oppressive, hierarchical social and religious order was not accepted, and from the 17th century onwards, the social history of Chhattisgarh is marked by the process of questioning and protests in the form of a number of socio-religious reform movements. These movements established a tradition of protest and have played a critical role in creation of the identity of Chhattisgarh, Initiated by sects like the Satnam Panth, the kabirpanthis and the Raedasis spread over all over Chhattisgarh, they carried the message of equality. Often the spread of these movement was within the boundaries of Chhattisgarh and therefore these movements contributed indirectly towards creating a regional consciousness.

An illustrative case would be the Satnam Panth, which emerged as sectarian formation, primarily reconstituting a small number of dalit groups by incorporating them as Satnamis, The Satnam Panths was an attempt to negotiate and cope with the cultural and economic processes in Chhattisgarh in the nineteenth century. It was a new sect, formed primarily amongst the poors of Chhattisgarh in the second decade of the nineteenth century and was led by Ghasidas, a humble farm worker. This community constituted a significant proportion, a little less then one sixth, of the total population of Chhattisgarh. They either owned land or were sharecroppers and farm workers.

The new sect was given the name of Satnam and its followers were expected to believe only in the formless - Satnam or the true name. Gradually, the followers of this sect were given the name satnamis. Satnamis abstain from meat, liquor, tobacco, certain vegetables and red pulses. Satnam Panth rejected the deities and idols of the Hindu pantheon. The panth preaches a casteless order. Guru Ghasidas initiated a Guru parampara in the sect, which became hereditary. The main religious centres of the sect in Chhattisgarh are Bhandar and Girod.

In the nineteenth century a new system of property rights and revenue collection known as the malgujari settlement was intorduced in Chhattisgarh. The new system was implemented with the sole purpose of expropriation and exploitation of marginal farmers, sharcropers and farm servants by the upper caste Malgujars. Satnam Panth and its followers responded to this exploitative system through various strategies.

In several cases the Satnamis deserted villages or continued with the process of Lakhabatta or the periodic redistribution of land, despite the implementation of the new system. Their united challenge to the upper caste Malgujars over the issues of rent and loss of land in the last decade of the nineteenth century was a reflection of the solidarity of Satnamis . This form of protest and response to the new system or property rights and malgujari settlements was widespread among the Satnamis of Chhattisgarh.

The primary concern of the Anglo Maratha politics in the Nineteenth century was of expropriation and consolidation of power. Guru Ghasidas the founder of the Satmani sect realised this. He believed that the politics of the Anglo-Marathas was deprived of morality. He worked towards uniting all downtrodden persons to morally oppose the immoral politics of the British The people of Chhattisgarh realised the potential threat of the British and were terror struck by the exploitative nature of their policies. Despite this, they were unable to unite under one flag to oppose the British. It was at this juncture that Ghasidas made efforts to unite the people of Chhattisgarh through the ideology of equality and non-violence.

Other sects emerged in response to the hierarchical social order and linked Chhattisgarh to other social reform movements in the country. However the regional specificities of these sects remained unaltered.

Kabir Panthis for example, are largely recruited from dalits and have a substantial presence in Chhattisgarh. The followers of this sect adhere to the teachings and principles of Kabir, the revolutionary social reformer saint poet of the sixteenth century. The centres of Kabir Panth activities are monasteries which are placed in the charge of Mahants. In Chhattisgarh, Kabir Panthi monasteries are in Kudurmal, Kharsia, Champa, Hardi, Bangoli, Banni, Dhamdha, Panda, Tarai and Ratanpur. The Kabir Panth does not believe in caste hierarchies. However in contemporary times the Panth has been divided along caste lines. The only time that they do not adhere to caste hierarchies is in the presence of the Chief Guru on the birth anniversary of Kabir. All who desire to become members of the Panth are required to renounce polytheism and to acknowledge their belief in only one god. The Kabir Panth of Chhattisgarh are descendents of Dharmadasa, one of the disciples of Kabir who established the Panth in Chhattisgarh. There fore the branch of the Kabir Panth in Chhattisgarh is also known as Dharmadasa or Bhai branch.

The Ramnami Panth is small sect in Chhattisgarh with a membership primarily from the dalit community. This sect propagates the cult of Rama among the dalits and does not believe in Brahmins as a medium for worshipping god. Ramnamis are found chiefly on the southern side of the Mahanadi in Chhattisgarh. This sect is easily distinguishable as they carry a flute and put peacock feathers around their caps. Ramnamis as the name suggests chant the name of Ram. They of ten get their bodies tattooed with the name of Ram.

The social religious reformer Ramananda had a committed dalit follower from Chhattisgarh. His name was Ravi Das or Rae Das. Gradually, the followers of Rae Das formed a separate sect and started calling themselves Rae Das Panthis or simply Raedasis. A striking similarity between all these sects is that the followers are drawn mostly from the Dalit communities. Secondly all these sects spread the message of equality.

The most widespread and important rebellion was the Bhumkal rebellion of 1910 that spread to 46 of the 84 parganas of Bastar. The term Bhumkal is significant as it refers to the social solidarity of the members of a clan that binds them to each other and to their specific Bhumor land. The basic reasons listed for the Bhumkal rebellion by historians clearly reaffirms the findings from earlier rebellions. It continued the tradition of tribal struggle for preserving and defending their traditions and their way of life and for reasserting their traditional rights on forests, land and natural resources. One of the main reasons for the rebellion is given by Standan dispossession of traditional forests and land resources had been the most important cause of the Bhumkal rebellion.

In 1908, the forests were first made reserved forests and the contractors given rights to take timber and wood for railway sleepers. This deprived the tribals of one of their main sources of their livelihood. Leasing out of liquor monopolies also aggravated the situation, as the locally made country liquor was declared illegal. The introduction of education and schools was seen by the tribals as an attempt by the State to subvert their culture and therefore became a precipitating factor. Finally, the brutality and exploitation by the police, which included begar by the officials culminated in the Bhumkal rebellion.

## Tribal Rebellions

Chhattisgarh is generally perceived as a tribal dominated state. Although this is factually incorrect it does reflect the significantly high proportion of tribals in the region. It also underscores a fundamentally important point that the tribals in Chhattisgarh have been able to retain their culture and traditional way of life despite the all pervasive influence of forces of modernity. While tribal people constitute 7.8 % and 23 % of the total population of India and Madhya Pradesh respectively they constitute 32.5 % of the population of Chhattisgarh.

According to the 1991 census the tribal population in the then districts of Chhattisgarh was Durg -12.6 %, Raipur -18.6%,

Rajnandgaon -25.3 %, Bilaspur -23.4 % Surguja -54.8 %, Raigarh - 45.5%, Bastar -67.7 %. The various tribes in the Chhattisgarh region are Gonds, Muria, Bhumja, Baiga, Kanars, Kawars, Halbas etc. A few of these tribes particularly the Gonds have influenced by the Hindu tradition and have in turn influenced local practices in the Hindu tradition as well. Other tribes like the Kamars and the Baigas have largely been untouched by the mainstream and have retained more of their traditional culture and way of life.

Chhattisgarh has withnessed several tribal rebellions starting from the late 18 century through the 19 century to the first few decades of the 20 century. Some of these tribal revolts were localised while others were more widespread. Geographically too, the rebellions were not centered in one region, in some of them precipitating factors were immediate and local in nature and in some the revolt took its time to brew. However the central narrative of these rebellions remained largely common and unchanged. All these rebellions were focussed and asserted the traditionally inalienable right of the tribals on the local resources land and forests. Often the mobilisation was around the issues of tradition culture and the tribal way of life. These rebellions were also protest against an alien system of governance and an alien political, economic and social order that had been forced upon them by the British. These tribal rebellions, although they predominantly took place in Bastar were spread across the various tribal areas of Chhattisgarh as well. The assimilation of this tradition of protest and rebellion by the tribals will be critical in any attempt to forge a Chhattisgarh identify and for evolving a vibrant and inclusive Chhattisgarh ethos. An understanding of these rebellions and integrating them in the new Chhattisgarh ethos will contribute to the future and the success of the new state. In this section we shall briefly discuss the tribal rebellions of Chhattisgarh.

The key tribal rebellions are listed:

1. Halba rebellion (1774-79)

2. Bhopalpatnam Struggle (1795)
3. Paralkot rebellion (1825)
4. Tarapur rebellion (1842-54)
5. Maria rebellion (1842-63)
6. First Freedom Struggle (1856-57)
7. Koi revolt (1859)
8. Muria rebellion (1876)
9. Rani rebellion (1878-82)
10. Bhumkal (1910)

The Halba rebellion is a very important event in the history of Bastar as it was responsible for the decline of the Chalukya dynasty, which in turn created circumstances that first brought the Marathas and then the British to the region. The rebellion was initiated in 1774 by the governor of Dongar, Ajmer Singhwith the intention of establishing an independent kingdom at Dongar. The Halba tribe and Halba soldiers supported him. However, the fundamental reasons for the rebellion were economic in nature. There had been a prolonged famine, which had severely affected the people who had very little cultivable land. The presence of Maratha forces and the terror caused by the East India Company in these adverse circumstances precipitated the rebellioin. The stronger armies of Bastar supported by the British and the Marathas crushed the rebellion. A massacre of Halba tribesmen followed the defeat of the Halba army. However, the revolt created conditions for the decline of the Chalukya dynasty which in turn significantly altered the history of Bastar.

The Paralkot rebellion was representative of the resentment felt by the Abujhmarias against the invasion of outsiders, primarily the Marathas and the British. This rebellion was supported by the Abujhmarias and was led by Gend Singh a fellow Abhujmaria. One of the objectives of the rebellion was to establish a world free of loot, plunder and exploitation. The presence of the Marathas and the British threatened the identity of the Abujmarias and they resisted this through organising the rebellion of Paralkot in 1825. The rebels were opposing the taxes levied by the Maratha rulers. In essence this rebellion was directed against the foreign interference and control of Bastar and wanted to re-establish the freedom of Bastar.

The rebellion of Tarapur (1842-54) was once again the assertion of the tribals against the invasion of their local culture and the tampering with their traditional principles of social, economic and political organization. It started with an opposition to taxes levied under the pressure of Anglo-Maratha rule. For the tribals, these experiences of coercive taxation were alien and new, and therefore they opposed them. The local Diwan became a symbol of oppression and bore the brunt of tribal anger.

The Maria rebellion, which lasted nearly 20 years from 1842 to 1863, was seemingly in favour of an inhuman practice of human sacrifice. In reality the revolt was against the insensitive and intrusive handling of tribal faith. The Anglo Maratha combine did not hesitate to enter and pollute the temple of Danteswari. The facts clearly indicate that this rebellion was more defensive in nature and was waged by the tribals to protect their land and tradition.

Furer Hamendorf writes all these rebellions were defensive movements, they were the last resort of tribesmen driven to despair by the encroachments of outsiders on their land and economic resources What is surprising is not the occurrence of uprisings, but the infrequency of violent reaction on the part of the aboriginals to the loss of their ancestral lands and to their economic enslavement. Hutton extends the analysis and writes early days of British administration did great detriment to the economic position of tribes through ignorance and neglect of their right and customs.

Bastar was also actively involved in the First War of Iindependence of 1857 with Southern Bastar as the centre of the revolt. Under the leadership of Dhruvarao a batle was waged against the British. He belonged to one of the Maria tribes called Dorlaon and was supported by his tribesmen.

Later in 1858, the Gonds challenged the British in several battles. In 1859 a very important rebellion began to take shape in Southern Bastar with the tribals refusing to let contractors undertake cutting of Sal trees. The people of these Jamindaris were called Kois. This rebellion was against the decision of the British to give contracts for cutting forests to contractors from Hyderabad. These contractors were also responsible for the exploitation of the tribals. The local tribals in 1859 decided that they would not allow the felling of a single tree. The British took this as a challenge to the might of the empire and used coercive methods to continue the felling of trees. This rebellion was loud and clear assertion by the tribals of their inalienable rights of the tribals on their forests and natural resources.

In 1867, Gopinath Kapardas was appointed the Diwan of Bastar State and was responsible for large scale exploitation of the tribal population. Tribals from different parganas jointly requested the King to remove the Diwan but the King did not concede to these demands. This led to the Muria Revolt of 1876 The rebelling tribals surrounded Jagdalpur on 2 March 1876; the King with great difficulty was able to inform the British forces. Finally a strong British army sent by the Resident of Orissa, crushed the rebellion.

## Tribal Crafts

Chhattisgarh is famous for traditional craft products made out of bamboo, wood etc. The folk paintings of Chhatisgarh depict the living expressions of the people, intrinsically linked with the socio-cultural ambiance of the area. They are not mere decorations but also spontaneous outpourings of religious devotions. The main craft produce of the State include Bamboo work, Wood carving, folk painting and folk Jewellery.

### *Bamboo Work*

Bamboo thickets are common sight in the State and tribals of Chhattisgarh have been putting their craftmanship to work. Craftsmanship of Chhattisgarh tribals can be seen from varying articles of craft produce they make out of bamboo. Articles for daily as well as decorative use are produced by these artisians. Some of the will known Bamboo produce include agricultural implements, fishing traps, hunting tools and baskets.

### *Wood Carving*

The woodcarving art has been flourishing in Chhattisgarh from time immemorial and one can find beautifully carved wooden products designed by the craftsman of the State. The skillful craftsmen of the State carve beautiful wooden ceilings, doors, lintels etc using different kinds of wood like shisham, teak, dhudi, sal and kikar. The craftsmen also make pipes, masks, doors, window frames and sculptures.

### *Painting*

Traditional wall paintings of the State is associated with rituals. Floors and walls are painted with colours and in almost every instance the depiction being associated with some ritual. Pithora paintings is a common traditional art form. These paintings originated in the tribal area of the Central India which is presently Madhya Pradesh and Chhattisgarh and depicts the offering to gods. These paintings are usually done on the occasion of marriages, child birth and other occasions of fulfillment of wish etc. Most of these paintings has a horse as it was considered auspicious to sacrifice a horse. In most of these tribal houses one can find pithora paintings. They are colorful and use natural colors.

## Tribal Tourism

If we talk about tribal tourism, then Chhattisgarh is one of the most fascinating tourist destinations of not only in India but the world. Known for its exceptional scenic beauty and unique and rich cultural heritage, Chhattisgarh has always been synonymous with tribes and tribal culture. Over one third of the state population is of tribes, most of them inhabiting in the thickly forested areas of the famous Bastar region. The tribes of Chhattisgarh are unique in their lifestyles and have beautifully retained their own culture and traditions for centuries.

Bastar is the largest tribal district of Chhattisgarh with over 70% of its total population comprising of tribals, which is about 26.76% of the total tribal population of Chhattisgarh. There are several tribal castes in Chhattisgarh with Gonds of Bastar being the most prominent among them. The Gond Tribes are well known for their unique Ghotul system of marriages, in all over the world. Other major tribes of Chhattisgarh region include the Baiga, Korba, Abhuj Maria, BisonHorn Maria, Muria, Halbaa, Bhatra and Dhurvaa tribes. The tribes of Chhattisgarh are known for their unique and distinctive tribal culture and each tribal group has its own distinct culture and enjoys its own unique traditional living styles. They differ from each other in their costume, eating habits, customs, traditions and even worship different form of god and goddess. Undoubtedly, Chhattisgarh is the most important tribal destination in India and the region has a great potential for tribal tourism.

The tribes of Chhattisgarh region are also known for their passion for dances and music, which are the most important amusements and a part and parcel of their day-today life. The tribal women of the Chhattisgarh region love to adorn themselves with plenty of ornaments made of cowries, beads, shells, bones, feathers, mixed metals, copper and bronze. The Chhattisgarh tribes are also known for their beautiful arts and crafts. Among festivals, Dusshera is the most important festival of the region but it's different from the north Indian Dusshera. Dusshera Festival of Bastar tribes is celebrated with much enthusiasm in Chhattisgarh every year when all the major tribes of the region gather at the Danteshwari Temple at Dantewada to worship the goddess Danteshwari. Undoubtedly Chhattisgarh is an undiscovered paradise, offering a tourist destination with a difference.

## Chhattisgarh Tribal Development Programme

India is a vast and diverse country, which is also a home for over one-fourth of world's absolute poor. IFAD, therefore, focuses on using its limited resources to develop innovative approaches that have a catalytic effect in leveraging additional resources for assisting the most vulnerable groups. The proposed programme has defined its target group and geographical area on this basis and has built on the experiences of the programmes, which are nationally funded as well as assisted by donors, such as DFID and GTZ, particularly in the area of rain fed farming and watershed management, and has combined these approaches with IFAD's own experience in India with participatory development process through the development of community based institutions. This is the first project in India to adopt watershed management as an intervention methodology.

Among the social groups in India, scheduled tribes (STs) have the highest proportion of the poor. While they account for only 8% of the total population, they comprise 40% of the displaced population. Literacy rate among STs is only is less than half of the general population, and that of rural tribal women about one-fourth. The Government of India has allocated significant amount of resources for tribal development, but the impact has been rather limited. The approach adopted has been more welfare-oriented, and there has been less emphasis on the issue of empowerment. This programme proposes to use the opportunity created by the recent constitutional amendment concerning the extension of the Panchayats Act to Scheduled Areas and would assist the state governments in putting into practice the principles established by this act in empowering the local communities and in establishing collaborative relationships with communities for designing resource management strategies which meet their perceptions and aspirations.

The proposed programme would cover two of the three states with the highest proportion of tribal population of India viz. Madhya Pradesh (MP) and Bihar. The target groups would comprise all households in the selected villages, i. e. villages with tribal, Primitive Tribal Groups (PTGs) and scheduled caste population of not less than 50% of the total population where the majority of the households live below the poverty line. The objective of the Programme would be to develop and implement a replicable model that ensures household food security and improves livelihood opportunities and overall quality of life of the tribal population based on the sustainable and equitable use of natural resources. To achieve this, the Programme would: i) empower tribal grassroots associations and users' groups, including women and other marginal groups; ii) promote activities which generate sustainable increases in production and productivity of land and water resources; and iii) generate sources of income outside of agriculture, particularly for the landless.

The basic approach would be to promote processes of awareness generation, legal literacy, social analysis and mobilisation for self-selecting group formation among disadvantaged women and marginalised groups. The programme would support initiatives identified, planned and implemented by beneficiaries and would provide the required resources and support. The resources would be managed directly by the beneficiaries after appropriate training and capacity building. These would be supplied through NGOs with a proven experience in applying such approaches.

The proposed programme would have three main components. Under the beneficiary empowerment and capacity building component, the programme would finance broad based awareness raising of tribal rights and of gender and equity issues, legal and managerial strengthening, and technical training. Similarly, under livelihood systems enhancement, the programme would finance all production-related activities as well as enabling measures, namely land and water management/ watershed development, including community-based small infrastructures; production systems improvement; rural micro-finance; and health and nutrition. Under the programme management and implementation component, the programme would finance salary and allowances for Programme Implementation Unit (PIU) staff at District level, the relevant running costs for the Tribal Development Society and a skeleton Programme Management Unit (PMU), a legal defence fund, specialised and baseline studies, training for the staff and the development of training material, exposure visits, study tours, and technical assistance, and the costs of capacity building of facilitating NGOs and their contractual support services.

A gradual and phased approach would be adopted to allow for the satisfactory empowerment of Gram Sabhas and for building up grassroots institutions. Therefore the programme would be carried out in two phases - a pilot phase and a scaling up phase- with a reassessment and evaluation at the end of the pilot phase and three years after commencement of the scaling up phase. It is envisaged that the programme would be completed over a eight year period.

The total programme cost over nine years, inclusive of contingencies, duties and taxes, is estimated at INR 2 276 million (USD 41.7 million). The programme funds, forming part of IFAD's assistance, having passed through the Government of India would be received by each Tribal Development Society (TDS, who would then release the funds to the districts programme implementation units (DPIUs). The DPIU would release the funds related to the NGO capacity building and overhead costs directly to the NGOs. The funds planned for the activities to be undertaken by the communities would be passed on either to special purpose committees to be established under the programme, or to the Gram Sabha.

The programme would be managed by involving Community-based Organisations, Tribal Development Society, Programme Management Unit, District Programme Implementation Units, Non-Governmental Organisations, and relevant line agencies belonging to the government of both States. At the village level, the Gram Sabha (GS) would be the basic unit for planning, co-ordinating and monitoring programme activities. The programme would finance the establishment of a comprehensive M&E framework comprising a computerised programme management system (CPMS) and a MIS, a participatory process monitoring system based on annual beneficiary workshops, periodic planning and budgetary process, a mid-term review and impact assessments systems. Participatory M&E mechanisms would be designed to enable the communities to monitor and evaluate their own performance, identify constraints and take corrective measures, when needed. Since the programme's activities would be demand driven, an environmental screening system (ESS) would be set up a screening procedure of all requests for financing emanating from Gram Sabhas/users' groups.

The programme would benefit an estimated 74 000 households located in 1 080 natural villages: over 51 000 households would be located in Madhya Pradesh, the remainder in Bihar. Almost 6 000 families form the primitive tribal groups (PTGs) are expected to benefit from programme interventions. With an estimated average household size of 5, there would be almost 370,000 beneficiaries. Over a 20 year period, the economic rate of return is estimated to be 14.2% for the programme aggregated over both states. While this ERR is not high, it represents reasonably good returns for a situation where grassroots institution development and capacity building is a primary focus.

The programme has a number of risks. Failure to promote community participation through creation of local leadership would cause the programme to degenerating into a conventional tribal development programme and this is the principal risk to the Programme. Secondly, the NGOs in the region, especially those in MP, are relatively inexperienced. Risks are also associated with provision of services required under the programme like Farmers Field School. Lastly, the program involves changing relationships within the development process and overcoming dependency attitudes of communities. As mentioned, most tribals have become overly dependent on Government subsidies while the proposed program expects beneficiaries' contributions in practically all the activities envisaged. This could be a risk for the program.

# 4

# Tribes of Jharkhand

The state of Jharkhand was born on 15th November 2000 out of Bihar State in India. It has a total population of about 26 million people. Its total land area covers around 80,000 Sq.Kms. of plateau of uneven topography. It is literally a mine of all the important minerals and forest resources of the country. This has led to industrialization at a very fast space. The word "Jharkhand" is originated from original tribal language, which means land of Jungles. Jharkhand is considered as a rich state because of it minerals.

Jharkhand is separated from Bihar in 2000 but the movement started in early 1900s and since then the demand of separate state was alive. The good tribal rulers rule the area and are known as the Munda Raja. Munda raja are still existing in this region. During the Mughal Empire, the Jharkhand region was known as "Kukara" region. This area came under British after 1765 and known as "Jharkhand".

There are more than 30 distinct Adivasi communities listed as "scheduled tribes" living in Jharkhand. Among them the most dominant communities are the Santals, the Oraons, the Mundas, the Hos and the Kharias. All these have their distinct language and culture. These major tribes are all settled agriculturists.

Jharkhand has a distinct identity historically. Jharkhand is a name given by the Mogul Emperors when they came in contact in the 15th century. It means a forest tract because at the time it was a dense forest of majestic sal tree full of wild animals including elephants, tigers and snakes. Historically the region was administratively divided into 4 areas : the Santal Parganas, Chotanagpur, Kolhan and Palamau all of which may have originated from the self governing village councils.

In the course of time people from outside came as traders and service holders in the traditional system of government. With them came much of the cultural influence and values. But it was during the British administration that the people got uprooted from their land because the administration gave recognition to those rights on land which were supported by documents issued by it.

The Adivasis of Jharkhand still cherish the aspiration for a decentralized governing system in which each citizens will have an equal rights over the decision making process. However, things have changed and there is uphill task despite the birth of a new State of Jharkhand.

## Tribal Communities

Some of the importance tribal communities living in Jharkhand are the following:

1. Jharkhand
2. Asur
3. Baiga
4. Banjara
5. Bathudi
6. Bedia
7. Binjhia
8. Birhor
9. Birjia
10. Bhumij

11. Chero
12. Chick Baraik
13. Gond
14. Gorait
15. Ho
16. Karmali
17. Kharia
18. Kharwar
19. Khond
20. Kisan
21. Kora
22. Korwa
23. Lohra
24. Mahli
25. Mal Pahariya
26. Munda
27. Oraon
28. Parhaiya
29. Santhal
30. Sauria Paharia
31. Savar

Some of tribals came from the East through Assam; others from the North-West by way of the Khyber Pass through Baluchistan. These latter were the Dravidian speaking tribes, one branch of which found final refuge in the wild country that was Jharkhand. These were the Oraons. The former include the Munda, who claim they were the very first settlers in Chotanagpur.

Today the Munda, the Oraon, the Kharia, Ho and Santhal, the five largest groups of tribes on the Plateau, are included among the 29 Scheduled Tribes listed by the Government of India. They have found "a lodging place in the turbulent mass of Indian civilization".

These three tribes - Munda, Oraon, Kharia - speak their own dialects, have their own racial features, follow customs peculiar to themselves, withal living together on the Chotanagpur Plateau. They have many things in common: a lingua franca known as Nagpuria or Sadri; Sacred Groves of Sal; ritual Hunts, Sacrifices, Festivals, Witchcraft Practices. All three Tribes are made up of exogamous septs, forbidding marriages between the same septs. Among the Tribes marriages are endogamous, restricting marriages within the tribe.

The centre of their culture is the village, depending on which members of what tribe are in the majority. Each village has its own Sacred Grove, thje Sarna, consisting of five or more Sal trees that are left standing when the forest was felled to give place to huts and fields to form a new village. In the village is the Akhara or Dancing Square meant solely for the young men and women of the village. In the fields of the village is the original water-hole, the Danri, whose water is necessary for marriage rites and for divination. If the clans do not meet at the Jatras or fairs as they used to do in times past, the confederacy of certain villages gather together on the high fields of Murma and Lohardaga every year, there to sing and dance the live long day and the long night through.

### Baiga

The Baigas are courageous woodsman and hunter. Till fairly recently the Baigas practiced 'dahiya' cultivation, that is, slash and burn. Thousands of squire miles of sal forests have been clean destroyed by them in the progress of their dahiya cultivation, the ground being afterwards occupied by dense scrub of low sal species springing from the stumps.

### *Gonds*

With over four million people, they are the largest tribe in Central India. The Gondi language is related to Telugu and other Dravidian languages. About half of Gonds speak Gondi languages, while the rest speak Indo-Aryan languages including Hindi.

The Gonds are traditionally agriculturalists; some practice shifting cultivation, while others raise cereals or herd cattle. Gond society is highly stratified and does not conform to the usual image of egalitarianism among tribals. The Gonds belong to a category of very large tribes (also including Santals and Bhils) that have traditionally dominated the regions in which they have lived. However, like other Adivasis, the Gonds have suffered from increasing landlessness since the 1960s.

Traditional Gond religion involves a distinct pantheon of gods and spirits, which many Gonds practice along with Hinduism. Gondwana or "land of the Gonds", is a loosely-defined area of southeastern Madhya Pradesh, eastern Maharashtra, and parts of Chhattisgarh, Orissa, and northern Andhra Pradesh. The region was home to several Gond kingdoms from the 15th century to the mid-18th century, when the Marathas expanded into the region from the west. The region gave its name to Gondwanaland, the ancient southern supercontinent which comprised present-day Africa, South America, Australia, India and Antarctica.

Commission after commission on the "language question" has called for instruction, at least at the primary level, in the students' native tongue. However, state governments have often demanded the introduction of regional language instruction in Gondi areas. Primary schooling among the Gonds of Andhra Pradesh, for example, began in the 1940s and 1950s. The government selected a group of Gonds who were semiliterate in Telugu and taught them the basics of written script. These individuals became teachers who taught in Gondi, and their efforts enjoyed a measure of success until the

1970s, when state policy demanded instruction in Telugu. The switch in the language of instruction both made the Gond teachers superfluous because they could not teach in Telugu and also presented the government with the problem of finding reasonably qualified teachers willing to teach in outlying tribal schools. Gonds frequently are reluctant to send their children to school, needing them to work in the fields instead.

### *Mahli*

Mahali people traditionally earned their livelihood by selling articles made of Bamboo. Some typical articles made by them are: Machi (a small bench), umbrellas, soop (used in kitchen, to remove dust from cereals), sop and chatai (for lying down and sleeping), raincap (special cap covering head, and upper back for protection from rains during work). They typically have a tattoo of their name on their hand.

### *Oraon*

The Oraon people inhabit various places of Jharkhand. Traditionally they depended on the forest for their ritual and economic livelihood, but in recent times they have become mainly settled agriculturalists. Small numbers of Oraon have emigrated to the northeastern part of India, where they are mainly employed as labourers on tea estates.

The Oraon language, Kurukh, belongs to the Dravidian family, and is most closely related to Brahui and Malto (Paharia). The Oraon people have a rich and vast range of folk songs, dances and tales, as well as traditional musical instruments. Both men and women participate in dance, which are performed at social events and festivals.

### *Santals*

The Santals are the largest tribal community in India. They speak Austro-Asiatic language called Santali .They are found mainly in the states of West Bengal, Bihar Jharkhand and Orissa .

On 30 th June 1855 two of the most revered Santal rebel leaders Sidhu and Kanhu Murmu mobilized 10000 Santals and declared a rebellion against the mighty British Colonists. The day is still celebrated among the Santal community with great respect and spirit for the thousands of the Santal martyrs who sacrificed their lives along with their two celebrated leaders to get Freedom from the oppressive rule of the Jamindars and the British operatives. Though the revolution was brutally suppressed, it marked a great change in the colonial rule and policy.

The Santali culture rich in many aspects are attracting many scholars and anthropologists for further research.The Santal philosophy and way of life is well reflected in their traditions, rituals, social structure and religion. The Santali literature just like any other community has mythology, poetry and songs, their aesthetic worldview is depicted in the paintings and artworks in the walls of their houses .The mythology states the creation theory and the stories of the Great Santal ancestors Pilchu Haram and Pilchu Bhudi.The first attempt to study the Santali culture was done by the Christian missionaries the most famous of them was the Norwegian-born Reverend Paul Olaf Bodding. It is really a matter of great pride for the Santals that they did not gave up their language, and that the Santali language was not obliterated and continues to remain although India suffered so many foreign invasions and intrusions.

Santal community is devoid of any caste system and there is no distinction made on the basis of birth. They believe in supernatural beings and ancestral spirits. The Santali rituals mainly comprise of sacrificial offerings and invocations to the bongas (spirits).The Santals have a very traditional system of governance called Manjhi –Paragana system which may be compared to the Local Self Governance in today's civilization. This body is responsible or authorized for taking decisions to ameliorate the village socio economic condition.

### Mundas

The Mundas are known in different names in the society such as Buno, Soultal, Kuli and Sarder. But they have their own customs and functions. They are the followers of the 'Sanatan' (original form of Hindu) religion. They follow all the religious customs of Sanatan. They were the worshipers of the god 'Shiva' (symbol of energy and life) in ancient time but now they worhip different gods and goddesses like the Hindus. Though, once the society of Mundas was mother dominated, now the families are father dominated. They have their own 'Morol' (chief of clan) and 'Raja' ( king ). A Morol dominates a clan and the Raja dominates a good number of clans. The Morols and the king give directives in their social and religious life.

There is a similarity between the Mundas and the Saotal in their physical structure. They are blackish, curly haired and dwarf in size. They are very industrious but with the passage of time their physical structure underwent significant changes. Some Mundas of new generation are as like as the Bengalis.

There is a similarity between the Saotal and the mundas in their way of taking foods. Like Saotal, the Mundas eat frogs. snakes. rats, wild animals, shells, snails and earthworm. But now a days, they have made some changes in their food items. They entertain their guests by giving them Tari (a kind of wine that is made from palm juice ) and Haria ( a kind of wine made from soaked rice). They themselves also drink Tari and Haria. But now a days, a change has come in their food habit as they are facing pressure of their surroundings. As the alternative food they are eating the foods that are eaten by the Hindus.

As it stands today, most of the Mundas are landless. Most of them have no land of their own. Some live in either on an open land or on others lands. In ancient time, the landlords who have used Mundas to cultivable their land by cutting the trees and bushes of sundarbans by hand made axe, gave the Mundas some land. From the ancient time this tribe is deprived of the light of education. The Mundas never come forward to be educated or the government or any other social organization did not come forward to educate them. Their social and surrounding condition also do not permit them to be educated. Very recently some non-government organizations have taken initiative to educate the children of the Mundas. Some Mundas are sending their children to school but they are very few in number. The Mundas have a language of their own. But they do not know about it's letters.

The house of the Mundas are made of mud. They live in damp and dirty environment. There is a lack of cleanliness among them. They are used to take overnight and rotten food. They give birth a lot of children. After their birth, the children grow up in an unfavorable environment. When they become ill, they depend on exorcising of evil spirits by uttering charms rather than taking medicine. As they are unaware about nurition, foods, pure drinking water and sanitation, their children grow up in an unhealthy environment.

## Tribal Population

Jharkhand has a population of 26.90 million, consisting of 13.86 million males and 13.04 million females. The sex ratio is 941 females to 1000 males. The population consists of 28% tribals, 12% Scheduled Castes and 60% others. There are 274 persons for each square kilometer of land. However, the population density varies considerably from as low as 148 per square kilometer in Gumla district to as high as 1167 per square kilometer in Dhanbad district.

Jharkhand has remained a home to a number of tribal communities since time immemorial. Infact, in some of the districts of Jharkhand, the tribal population predominates, the non tribal one. Jharkhand has 32 primitive tribal groups. These are the Asur, Baiga, Banjara, Bathudi, Bedia, Binjhia, Birhor, Birjia, Chero, Chick-Baraik, Gond, Gorait, Ho, Karmali, Kharwar, Khond, Kisan, Kora, Korwa, Lohra, Mahli, Mal-Paharia, Munda, Oraon, Parhaiya, Santal, Sauria-Paharia, Savar, Bhumij, Kol and Kanwar.

*Table 1. Tribal Population profile in Jharkhand*

| Tribes | Population | % in Tribal population | literacy within tribe |
|---|---|---|---|
| Asur | 7783 | 0.13 | 10.62 |
| Baiga | 3553 | 0.06 | 4.22 |
| Banjara | 412 | lowest | 12.38 |
| Bathaudi | 1595 | 0.03 | 16.93 |
| Bedia | 60445 | 1.04 | 10.82 |
| Bhumij | 136110 | 2.35 | 16.45 |
| Binjhia | 10009 | 0.17 | 14.52 |
| Birhor | 4057 | 0.07 | 5.74 |
| Birjia | 4057 | 0.07 | 10.50 |
| Chero | 52210 | 0.09 | 17.30 |
| Chick Baraik | 40339 | 0.69 | 20.17 |
| Gond | 96574 | 1.66 | 20.00 |
| Gorait | 5206 | 0.09 | 16.61 |
| Ho | 536524 | 9.23 | 17.71 |
| Karmali | 38652 | 0.66 | 13.30 |
| Kharia | 141771 | 2.44 | 24.86 |
| Kharwar | 222758 | 3.83 | 17.22 |
| Khond | 1263 | 0.02 | 15.99 |
| Kisan | 23420 | 0.40 | 13.41 |
| Kora | 33951 | 0.58 | 9.28 |
| Korba | 21940 | 0.38 | 6.14 |
| Lohar | 169090 | 2.91 | 12.71 |
| Mahli | 91868 | 1.59 | 12.74 |
| Mal Paharia | 79322 | 1.37 | 7.58 |
| Munda | 845887 | 14.56 | 22.16 |
| Oraon | 1048064 | 18.05 | 23.28 |
| Parhaiya | 24012 | 0.41 | 15.30 |
| Santhal | 2060732 | 35.47 | 12.55 |
| Sauria Paharia | 30269 | 0.68 | 6.87 |
| Savar | 3014 | 0.05 | 9.55 |
| Unspecified | 6660 | 0.1 | 3.94 |
| Total | 5810867 | 100.00 | 16.99 |

The geographical area now comprising Jharkhand was previously part of Bihar. The area has witnessed migration of people from the adjoining areas of Bihar and West Bengal for last several decades. Industrial and mining centres like Jamshedpur, Dhanbad and Ranchi have attracted people from all parts of India.

Hinduism, Islam and Christianity are the three religions that came in through immigrants. The tribal comunities of Jharkhand have their own spiritual beliefs, commonly called Sarna. During the colonization process the tribal religious beliefs were looked down upon as pagan and inferior. Through overt and covert conversions and other influences at assimilation, the Christian missionaries have contributed much for the demolition of many of the tribal Sarna beliefs.

## Tribal Religions

Most of the tribes of Jharkhand were nature worshippers before converting to more institutionalised religions like Christianity and Hinduism. Around 17% of the tribal population of Jhakhand practise Christianity. The tribals rationalise the forces of nature by endowing objects of nature with supernatural qualities and worship them as manifestations of the Supreme Being.

### *Impact of Christianity on Tribes*

The present state of Jharkhand, which was carved out of Bihar in November 2000, is a part of Chotanagpur plateau of Indian peninsula. Its complex social condition provided unique opportunity to the various socio-religious and anthropological groups for carrying out their intellectual pursuit in this most diverse cultural and linguistic area of central India. But in the process of their academic romanticism the homogenous character of the tribal society got disturbed. The social scientists, who believe in the history based on Christian tradition, projected the tribes inhabited in this region as indigenous people. In fact the tribes of separate ethnic races settled here in course of their migration from different geographical regions of the subcontinent and as such the theory of their indigenous character became a debatable issue.

The respective dominant groups almost everywhere in the world have significantly used religion as tools to strengthen the mechanism for maintaining their hegemony in the society. Accordingly, colonial and imperialist forces of western world also used Christianity for furthering their colonial and cultural interest among the hapless multi-ethnic tribes settled in this region for centuries.

Advent of Christianity in Jharkhand dates back to 1845, when the first four Christian Missionaries from Germany established the Gossner Evangelical Lutheran Church in Ranchi, the present capital of Jharkhand State. Gradually, the Churches of other denominations like Anglicans and Roman Catholic established their foothold in this region. These missionaries under the patronage of British colonial power gradually and steadily launched a cultural invasion on racially different tribes through proselytisation. They successfully used religion as a mechanism to expand the hegemony of church among the 'indigenous' people of the area. Their zealous attempt to denunciate the socio-religious faith of the tribal people had the sole purpose to manipulate for the imposition of the Christian tradition of west in central India. In due course of time they succeeded to a considerable extent in imposing their moods, concepts and images on these 'indigenous tribes', though, it created a quagmire in the homogenous tribal society. Thus, contrary to the myth that the missionaries came to the area with caring and sharing philosophy - they were caring only for those who changed their socio-religious loyalty from SARANA (Sacred groves as place of worship by the local tribes) to GIRJA (Church).

Initially, the 'Bible came in conflict with sword'. At the initial stage even revolt by Birsa Munda (1890-1895) popularly known as Birsa Bhagwan among the tribal people of

Jharkhand was an anti-Christian missionary movement, which was later projected as part of National Freedom Movement. Birsa even took exception to Christian Sunday as day for rest and prayer and substituted it with Thursday for the socio-religious congregation of his followers.

Though, in comparison to Hinduism, Christianity was a recent phenomenon in this region, the latter left a deep rooted and long-term impact on tribal mind and life. In fact the work of Christian missionaries not only covered the religious domain but it also influenced the socio-political life of the tribes settled here. The land and forest, which belonged to the community, were the only source of their livelihood. But with commercialisation of these sources of their survival through introduction of Permanent Settlement Act by the then British Government, people lost their sources of livelihood. Taking advantage of their plight, the Christian missionaries intervened in the issue and helped the affected people to some extent by taking the British power into confidence. In the bargain they succeeded in converting a sizeable section of local inhabitants.

After establishing their foothold in the region Christian missionaries gradually monopolised the education as Church subject. With the patronage of British imperial power they succeeded in creating a dominant group within the tribal community through allurement and some philanthropic and social activities. Gradually they alienated the converts from the rest of their community members and forced them to accept the cultural tradition of the west at the cost of forgetting their respective socio-cultural tradition. In the process of such social transformation however, Christianity left a deep rooted negative impact on the life and mind of the tribal people, which may be described as under:-

— Contrary to the collective outlook of tribal society, individual approach to life became prominent particularly among the converts, who represented the tribal elite.

— Community ownership of land and forest, which was the traditional means for subsistence was lost due to their commercialisation and barter economy was replaced by the market economy of the west.

— Practice of making social decision on the basis of consensus, which was a form of tribal democracy, was replaced by the concept of democracy with Christian tradition.

— Puritanism and conservatism of Christianity replaced animism, which was an underdeveloped form of liberal Hinduism.

By the time India attained Independence, the Christian missionaries successfully expanded their base among the different tribes of Chotanagpur and also created church leaders from within the respective community. Switching over from socio-religious to politico religious mode for expanding their hegemony over the tribal people, Christian missionaries utilised the services of the converts to keep their community members away from their emotional integration with rest of the population of the country. These leaders, who became the privileged group due to their education in western pattern subsequently, emerged as a viable force to guide the political movement of tribal people for a separate tribal land of Jharkhand. It may be worthwhile to mention that almost all the leaders of Jharkhand party, which emerged as a political outfit of the tribals in 1949, were Christians.

Unfortunately, the political dispensation of the country in post-colonial India never tried to understand the socio-cultural condition of the different ethnic groups particularly the tribals and allowed them to play in the hands of the alien forces responsible for the protracted unrest in the region. Taking advantage of the situation, Christian missionaries made concerted efforts to keep the tribals alienated from the mainstream polity of the country. However, heavy influx of non-tribal population from the plains of Bihar following industrialisation and consequential urbanisation of the area and successful operation of the then Congress Government to win over the leaders of the movement thwarted such attempt of the missionaries at least temporarily.

By mid sixties Hindu revivalists also took an initiative to establish their foothold in the region. They also opened schools and other socio-religious centres parallel to Christian institutions. Banking upon Sanskritisation model of anthropology, which was even supported by some foreign anthropologists that the tribes of the region have been the followers of Hinduism, the forces of Hindutva launched an aggressive campaign against the Christian missionaries.

By mid eighties Jharkhand movement reached a low ebb and proselytisation programme of the Christian missionaries was substantially contained due to planned opposition of Hindu revivalists. Besides, the Hindu revivalists succeeded in re-conversion of sizeable number of tribals and as a result the Christian missionaries suffered from a sort of frustration and demoralisation. In 1986, however the visit of Pope to Ranchi and other parts of India was a moral booster for the Church functionaries.

Taking up the challenge of the forces of Hindutva as an alarm signal, the Christian missionaries made some tactical changes to counter their adversaries. They switched over from socio-religious activities to politico-religious mode and even joined hands with the forces of Left extremists. Christian missionaries always treated the Communists as untouchables. However, when western lobby pampered the Left extremists for their anti Russian stand, Christian institutions also gave them shelter in Church sponsored voluntary organisations. The move was to fight against the growing influence of the Hindu revivalists among the tribals.

Another tactical move of Christian Missions was tribalisation of Christianity in one hand and Sanskritisation of the names of their institutions on the other. Giving Hindu names to the converts during Baptisation, allowing the women folk to imitate their Hindu counterparts in dress/ gestures,

Sanskrit names to various Christian institutions like Nirmala College, Satya Bharati, Nirmal Hriday, Jan Vikas Mandal and Vikas Maitree and allowing the converts for participation in animistic celebration of non-Christian tribals were part of such tactical move of the missionaries.

Missionaries with the support of the Leftist forces, who subscribe to the modernisation theory of anthropology that the tribes of the region were indigenous settlers, created a situation, which led to confrontations between the tribal Christians and the Hindu-non-tribals. Such Christian-Hindu encounter accelerated the process for turning incendiary, which gradually widened the ethnic divide in the region. Taking advantage of the situation, foreign funded organisations like Indian Social Institute, an outfit of Roman Catholic Mission, William Carries and others with lot of financial resources in their possession accelerated the process of tribalisation of Jharkhand politics. They organised seminars and workshops for propagating the alleged plight of the tribals and training camps for the target group of tribal youths for their infiltration in various Social Actions and Christian Actions Groups.

With a view to mobilise the tribal people against various development projects launched by the Government in the region, Christian missionaries highlighted the danger of further influx of non-tribal population with such projects. They created apprehension of displacement in tribal mind and abandonment of their 'Sarana and Sasan' (the places of worship). Tribal political leaders on the other hand were convinced that influx of non-tribal population would adversely affect the demography of the region, which consequently would affect the hegemony of tribal voters in the constituency. They accordingly organised seminars, symposia and workshops to oppose the various developmental projects like Koel Karo Hydel project, Kutku Dam project and Paras Dam project initiated in the region by the government. The move was to counter the attempt of the contemporary governments of post-colonial India to integrate the tribes in the mainstream developmental process of the country.

Competitive experiments of Westernisation and Indianisation of the tribals by the respective forces created confusion in tribal society and thereby prompted a new generation of tribal youths to adopt the path of extreme tribalism. They wanted tribal veto in each and every process of development in the region. Meanwhile a new concept of applied anthropology with a theory that tribals were indigenous people of the land with separate nationality gave a new issue of tribal nationalism to tribal youths.

Any attempt on the part of the Government for scientific transformation of tribal society was viewed by the new generation as its ethnocentric bias against the growing urge of tribal nationalism. This new concept being closer to modernisation model of anthropology and an ingredient of westernisation also supported the theory of the Leftists that India was not one nation but a combination of several separate nationalities. It therefore, suited the politico-religious design of the Christian missionaries in containing the process of re-conversion by the Hindu revivalists.

Tribals of Jharkhand are now passing through a serious transition both socially and politically. They are not found content even with creation of new state of Jharkhand. On one hand the advent of Christianity disintegrated their life style and on the other the concerted effort of Christian missionaries to maintain their cultural hegemony over them gradually changed their outlook. The Christian converts within the community interpreted their indigenous life style befitting to Christian tradition without taking into account the negative impact of proselytisation, westernisation and de-tribalisation of the community.

Christian-tribal leaders, who on account of their education were more vocal than others, dominated Jharkhand politics for a long time. However, in due course of time, when non-Christian leadership started showing results, it turned into political as well as civilisational conflict. Accepting the Christian tradition, the community-centric tribal society became individual centric, which led to ethnic conflicts. Instead of strengthening the country with the concept of Indian nationalism, concept of tribal nationalism became the socio-political ideology of the people. Dr.Nirmal Minz, a noted tribal church leader in his write-up - "Passing Scene of Chotanagpur" consciously avoided these negative impacts of Christianity on the homogenous life style of tribal society.

The politico-religious march of the Christian missionaries and their encounter with Hindu-revivalists pushed the people of Jharkhand to a position, which has enormous potentiality to widen the ethnic divide in the region. Political parties with their eyes on votes are no more interested in social integration of tribals with non- tribals. Urge for tribalisation of Jharkhand, which is a reflection of accumulated hatred against non-tribals has deeply penetrated the tribal mind.

Instead of making a concerted effort to develop an institutional mechanism to thwart the attempt of divisive forces in the region, the political leadership in the state is helping them due to their vote bank politics, which is apparently a danger signal for peace and harmony in the state. This is the reality of the ongoing problem in Jharkhand State and the Centre needs to pay more attention to the current conflict.

## Challenges to Customary Rights of Tribals

According to prominent historians like SC Roy, the Mundas were spread all over the north of India in the 3rd Millennium BC, and they were constantly on the move. Their wanderings were some times due to natural causes, but often due to invasion by outsiders. The Mundas fled to the hilly regions to preserve their independence and identity. At one time, they inhabited what is presently Punjab. Later they came down to Utter Pradesh, then to Bihar and finally they settled in Chotanagpur or Jharkhand.

The Oraons, representing the Dravidian tribes, were originally in the Konkan region of what is presently Karnataka. Later they moved towards Maharastra, Bihar and finally to Chotanagpur a few centuries after the Mundas.

The Santhal tribe had lived prosperously for some centuries in the Champ region (now in Chattisgarh). Later they moved towards Bhagalpur, and finally to Saont in Midnapur, from which they derived the name Santhal. The Adivasis inhabited the Gangetic plains during the pre-Vedic period and were an agrarian society. When the pastoral Aryans invaded the Gangetic plains they succeeded in conquering the fertile area since they had horses which enabled them to be more mobile.

One of the main characteristics of the Adivasis in the course of their history of struggle with alien cultures was the fact that they were always away from the centre of power, they were frequently on the fringes. In the era of small kingdoms developing into empires such as the Magadha empire and the Ashoka Mauria during the 800 BC, and the Guptas and Cholas around 10th and 12th AD, evidence of the marginal existence of the Adivasi community is to be found. In all the records we find references to Adivasi people as dasyu, danavs, rakshasha and savage, etc.

The Aryan people were more dominant and aggressive. They had a monarchical system of governance based on the varna system and a standing army with fighting skills. Egalitarian Adivasi communities did not have a kingship system, since it was based on hierarchy — a concept alien to the tribal ethos. Instead of Kingship the Adivasis had clan groups among the Kily system -- the clan system. This later developed into the Khutkati system. Nor did they have a standing army, since the self-sufficient Adivasis communities did not have a division of labour based on workers and non-workers.

Marginalisation of the Adivasis continued during the medieval period. During this period, the Muslims came to India, as early as 711 AD, as a part of an expedition led by the Arab General Muhammad bin Qasim. Shortly thereafter, Sindh, part of lower Punjab, was incorporated into the Arab Umayyad Caliphate. In the course of time, the Muslims conquered a number of Hindu kings. However, the Muslim Emperors were not interested in invading the Adivasi areas, except for collecting malgujari – tax. Even during this period, the Adivasis continued their traditional system of socio-cultural and political governance - the Parha and the Manki Mundua system. This was the basis of the social union among the Adivasis in Jharkhand.

Kingship developed amongst the Adivasis as a result of the necessity to protect their natural and livelihood resources from alien predations and to pay taxes to more powerful emperors. The kings would appoint someone from amongst their kin to be an agent to collect tax. The revenue thus collected was then used for paying the taxes to the emperor. The Nagbashi Rajas, the Jaria garh Raja, the Ratu Raja, etc., were amongst some of these small kings. They would collect malgujari from the people to pay to the Emperors. This system of kings can be seen in the Oraon areas, in the western region of Jharkhand.

This kingship system was resisted by the Adivasis. The Hos resisted the malgujari, and so too did the Santhals and the Mundas. This resistance became more prominent during the British rule in India which resulted in the Chotanagpur Tenancy Act, the Santhal Parganas Tenancy Act, and the Wilkinson Rule. These rules and Acts recognised the distinctiveness of the social-cultural and political institutions of the Adivasi people. They also provided the British government with a better way of collecting tax from a people who refused to part with the lands that had been cleared and cultivated for several generations. It is clear that the customary system of self-governance of the Adivasis has existed and evolved in the course of the history as far back as we can trace it. Their customary practices have been one of the main strengths of the Adivasi people. This is how they have been able, in the past, to resist outside forces encroaching into their freedom.

***Disempowerment***

The economic effects of forcible incorporation of Adivasis into a stratified market economy have been well recorded. However, as well as the economic exploitation and land alienation, the incorporation and subordination of the Adivasi society in to the market economy, has led to the destruction of the community as a whole. This disempowerment was done through a very conscious destruction of the Adivasi institutions of governance.

In the case of Jharkhand, with the establishment of British rule we find a conscious effort to destroy the traditional Adivasi institution of self-governance, self-regulation, such as Munda Manki system and the Parha system. These representative institutions were supplanted by a new set of institutions to enable the British not only to appropriate the economic and labour resources of the Adivasi communities in the form of land revenue and indentured labour, but also to make these new institutions independent of the control of the Adivasi community.

It is no accident that unlike the Munda Manki system, which was communitarian and not necessarily hereditary, the new system was always based in an individual authority and in several cases hereditary. These offices of revenue extraction were vested with authorities of a feudatory chief or raja. Apart from the system of revenue and labour extractions a new and bureaucratic civil and criminal administration was also set up.

Bureaucracy, police and courts were encountered by the Adivasi communities for the first time. These institutions not only destroyed the Adivasi communities, since they were completely out of the control of the society, they also eroded the communitarian principles that permeated the self-regulatory mechanism of the Adivasi society. The impact of this ethos was evident in the mechanism of dispute settlement in the traditional Adivasi institutions.

In the case of disputes, such as inter-clan clashes, murders or debts, the emphasis of the community panchayat was on justice, rather then judgement or punishment. All this changed with the advent of the modern bureaucracy that was based on individualism and impersonality. The Adivasis notion of justice was replaced by the modern binary of crime and punishment. The inability of the Adivasi people to grasp this subtle but deadly shift often led to tragic consequences. In the initial year of the establishment of police stations there are several recorded instances of the Adivasi warriors reporting to the police station with the body of their victims.

What has been patronizingly recorded by the police officials as the "innocence and simplicity of the savage tribals" was in fact the result of the failure of the Adivasi communities to understand the full import of the modern judicial principle of crime and punishment. Rather then endeavouring to resolve the cause of acrimony between the Adivasi individuals or groups so that harmony could once again be restored, as was the traditional custom of the Adivasi panchayat, the modern institutions resorted to punitive action, since for them an individual was solely responsible for its acts of omission and commission.

The Adivasi mechanism of grievance redress was therefore trespassed and violated. Furthermore, in its dealings with modern bureaucracy, judiciary and police the Adivasi notion of self-respect was violated. The elitist attitude of the colonial and Indian mindset was largely responsible for this. It either treated the Adivasi as a barbarian or as a simple or genial savage who was incapable of taking care of himself.

Apart from the attitude of the officials, the mystifying processes and functions of these new institutions made it impossible for the Adivasis to engage with these institutions on an equal footing. Official work during the colonial period was done entirely in English and in the post independence era in Hindi. Given the preponderance of these non Adivasis languages, the Adivasis were either compelled to learn the language of their conquerors and the attached cultural baggage or depend on the non-Adivasis in their efforts to seek justice from the modern institutions.

Either way, the Adivasis lost their autonomy, self sufficiency and self respect. It is not an accident therefore that in every Adivasi protest institutions of police, judiciary and bureaucracy were made targets of attack. It is worth noting here the curious case of the shooting of an arrow by Birsa Munda on a seminary in Sarvada to mark the beginning of his protest. This act has been interpreted by certain communal minded people as an attack on the religious beliefs of the inmates of the seminary. However, if the intention of Birsa was to destroy the seminary rather then shooting a single arrow from a great distance he would have organised a full fledged raid on the institution.

However, what a western anglophile failed to recognise is that the problem of Adivasis is not only the inability to successfully represent their case in the modern institutions, but the very act of incorporation of the Adivasi society within the modern institutions. The arrow shot on the pastor by Birsa was not aimed at his religious belief, but was intended to draw a line of demarcation between the Adivasis desire to retain their traditional autonomy and the desire of an anglophile to facilitate an easy and civilised way of coopting the tribal community into the modern system.

Oral tradition as a basis of customary practices The Adivasi customary practices evolve from the praxis of oral traditional. In other words, the culture defines the customary practices. It is reflected in what people give value to and what they value. The event is important rather than the time in which it took place. It is not important that it is published but that it is remembered and recounted through the generations. The past is not a catalogue of facts but an encoding of events as the marker of Adivasi valor, justice, dignity, etc. Oral traditions are expressions of communality and community unlike the written script which becomes individual and personal.

The manner in which the Adivasi oral traditions were weakened was through the imposition of the written script by the ruling class. So today any and everything has to be written down in order to have validity. Whatever is unwritten and oral has been put in the category of myths and superstition. Once the commonality of the material resources gets privatised there will be an adverse impact on social relationships among the members of the society and a very negative influence on the cultural values and attitudes of the people. This is precisely what the British did by introducing the individual patta system.

This is exactly what happened to the Adivasi in India and in Jharkhand. As a result communalism is replaced by individualism. Common property becomes private property. Co-operation becomes competition. Consensus in decision making becomes majority decision. Equality among the members of the community becomes inequality. When India became independent the local ruling class, which was largely non Adivasi and which hailed from north Bihar, and whose language was Hindi, systematically imposed Hindi on the Adivasi people of Jharkhand.

Thus Hindi was made a necessary language both at the level of administration as well as in the formal education system. As a consequence, the children who started to go to primary school had to learn Hindi. The Adivasi school-going children did not fare well in Hindi because they did not speak it at home, whereas the non-Adivasi children, whose mother tongue was Hindi, did much better at school.

Hindi was also propagated to lessen the importance given to English. In this effort however the independence government largely failed because English continued to hold its sway in college and university education. The net consequence of this language policy was that Adivasi languages suffered from a double assault from government patronized Hindi and elite patronized English. National development leading to underdevelopment of the Indigenous people India has one of the largest indigenous populations in the world. Adivasis in India form nearly 8 percent of India's total population.

In the state of Jharkhand, during fifty years since independence, the Jharkhand land and the Jharkhandi people have been in a process of being reduced to shambles in several respects. The region consists of 79,714 sq kms of land with 2,69,09,428 population of whom 30 percent are indigenous Adivasis, whereas they were 60 percent at the start of the last century. Due to displacement process the indigenous people of Jharkhand are perhaps the worst hit, other wise this region is the richest region in the whole country in terms of natural resources, viz. timber and several kinds of minerals drawn from far flung areas. The planners of India's 5 year plans adopted a policy of positive discrimination towards Adivasis by providing them with certain extra facilities.

## Tribal Festivals

### *Hal Punhya*

Here the cultivation year begins with the fall of winter. The first day of Magh month which is known as Akhain Jatra or Hal Punhya, means the beginning of ploughing. The farmers, to symbolize this auspicious morning plough two and half circles of their agricultural land. This day is also considered as the symbol of good fortune.

### *Sarhul Festival*

The Sarhul festivals is the worship of the village deity who is supposed to be the protector of the tribes. Unless the deities of their village are pleased on them they can not be safe and prosperous. The festival is very popular for its festive mood. The whole region is highly charged with dance and song, food and drinks. It is celebrated in the spring season when the sprouting Sal gets greener and Sal trees blossoms with its flower called Shalony or Shalai.

This is the symbolic flower of Sarhul. The village deities are worshipped with this flower. The Shalai is also a symbol of friendship and brotherhood which the tribal priest distribute in every house of the village. The Prasad or offering of this festival is known as Hadia or Diang, immensely popular wine made of stale rice. Men & women get absorbed in nature with gay and over whelm with joy.

### *Bhagta Parab*

Bhagta Parab namely the festival of the devotees, comes in the end of spring season and in the beginning of summer season. Among the tribal, it is popularly known as worship of Budha Baba because here it has got its own meaning and procedure of worshipping. Bhagta or devotees observe fast for the worship. In the evening they carry their village priest called Laya from bathing pond to the temple.

It is a peculiar sacrificial scenario when the Laya gets out of the pond after bathing the devotees make a chain, locking their thighs with each other and come forward to offer their bare chest to Laya for walk over. After the evening worship, devotees take part in dynamic and vigorous Chhau Dance.

The next day, a primitive sports of bravery is observed. The devotees pierce hooks on the back of their skin and get tied at one end of a long horizontal wooden pole, which is hanging on the top of a vertical Shal wood pole, at a height of about 30 feet or some times 50 feet. Now the other end of the horizontal pole which is connected with a rope, pulled around the pole by the people and the tied devotee display the breath taking dance in the sky.

### *Rohin*

This festival is perhaps the first festival of Jharkhand. It is a festival of sowing seeds in the field. Farmers starts sowing seeds from this day but there is no dance or song like other tribal festivals but just a few rituals. There are some other festivals like Rajsawala Ambavati and Chitgomha are also celebrated with Rohin.

### *Karam*

The another extensively celebrated festival is Ind-Karam which is held on the 11th day of the phases of moon in Bhadra month. It is the festival of youthfulness and for the youth. The youth of villages get together in the forest. Where they dance, sing and collect fruits and flowers for the worship of the deity known as Karma Devta. At the evening, when the worship is over, dancing and signing go all through the night. The entire plateau resounds with dance of damsel, song of spirit and joy of juvenalia. It is indeed a rare example of such a vital and vibrant youth festival.

At the same time, the unmarried girls celebrate the Jawa festival, which has its own kind of dance and songs. This is held mainly with an expectation of fertility and better household. The unmarried girls decorate a small basket with germinating seeds. It is believed that the worship for good germination of the grains would increase the fertility as well. The girls also offer a green melon to the deity as a symbol of 'son'. This reveals the primitive expectation of human being, i.e grain and children.

### *Bandna*

Perhaps the most popular festivals is Bandana Parab during the black moon of Kartik month (Kartik Aamavashya). This festival is mainly for the benefit of animals and symbol of animal worship. The songs of this festival are called Ohira. Farmers clean their animals, feed them well, give them complete rest, decorate and ornate them.

They sing songs of admiration as an acknowledgement for their contribution. The primitive people believe that animals also have spirits which might harm or benefit them. So as to pacify these spirits as well as for better performance they worship their animals. The alluring of the week long festival takes place on the last day. Bulls and buffalos are chained to a strong pole and they are attacked with a dry animal hyde. The angry and excited animals hit the dry skin with its horns and the crowd enjoy looking at its vigorousness, anger and excitement. A unique aspect of Bandna is the wall embellishment with the folk painting.

***Tusu Makar***

Here the most common festival is Tusu or harvest festival comes during the winter in the last day of Poush month. It is also for the unmarried girls. For them Tusu is super excellent with grace and elegance who may fulfil their desire. Though there is no history behind this festival, there are some ritual custom and what it has its tremendous store of scintillating songs full of life and taste.

***Bandna***

Bandana is one of the most famous festivals celebrated during the black moon of month of Kartik (Kartik Aamavashya). This festival is mainly for the animals. Tribals are very close with animals and pets. In this festival, people wash, clean, paint, decorate feed well and put ornaments to their cow and bulls. The song dedicated for this festival is called Ohira which is an acknowledgement for animal's contribution in their day-to-day life. The belief behind this festival is animals are integral part of life and have souls as human being do. The most exciting day of the bandana week is the last day. Closured Bulls and buffalos are chained to a strong pole and they are attacked with a dry animal Hyde. The angry animals hit the dry skin with its horns and the crowd enjoys. Generally the colour used for decorating animals are natural colours and the is artwork is of folk type.

## Tribal Arts

Indigenous art of Singhbhum, originated with folk spirit of Jharkhand. So, it is undividable from original Jharkhand folk art. The heritage of art maintained by the indigenous people of Singhbhum transmit the imagination about their evaluation and existing along with the concept of beauty. It is wrong to formulate that folk art in general do not have any aesthetic aspect and it is just a utilitarian object. So is the case of Singhbhum. The folk art of Singhbhum embraces articles of daily use as well as those made on special occasion such as wedding and funerals. The basic purpose of all folk art around the world is ritualistic. Creation of art is underlined with certain rituals be it mask, ancestors statues, utensils or even fetishes, knitting, matting, weaving, basketing, wood craft, earthen wares etc.

### *Folk-Song*

Akhariya Domkach, Dohari Domkach, Janani(Woman) Jhumar (Anganai), Mardana(Man), Jhumar, Phagua, Udasi, Pawas, Daiddhara, Pahilsanjha, Adhratiya (Midnight), Bhinsariya (Morning), Pratkali, Jhumta

The tribal communities of Jharkhand date back 5000 years, according to some historians, proven by the cave paintings discovered in the region.

Dance and music make up an integral part of their social interaction, which is true of most tribal societies all over the world. "Sarhul" is the most celebrated tribal festival of the region when they worship the Sal tree with much dance, music, drinking and camaraderie.

"Paitkar' painting in scrolls and elegant stone work are delicate and intricate handicrafts of the region that rarely find their way to the market for lack of sponsorship. Woodwork, bamboo crafts, metal work and toys are widely made by the tribes of the region.

The most important among them are their wall embellishment and mask for Chhau dance. Since the area of their art is under rapid extinction due the displacement, they are on the verge of degradation. Traditionally they used various art forms. Among them body painting (tatoo), stone cutting, bull painting (during Bandna) folk painting fresco, sculpting horse, elephant etc. for the ritual purpose. Also they used to craft some totemic images in the wood. Decoration of wall is very common art.

The methods and materials used are traditional and handed down in the families, generation after generation and still persist with little alteration. It is unsophisticated of even rough hewn, often with bold colours. The quality of freshness, spontaneity, sincerity and simplicity of their art are appreciable. The type of decorative designs have characteristic of new stone age or Neolithic.

## Crafts

### *Scroll Painting*

Rapidly extincting community of folk painters of the district known as 'Paitkar' make scroll painting. Mainly they illustrate the primitive concept of "life after death".

### *Chhiy Mask*

The mask made of Papier machei in Singhbhum has its own significance. Papier machei of Kashmir is famous for house wares and decorative items with delicate painting and papier machei of Madras is well known for large size sculpted images. The papier machei of Saraikela and Charinda is popular for the mask for Chhou Dance. The methods and materials are separate from each other.

### *Wooden Work*

The Jharkhand region was also known as Jungle Mahal because of its dense forest which is inherent. The forest is rich with quality wood and the wood is used for producing the equipment required in housing, farming, fishing etc. for survival. The artisans of some villages went a step ahead and have explored creativity as well in their art, like beautifully decorative door panels, toys, boxes, and other household articles. Chhuthar, the carpenter community is engaged in this trade. Others are also skilled in this trade.

### *Bamboo Works*

The bamboo found in this thick forest is of a special quality. These bamboos are thin but strong and flexible. The artisan of Jharkhand use these bamboos in different artifacts like, basket, hauting & fishing equipments. Besides the Mahlis, Kharia's in some villages have taken this trade for their survival. Particularly, the fishing cage made by the Kharias are excellent.

### *Pottery*

Broken pieces of potteries are found in the bank of Subernarekha in Dulmi are of good quality with design and painting on it, reveals its trend.

### *Weaving*

The community surviving in jungle by fishing and hunting have a high quality of weaving skill, eg. dress materials and nets for hunting and fishing are very intricate with fascinating patterns. Still these weavers, called Tanti, make typically designed dress for Santhal.

### *Ornament*

Tribals are very fond of ornaments all over the world. So the tribal of this area inherently use various types of ornaments, like the ornaments made of bead, precious stones metals like gold and silver. Design is very simple like their art. Moal a rounded pipe of silver on feed, flats waste girt, spiral silver wires on wrist and arm, wide variety of necklace, ear ring etc

### *Weapon*

In the area weapon art is not much conventional but very common and similar to the primitive people. The black smiths produce all required tools and weapons for agriculture and safety.

### *Ritualistic Offerings*

The people of this area are totemic so they use several ritualistic offerings like clay made horse, elephants etc. to pacity their village gods and goddesses.

### *Stone Carving*

Even a few years back the tradition of stone carving was alive. Some families who were well skilled are not showing up any more, only few artisan are seen in the district.

### *Metal Work*

Besides agricultural implements, hunting tools and weapons are the product by the blacksmith. The Malhar and Thentri communities are expertise in metal casting, mainly producing house wares. Malhar are nomadic but the Thentris are settle amidst the tribes in the district.

### *Toy Making*

In the hilly regions of Jharkhand and around its capital city Ranchi, there dwell families who, for generations have revelled in toy making. Their wooden cut outs, glossed with an eye-catching canary paint depict the nature around. Of course the sizes are miniaturised for they are really playthings for children that have wheels for mobility or detachable limbs that allow free acrobatics manipulated by the pulling of string. These agile puppets are usually made from palm leaf slivers painted with pink dots and finger paintings, giving the right accents to a day of fun and frolic.

The love of the people of Jharkhand for the grand weddings and their accompanying fanfare is reflected in the toys also. The toy traders recreate the wedding of Lord Rama or the elephant god Ganesha in the toys. The lord as a groom is draped in a canary yellow lower garment or dhoti, the typical wedding finery for a bridegroom.

The tinges of gold on the garment and the veiled face of the toy bride complete the ambience. Of the scenes of nature nothing pleases these craftsmen more than the sight of a flock of brilliant parakeets in paddy green feathers. The contrasting red of the beak is a bonus that few can overlook. But the bird is not a boring depiction of its realistic form. Only the colours of the bird are copied and then re-designed in folk art forms of well- defined lines and frozen posture forms.

# 5

# Tribes of Orissa

Geographically, Orissa in Eastern India is divided into two parts: the coastal belt near Bay of Bengal, and the hilly regions. Orissa has a total population of 3,68,04,660 according to the census of 2001. The total number of persons in the scheduled tribe population is 81,45,081. The tribals are the indigenous auto-ethonous people of the land who occupy the relatively more inaccessible regions of forests and hills. As a result, we find tribes who, for centuries, lived far away from the mainstream in their relatively isolated, inaccessible, less fertile and less agriculturally productive regions of forests, hills and mountains. During the British India period, with the introduction of land rent system, the immigrants, Jagirdars and zamindars, forced many tribals to pay high rents or to render unlimited amount of forced labour. Such exploitation further forced many tribals to settle in more inaccessible regions of hills, thus isolating themselves from the mainstream.

Since prehistoric days the land of Orissa has been inhabited by various people. The earliest settlers of Orissa were primitive hill tribes. Although prehistoric communities cannot be identified, it is well known that Orissa had been inhabited by tribes like Saora or Sabar from the Mahabharata days. Saora in the hills and the Sahara and Sabar of the plains continue to be an important tribe distributed almost all over Orissa. Most of the tribal people have been influenced by Hindus and have adopted Hindu manners, customs and rituals. Bonda Parajas of Koraput district are the best example of these tribes.

Most of the tribal people and much of the population in Orissa belong to the Australoid group in racial history, while most of the general population belong to the broad-headed Alpinoid type. Besides this, a sprinkling of Mediterranean type is found in the general population.

Orissa had a high percentage of scheduled castes and tribes which together make 9.78 million. The scheduled tribes are concentrated in two belts. The northern belt comprises the district of Mayurbhanj, Keonjhar and Sundargarh. The southern belt consist of the district of Koraput, Ganjam and Phulbani. A large percentage of the tribal population in these districts have their own oral tribal languages and they do not know Oriya. The most important of these languages are Mundari, Santali, Saora and Kui / Kuvi.

There are four cultural regions within the present boundaries of Orissa. The north-eastern areas bordering on Bengal have been influenced in dress, food, habits, languages, social customs and festivities of Bengali culture and language. The southern parts of Ganjam and Koraput districts have a sizable Telugu-speaking population and have been influenced in language, food habits, dress and marriage customs by the Andhra culture and language.

## Tribal Communities

According to 1991 Census, in Orissa the total strength of tribal population is approximately seven million which constitutes 22.21% of the total population of the State. There are sixty-two tribal communities speaking various tribal languages as mother tongue in Orissa, as recognized by the Indian Constitution under article 342 of Section 4. They are:

1. Bagata
2. Baiga

3. Banjara, Banjari
4. Bathudi
5. Bhottada, Dhotada
6. Bhuiya, Hbuyan
7. Bhumia
8. Bhumij
9. Bhunjia
10. Binjhal
11. Binihia, Binjhoa
12. Birhor
13. Bondo Poraja
14. Chenchu
15. Dal
16. Desua Bhumij
17. Dharua
18. Didayi
19. Gadaba
20. Gandia
21. Ghara
22. Gond, gondo
23. Ho
24. Holva
25. Jatapu
26. Jung
27. Kandha gauda
28. Kawar
29. Kharia, Kharian
30. Kharwar

31. Khond, Kond, Kandha, Nanguli Kandha, Sitha Kendha
32. Kisan
33. Kol
34. Kolah Laharas, Kol Laharas
35. Kolha
36. Koli, Malhar
37. Kondadora
38. Kora
39. Korua
40. Kotia
41. Koya
42. Kulis
43. Lodha
44. Madia
45. Mahali
46. Mankidi
47. Mankirdia
48. Matya
49. Mirdhas
50. Munda, Munda Lahora, Munda Mahalis
51. Mundari
52. Omanatya
53. Oraon
54. Parenga
55. Paroja
56. Pentia
57. Rajuar
58. Santal

59. Saora, Sever, Saura, Sahara
60. Shabar, Lodha
61. Sounti
62. Tharua

Linguistically the tribes of India are broadly classified into four categories, namely:

(1) Indo-Aryan speakers,
(2) Dravidian speakers,
(3) Tibeto-Burmese speakers, and
(4) Austric speakers.

In Orissa the speakers of the Tibeto-Burmese language family are absent, and therefore Orissan tribes belong to other three language families. The Indo-Aryan language family in Orissa includes Dhelki-Oriya, Matia, Haleba, Jharia, Saunti, Laria and Oriya (spoken by Bathudi and the acculturated sections of Bhuyans, Juang, Kondh, Savara, Raj Gond etc.). The Austric language family includes eighteen tribal languages namely, Birija, Parenga, Kisan, Bhumiji, Koda, Mahili Bhumiji, Mirdha-Kharia, Ollar Gadaba, Juang, Bondo, Didayee, Karmali, Kharia, Munda, Ho, Mundari and Savara. And within the Dravidian language family there are nine languages in Orissa, namely, Pengo, Gondi, Kisan, Konda, Koya. Parji, Kui, Kuvi and Kurukh or Oraon.

The tribes of Orissa though belong to three linguistic divisions, yet they have lots of socio-cultural similarities between them. These commonalities signify homogeneity of their cultures and together they characterise the notion or concept of tribalism. Tribal societies share certain common characteristics and by these they are distinguished from complex or advanced societies. In India tribal societies had apparently been outside the main historical current of the development of Indian civilization for centuries. Hence tribal societies manifest such cultural features which signify a primitive level in socio-cultural parameter.

## Tribal Habitat

A major portion of the tribal habitat is hilly and forested. Tribal villages are generally found in areas away from the alluvial plains close to rivers. Most villages are uniethnic in composition, and smaller in size. Villages are often riot planned at all.

## Tribal Economy

Tribal economy is characterised as subsistence oriented. The subsistence economy is based mainly on collecting, hunting and fishing (e.g., the Birhor, Hill Kharia), or a combination of hunting and collecting with shifting cultivation (e.g., the Juang,, Hill Bhuyan, Lanjia Saora, Kondh etc.) Even the so-called plough using agricultural tribes do often, wherever scope is available, supplement their economy with hunting and collecting. Subsistence economy is characterised by simple technology, simple division of labour, small-scale units of production and no investment of capital. The social unit of production, distribution and consumption is limited to the family and lineage. Subsistence economy is imposed by circumstances which are beyond the control of human beings, poverty of the physical environment, ignorance of efficient technique of exploiting natural resources and lack of capital for investment. It also implies existence of barter and lack of trade.

Considering the general features of their (i) eco-system, (ii) traditional economy, (iii) supernatural beliefs and practices, and (iv) recent "impacts of modernization", the tribes of Orissa can be classified into six types, such as:

(1) Hunting, collecting and gathering type,

(2) Cattle-herder type,

(3) Simple artisan type,

(4) Hill and shifting cultivation type,

(5) Settled agriculture type and

(6) Industrial urban worker type.

Each type has a distinct style of life which could be best understood in the paradigm of nature, man and spirit complex, that is, on the basis of relationship with nature, fellow men and the supernatural.

Tribes of the first type, namely Kharia, Mankidi, Mankidia and Birhor, live in the forests of Mayurbhanj, Keonjhar and Sundargarh districts, exclusively depend on forest resources for their livelihood by practising hunting, gathering and collecting. They live in tiny temporary huts made out of the materials found in the forest. Under constraints of their economic pursuit they live in isolated small bands or groups. With their primitive technology, limited skill and unflinching traditional and ritual practices, their entire style of life revolves round forest. Their world view is fully in consonance with the forest eco-system. The population of such tribes in Orissa though is small, yet their impact on the ever-depleting forest resources is very significant. Socio-politically they have remained inarticulate and therefore have remained in a relatively more primitive stage, and neglected too.

The Koya which belongs to the Dravidian linguistic group, is the lone pastoral and cattle-breeder tribal community in Orissa. This tribe which inhabits the Malkangiri District has been facing crisis for lack of pasture.

In Orissa Mahali and Kol-Lohara practise crafts like basketry and black-smithy respectively. The Loharas with their traditional skill and primitive tools manufacture iron and wooden tools for other neighbouring tribes and thereby eke out their existence. Similarly the Mahalis earn their living by making baskets for other communities. Both the tribes are now confronted with the problem of scarcity of raw materials. And further they are not able to compete with others, especially in the tribal markets where goods of other communities come for sale, because of their primitive technology.

The tribes that practise hill and shifting cultivation are many. In northern Orissa the Juang and Bhuyan, and in southern Orissa the Kondh, Saora, Koya, Parenga, Didayi, Dharua and Bondo practise shifting cultivation. They supplement their economy by foodgathering and hunting as production in shifting cultivation is low. Shifting cultivation is essentially a regulated sequence of procedure designed to open up and bring under cultivation patches of forest lands, usually on hill slopes.

In shifting cultivation the practitioners follow a pattern of cycle of activities which are as follows:

(i) Selection of a patch of hill slope or forest land and distribution or allotment of the same to intended practitioners

(ii) Worshipping of concerned deities and making of sacrifices,

(iii) Cutting of trees, bushes, ferns etc., existing on the land before summer months,

(iv) Pilling up of logs, bushes and ferns on the land,

(v) Burning of the withered logs, ferns and shrubs etc. to ashes on a suitable day,

(vi) Cleaning of the patch of land before the on-set of monsoon and spreading of the ashes evenly on the land after a shower or two,

(vii) Hoeing and showing of seeds with regular commencement of monsoon rains,

(viii) Crude bunding and weeding activities follow after sprouting of seeds,

(ix) Watching and protecting the crops,

(x) Harvesting and collecting crops,

(xi) Threshing and storing of corns, grains etc., and

(xii) Merry-making.

In these operations all the members of the family are involved in some way or the other. Work is distributed among the family members according to the ability of individual members. However, the head of the family assumes all the responsibilities in the practice and operation of shifting cultivation. The adult males, between 18 and 60 years of age under-take the strenuous work of cutting tree, ploughing and hoeing, and watching of the crops at night where as cutting the bushes and shrubs, cleaning of seeds for sowing and weeding are done by women.

Shifting cultivation is not only an economic pursuit of some tribal communities, but it accounts for their total way of life. Their social structure, economy, political organization and religion are all accountable to the practice of shifting cultivation.

In the past, land in the tribal areas had not been surveyed and settled. Therefore, the tribals freely practised shifting cultivation in their respective habitats assuming that land, forest, water and other natural resources belonged to them. The pernicious, yet unavoidable practise of shifting cultivation continues unchecked and all attempts made to wean away the tribals from shifting cultivation have so far failed. The colonization scheme of the State Government has failed in spirit.

In certain hilly areas terraces are constructed along the slopes. It is believed to be a step towards settled agriculture. Terrace cultivation is practised by the Saora, Kondh and Gadaba. The terraces are built on the slopes of hill with water streams.

Several large tribes, such as, Santal, Munda, Ho, Bhumij, Oraon, Gond, Mirdha, Savara etc. are settled agriculturists, though they supplement their economy with hunting, gathering and collecting. Tribal agriculture in Orissa is characterised by unproductive and uneconomic holdings, land alienation indebtedness, lack of irrigation facilities in the undulating terrains, lack of easy or soft credit facilities as well as use of traditional skill and primitive implements. In general, they raise only one crop during the monsoon, and therefore have to supplement their economy by other types of subsidiary economic activities.

Tribal communities practising settled agriculture also suffer from further problems, viz:

(i) want of record of right for land under occupation,

(ii) land alienation

(iii) problems of indebtedness,

(iv) lack of power for irrigation

(v) absence of adequate roads and transport,

(vi) seasonal migration to other places for wage-earning and

(vii) lack of education and adequate scope for modernization.

Sizable agglomeration of tribal population in Orissa has moved to mining, industrial and urban areas for earning a secured living through wage-labour. During the past three decades the process of industrial urbanization in the tribal belt of Orissa has been accelerated through the operation of mines and establishment of industries. Mostly persons from advanced tribal communities, such as Santal, Munda, Ho, Oraon, Kisan, Gond etc. have taken to this economic pursuit in order to relieve pressure from their limited land and other resources.

In some instances industrialization and mining operations have led to uprooting of tribal villages, and the displaced became industrial nomads. They lost their traditional occupation, agricultural land, houses and other immovable assets. They became unemployed and faced unfair competition with others in the labour market, Their aspiration - gradually escalated, although they invariably failed to achieve what they aspired for. Thus the net result was frustration.

The overall kinship system of the tribes may be label led as tempered classificatory. In terminology the emphasis lies on the unilinear principle, generation and age. Descent and inheritance are patrilineal and authority is patripotestal among all the tribal communities of Orissa.

Among the tribes there is very little specialization of social roles, with the exception of role differentiation in terms of kinship and sex and some specialization in crafts, the only other role specializations are Head-man, Priest, Shaman and the Haruspex.

There is very little rigid stratification in society. The tendency towards stratification is gaining momentum among several settled agricultural tribes under the impact of modernisation. The tribes of Orissa are at different levels of socio-economic development.

The position of priest, village headman and the inter-village head-man are hereditary. The village headman is invariably from original settlers' clan of the village, which is obviously dominant. Punishments or corrective measures are proportional to the gravity of the breach of set norms or crime, and the punishments range from simple oral admonition to other measures, such as corporal punishments, imposition of fines, payment of compensation, observance of prophylactic rites and excommunication from the community. Truth of an incident is determined by oath, ordeals and occult mechanism.

As regards the acquisition of brides for marriage, the most widely prevalent practice among the tribes of Orissa is through "capture", although other practices, such as, elopement, purchase, service and negotiation are also there. With the passage of time negotiated type of marriage, which is considered prestigious, is being preferred more and more. Payment of bride-price is an inseparable part of tribal marriage, but this has changed to the system of dowry among the educated sections.

The religion of the Orissan tribes is an admixture of animism, animalism, nature-worship, fetishism, shamanism, anthropomorphism and ancestor worship. Religious beliefs and practices aim at ensuring personal security and happiness as well as community well-being and group solidarity. Their religious performances include life-crisis rites, cyclic community rites, ancestor and totemic rites and observance of taboos. Besides these, the tribals also resort to various types of occult practices. In order to tide over either a personal or a group crisis the tribals begin with occult practices, and if it does not yield any result the next recourse is supplication of the supernatural force.

## Tribal Culture

Orissa occupies an unique position in the ethnographic map of India for having the largest variety of tribal communities.Although they are found in all the districts of the State, yet more than half of their total strength are found in the districts of Koraput, Rayagada, Naurangpur, Malkangiri, Kalahandi, Nauapara, Kandhamal, Baudh, Keonjhar, Sundargarh and Mayurbhanj.

The tribes of Orissa are at various stages of socio-economic development. At one extreme are the group which lead a relatively secluded and archaic mode of life keeping their core culture intact, while at the other extreme there are communities which are indistinguishable from the general agricultural communities.

Any society - tribal or otherwise, comprises of organised groups of people who have learnt to live and work together interacting in the pursuit of common goals. Each society has its own rules of business and tricks of trade which helps its people to define their relationship with one another and live and work together. Therefore a society is a going concern and functions and perpetuates itself on the basis of the rules for living together.

The tribal people express their cultural identity and distinctiveness in their social organisation, language, rituals and festivals and also in their dress, ornament, art and craft. They have retained their own way of managing internal affairs of the village mainly through two institutions namely, the village council and the youth dormitory. The dormitory is the core of tribal culture and it reinforces the age-old traditions. In Orissa this institution occurs among many tribal communities in some form or other.

The Juangs call it Majang and Darbar, the Kondhs call it Dindaghar, the Bhuyans call it Dhangarabasa and among the Bondos it goes by the name Ingersin. Of all the tribes the dormitory system is well organized among the Juang. Conspicuous in the village, the Mandaghar is the largest hut. It has wall on three sides and is open in front. The wooden parts and side walls are carried with decorative symbols depicting animals. The boys hang their changu, a flat tambourine like drum which is used at the time of dancing. In front of the Mandaghar is the small open space where dance takes place almost every night after the day's work is over. The dormitory is so to say a school of dancing and expression of the communal art of the people. The elders of the village assemble at the dormitory house every day for every important event in their corporate life. Here they discuss matters concerning the welfare of the village, settle the distribution of swidden and fix date and time for celebration of the village festivals, etc. In these respects the dormitory may be considered as the centre of social, economic and religious life of the village.

The amazing conglomeration of traditions, beliefs, sorrows and philosophies that together constitute and vitalise the rituals and festivals of the tribes, has descended from antiquity and has been preserved unimpaired to the present day. Every facet of their life covering round-the-year activities is intimately connected with religious beliefs and ritual practices. It is these aspects of their culture that give meaning and depth to their lives, and solidarity to their social structure.

The tribes believe that their life and work are controlled by supernatural beings whose abode is around them in hills, forests, rivers and houses. It is very difficult to standardize the

Gods and spirits as their composition continually changes when old ones are forgotten with the introduction of new ones. Their Gods differ from one another in composition, function, character and nature. Some are benevolent; some are neutral and some are malevolent. The malevolent spirits and Gods are cared more than their benevolent counter parts as they can bring misery.

Manipulation of environment being the main concern of the tribals, all the ritual acts are directed towards stimulating natural processes. Illness or misfortune is attributed to displeasure and malicious act of the Gods or ancestors. The sacrifice of different kinds of livestock accompanied by all the rites and ceremonials of fetishism is considered appropriate appeasement. Moreover, their extremely superstitious nature prohibits the undertaking of any enterprise unless the Gods are first appeased and the omens, after being carefully considered, are adjudged to be propitious.

Among the tribes there are religious functionaries who cater to their spiritual needs. For example, the hierarchy of priests among the Saoras may be divided into three categories. The Buyya is a priest who presides at agricultural festivals and offers sacrifices that especially characterize these occasions. The Kudan is a shaman who combines the functions of priest, prophet and medicine-man. The sacerdotal head among the Juang is called Nagam or Buita, Pujari or Sisa among the Bondos and Jani among the Kondhs. The post of these officials are mostly ascribed but not achieved.

The ceremonies and festivals of the tribes can be classified into two groups, that is, those that relate to the individual families and those that relate to the village as a whole. The ceremonies and rites relating to birth of a child, marriage, death are observed family-wise whereas those relating to various agricultural cycle, eating of new fruits, hunting, etc. are observed by the village community.

Some of the important festivals observed by the tribal communities of Orissa include Guar ceremony of the Saora,

Gotar of the Gadaba, Push Punei of the Juang, Kedu of the Kondh, Karam festival of the Oraon, Chait Parab of the Bondo and Magha Parab of the Santal.

With the advent of time, traces of borrowing from Hindu Pantheon and religious ceremonies are noticed among the tribes of Orissa. They have started worshipping Siva, Parbati and Lord Jagannath. Hindu festivals like Raja, Laxmipuja, Dasahara and Gamha are also becoming popular among them day by day.

The tribes of Orissa, despite their poverty and their pre-occupation with the continual battle for survival, have retained the rich and varied heritage of colourful dance and music forming integral part of their festivals and rituals. Among them, the dance and music is developed and maintained by themselves in a tradition without aid and intervention of any professional dancer or teacher. It is mainly through the songs and dances the tribes seek to satisfy their inner urge for revealing their soul. The performance of these only give expression to their inner feelings, their joys and sorrows, their natural affections and passion and their appreciation of beauty in nature and in man.

Although the pattern of dance and music prevalent among them vary from tribe to tribe yet there are certain features common to all. Tribal dances have some accompaniments by means of which the rhythm is maintained. This consists of clapping of hands or beating of drums or an orchestra of different instruments. Every dance is accompanied by a song which is sung by the performers. Both men and women, young and old dance and invariably sing but the accompanying orchestra or music is usually provided by the male members. Tribal dance is characterized not only by its originality and spontaneity but also for its wide range of movements. Many parts of the body such as head, back, arms, feet. finger, etc. are brought into play. Some of the tribal groups put on colourful dancing costume during their performance.

Like dance, the songs sung by different tribal groups differ from one tribe to the other. Among the tribes everyone is a musician and poet. When happily inspired, they can coin a song then and there and sing it. Like any others, when they see things of beauty and meet pleasantly, they exhibit this pleasure and happiness by composing songs. One finds in these songs humours, jokes, romance, satires, criticisms, acquisitions and anger. Though there is no modernity and fineness, their ideas being natural, the compositions are good, inspiring and melodious. On the occasion of performing Pujas and observance of festivals the songs sung are different. Such songs are adopted from the past so many years. These songs describe the history of gods, the process of creation and some epic stories.

The joy of free life find expression in tribal art and craft. It is through this endeavour their cultural self-image and aesthetic sensibility are visualized. The artistic skill of the tribal people is not only manifested in their dance and music but also in their dress and ornaments, wall-paintings, wood carvings and decorations, etc. The beautiful wall-paintings and floral designs of the Santals and the ikons of the Saoras which depict geometric designs and stylistic figures of plants and animals are the best example of tribal art. The multicoloured designs and relief figures of animals and human beings which decorate the walls of Mandaghar in Juang society are indeed works of very high order. Similar wall-paintings and decorations as observed among the Mundari group of tribals are also very attractive.

Some of the tribal communities like the Bondo and the Gadaba have their own looms by which they weave clothes for their own use. These hand spun textiles of coloured yarn are examples of best artistic skill of these people. So also among the Dongaria Kondhs the ladies are very much skilled in making beautiful embroidery work in their scarf. The tribal women in general and the Bondo, the Gadaba and the Dongaria Kondh women in particular are very fond of using ornaments. The Bondo women who are considered most primitive, look majestic when they wear headbands made of grass, necklaces of coloured beads and girdles made of brass on their bodies. All these are expressions of their artistic quality and aesthetic sense.

The tribal people turn out excellent handicrafts for their own use. The wood carving of the Kondhs, metal works by lost wax process among the Bathudis, cane and bamboo basketry works among the Juangs and Bhuyans, are all symbolic of artistic creation.

## Social Organisation of Tribes

The most fascinating feature of the Adivasis is their social system and its organisation.The traditional Adivasi society with its standard pattern or tribe, sub-tribe and clan is 8 cohesive unit in which the community spirit is dominant. It is this inter-personal, face-to-face relationship that endows them with a sense of belonging. Tribes like the Saoras, Kondhs, Gonds and Santals have spread out it to wide areas with the result that, sub-tribes have been formed claiming an independent cultural identity as with the Kutia, Dongria and Desia Kondhs, the Lanjia Saoras of Pultasing and the Sudh Saoras of the coastal districts, the plain Bondas and the hill Bondas. Each of these groups has developed and nurtured its own style of economic activity,social organisation and cycles of rites and rituals for separate identity.

The dan is the bigger unit and its number varies from tribe to tribe. The Juangs, Santals, Kondhs, Gadabas and Parajas are well known for their exogamous patrilineal totemic dan organisation. The Juangs have as many as 24 clans which have totemic names that are given after objects, trees, and food grains which point to a common ancestry and attitudes of reverence to the ancestors which act as a cultural bond among them. The Saoras, however, have an extended family called birinda descended from a common ancestor, and not a dan system. A Saora woman unlike other women of other tribes continues to belong to her father's family after marriage and not to her husband's dan.

The main organising principle of the Adivasi Society is kinship with little stratification embracing both consaguineal and affinal groups who use both classificatory and descriptive terms in their modes of address. The emphasis is placed on the unilineal principle, generation and age. The Adivasis accept inheritance and authority through the male line.

The growing-up socialization process of the Adivasis is extremely interesting, consisting as it does of practices that regulate life in a complex manner. The rites of passage comprising birth, puberty, marriage and death play a very important role in tribal society for which initiation and training are provided carefully. It is these rites that are introduced through youth dormitaries variously called Majang (Juang), Dindaghar (Kondh), Dhangrabasa (Bhuyan) or Ingerson (Bonda). The dormitory is a large hut closed on three sides and open in the front. It is used for training the youth in dancing as well as for holding village councils for discussing and deciding important matters concerning the village or communal welfare. The presiding functionaries in the village council are the headman and the priest. The former, variously called Naik (Juang), Pradhan (Bhuyan), Gomango (Saora) Majhi (Saonta), Munda (Ho), Budrik (Gadaba) decides the secular matters while the latter called Dehury (Bhuyan), Boita (Juang), Buya (Saora), Kartha (Oraon), Jani (Kondh) is responsible for decisions on religious and spiritual matters.

Along with the headman and the priest, the shaman, and the harospex, who can gaze into the stars and foretell the future, cbnstitute the governing elite of the village. Some tribes like the Juangs, Bhuiya, Gondsand Oraons have inter village councils, the head of which is the headman of the most important village usually a respectable person of age and experience. This council deals with inter village disputes and other matters pertaining to the village as an entity, not individuals. In most matters the decisions are accepted and implemented successfully. But this system is now under stress owing to the introduction of the modern Panchayat system often disturbing and dislocating the ancient ways of life.

## Staus of Tribal Women

The tribal women have a peculiar position and status in the tribal society. In some tribal societies, matrilineal and matriarchal systems exist. Most of the tribal organizations have clearly defined areas of work among the males and the females. Although the work domain assigned to woman is important in terms of sustenance of the family, yet viewed from the value rating of work, they are relatively low in the hierarchy of work domains.

Tribal women in Indian society have been contributing positively to the local economy by participating actively along with men in the pursuit of economic activities to earn livelihood. In reality, women are seen to do more hard work in the fields than women. They participate in all agricultural operations except ploughing. They work in all sectors of indigenous cottage industries, tribal arts, and production of artifacts.

In other words, they share major responsibilities in the production process. The division of work is heavily loaded against the tribal women, because, in addition to an equal or greater burden in the economic production process, she has to take the sole responsibility of household chores, which is a stupendous task. Child-rearing is also her sole responsibility. Tribal women working in the fields carrying child in the back is a common sight in the tribal areas. Nowhere will one find a tribal man carrying the child on his back while he works on the field. This kind of division of labour places women in a disadvantageous position compared to their non-tribal counterparts.

Among the non-tribals, except in few urban cases, men look after the financial aspects while women look after the household aspect and remain under the control of men. In the market place, tribal women are seen as vendors as well as buyers especially in the weekly market, a scene normally not found in non-tribal communities. The tribal woman has the freedom to choose her husband and often dates with boys without any restriction. Premarital sex is also prevalent in some community. This arrangement is conspicuous by its absence in non-tribal counterparts. Whereas her parents, due to the dowry system followed in marriage, consider the non-tribal girl as an economic liability, the tribal girl is considered as an economic asset. The concept of 'bride price' justifies this. A tribal groom has to pay bride price to the bride's father on marriage for the economic loss the father is going to face.

## Religion of Tribal Community

The religion of the tribal community is the resultant of traditions and beliefs that have come down to them from antiquity. The Adivasis like the Hindus are polytheists. The supreme deity, who is believed to be the creator of the world is a mythical figure, under whom there are a number of gods and goddesses often malignant in dispensation. The Adivasis rely on the village priests to please and propitiate their gods at the time of sickness, pestilence or for the yield of good crops and healthy Livestock good progeny.

Life crisis rites of different types, cyclic community rites like sowing of seeds, harvesting of crops, eating of the first corn, the performance of seasonal festivals like Guar (Saora), Gohar (Gadaba), Push Ponei (Juang), Kedu (Kondh), Karam (Cram), Chait Parah (Bonda), Magh Parah (Santal), other community rites, ancestral rites, occult practices are decided upon by the village priest. The influence of Christian and Hindu religions is seen in the celebration of Christian festivals like Easter, Good Friday and Christmas and Hindu festivals like Raja, Gamha Pumima, Durga Puja and Laxmi Puja and the worship of Lord Jagannath (originally a Savara deity), Shiva and Parvati. Their religion, which exhibits features of animism, animalism, anthropomorphism, nature-worship, fetishism, ancestor-worship is under the control, guidance and supervision of the village.

## Health Status

Despite remarkable world-wide progress in the field of diagnostics and curative and preventive health, still there are people living in isolation in natural and unpolluted surroundings far away from civilization with their traditional values, customs, beliefs and myth intact. They are commonly known as "tribals" and are considered to be the autochthonous people of the land. About half of the world's autochthonous people, comprising 635 tribal communities including 75 primitive tribal communities live in India. They are found in all states except Punjab, Haryana and Jammu & Kashmir. Orissa, the most picturesque state in eastern India, occupies a unique place in the tribal map of the country having largest number of tribal communities (62 tribes including 13 primitive tribes) with a population of 8.15 million constituting 22.3% of state's population. The primitive tribal communities have been identified by the Govt. of Indiain 15 states/union territories on the basis of (a) pre agricultural level of technology (b) extremely low level of literacy; and © small, stagnant or diminishing population.

Health is a prerequisite for human development and is an essential component for the well being of the mankind. The health problems of any community are influenced by interplay of various factors including social, economic and political ones. The common beliefs, customs, practices related to health and disease in turn influence the health seeking behaviour of the community. There is a consensus agreement that the health status of the tribal population is very poor and worst among the primitive tribes because of their isolation, remoteness and being largely unaffected by the developmental processes going on in the country.

Studies undertaken in the country indicate that the primitive tribes have distinct health problems, mainly governed by multidimentional factors like their habitat, difficult terrain, ecologically variable niches, illiteracy, poverty, isolation, superstition and deforestation. Hence an integrated multidisciplinary approach has been adopted by different researchers to study the tribal health problems.

Orissa Health Strategy 2003 has advocated for improving the health status of tribal population by reducing mortality and morbidity. It indicates that the tribal people suffer disproportionately from malaria, sexually transmitted diseases, tuberculosis, genetic disorders like G6PD deficiency, sickle cell anaemia as also nutritional deficiency diseases. These are some of the special health problems attributed to these communities. The situation analysis of health indices of the tribal population in Orissa are worse than the national average: Infant mortality rate 84.2; under five mortality rate 126.6; children under weight 55.9; anaemia in children 79.8; children with acute respiratory infection 22.4; children with recent diarrhoea 21.1; women with anaemia 64.9 per 1000.

A high incidence of malnutrition has also been documented in the tribal dominated districts of OrissaOrissa is one of the ten states in the country covered under the National Nutrition Monitoring Bureau (NNMB). According to the latest report of NNMB (2000 - 2001), Orissa continues to have second highest level of under nutrition among the ten states. When compared with the aggregate figures for chronic energy deficiency (BMI < 18.5) in adult men and women in these states the level is higher in Orissa. The prevalence of chronic energy deficiency (CED) in adult men in the state is 38.6% compared to aggregate of 37.4%, whereas the CED prevalence in the adult women is 46% against 39.3% aggregate figure. As malnutrition is known to potentiate susceptibility to death due to infectious diseases, the high mortality rate amongst the primitive tribes may be attributed to this. In a prospective study conducted in Bondo, Didayi, Juanga and Kutia Kondha primitive tribes of Orissa severe malnutrition (based on Gomez classification) was observed in 16, 19, 25.1 and 26.6% population respectively.

In a separate study conducted by Regional Medical Research Centre (RMRC), Bhubaneswar, 66% of primitive tribal population (6 - 15 years age group) of Mayurbhanj and Sundergarh districts was found to be malnourished. Similarly the chronic energy deficiency was found to be very high among Langia Saura (89.4%) and Kutia Kondha (88.9%) primitive tribes of Rayagada district of Orissa. Nutritional status of primitive tribes of Orissa was lower compared to other major tribes. Anthropometric analysis of other primitive tribes of the country revealed that 50% of the children in Pahariyas of the Rajmahal hills of Bihar were below 3percentile and below 90% of Harvard standard. It was found that 85% of Great Andamanese children (<6 years) were undernourished and more than 77% children and adolescents (<19 years) were stunted, wasted or both, while 38.8, 23.6 and 7.3% preschool children among Baiga tribes of Madhya Pradesh had mild, moderate and severe grades of malnutrition respectively.

The majority of Bondo, Didayi, Kondha and Juanga primitive tribes of Orissa had different grades of anaemia (as per WHO classification) as an important clinical manifestation. The severe anaemia (Hb<7 g/dl) ranged from 0.6 to 2.3%, moderate (Hb 7-9 g/dl) from 7.4 to 13.6% and mild (Hb 9-11 g/dl) 30.7 to 48.2% of population. Anaemia was more common in females than males. Another study reported 85% of Paudi Bhuyan primitive tribes of Sundergarh district to be suffering from different grades of anaemia. A cross sectional study conducted in Madhya Pradesh revealed severe anaemia in 40% of Abhujmaria, 29% of Birhor and 42.2% of Baiga primitive tribes. Majority (51.2%) of the anaemic primitive tribal population of Orissa showed microcytic hypochromic blood picture suggestive of iron deficiency anaemia. Statistical analysis revealed a positive correlation between hookworm infestation and anaemia possibly due to indiscriminate defecation, bare foot and lack of health awareness. An appropriate intervention resulted in the reduction of worm infestation and improvement of anaemia status in 51.2 and 34.8% of individuals respectively.

The demographic status of the primitive tribes has shown a declining or static trend. The demographic data of Juanga primitive tribe of Orissa revealed a marital fertility rate of about 6 and life expectancy at birth 35.9 years. A study carried out recently by RMRC, Bhubaneswar amongst four primitive tribes of Orissa, revealed an infant mortality rate (per 1000 live birth) of 139.5 in Bondo, 131.6 in Didayi, 132.4 in Juanga and 128.7 in Kondha (Kutia); a maternal mortality rate (per 1000 female population) of 12 in Bondo, 10.9 in Didayi, 11.4 in Juanga and 11.2 in Kondha tribe; the life expectancy of 48.7 years in Bondo, 57.1 years in Didayi, 49.6 years in Juanga and 50.7 years in Kondha; the crude birth rate (per 1000 population) of 18.31 in Bondo, 24.3 in Didayi, 22.3 in Juanga and 21.6 in Kondha tribe and the crude death rate (per 1000 population) of 19.2 in Bondo, 23.7 in Didayi, 21.2 in Juanga and 20.9 in Kondha population. The average number of pregnancies was found to be 5.09 in Kutia Kondha tribe.

The unhygienic and primitive parturition practices were mainly responsible for high maternal mortality. It was observed that among Kutia Kondha the delivery was conducted by the mother herself in a half squatting position holding a rope tied down from the roof of the house. This helped her in applying pressure to deliver the child. In complicated labour, obviously it might lead to maternal as well as child mortality. Similar crude birth practices were also found in Kharia primitive tribes. The selection potential based on differential fertility and mortality was found to be 0.668 in Lodhas of West Bengal and 0.524 in Sahariyas of Rajasthan. The demographic characteristics of the Baiga tribes of Madhya Pradesh has shown steady rise since 1901.

Forty-two percent of the populations were under 14 years of age and 89% were under the age of 40 years. The mean menarcheal age is 15.2 years and mean age at first marriage was 16.6 years. Age at menarche, marriage, breast-feeding and time interval between marriage and first conception are natural in this society.

### *Upper Respiratory Tract Infection*

After anaemia, the respiratory disease including upper respiratory tract infection was more commonly prevalent (14.9% in Bondo, 16.6% in Didayi, 13.6% in Kondha and 8.3% in Juanga) and accounts for a high infant mortality due to inadequate vaccination, lack of early diagnosis and prevention. Similar observations were made in Birhor (11.2%) and Sahariya (57.5% in children aged 0-4 years and 56.9% in children aged 5 -14 years) tribes of Madhya Pradesh.

#### *Malaria*

Malaria is the foremost public health problem of Orissa contributing 23% of malaria cases, 40% of Plasmodium falciparum cases and 50% of malaria deaths in the country. More than 60% of tribal population of Orissa live in highrisk areas for malaria. Though the tribal communities constitute nearly 8% of the total population of the country, they contribute 25% of the total malaria cases and 15% of total P.falciparum cases. Various epidemiological studies and malariometric surveys carried out in tribal population including primitive tribes reveal a high transmission of P.falciparum in the forest regions of India, because malaria control in such settlements has always been unattainable due to technical and operational problems. In a specific study conducted in undivided Koraput district, it was observed that the district is endemic for malaria and is hyperendemic in top hills where Bondo primitive tribes are residing. A prospective study conducted by RMRC, Bhubaneswar during 2000 - 2003 in Malkangiri,

Kandhamala and Keonjhar districts, showed slide positivity rate (SPR) of 14.2% in Bondo, 14.4% in Didayi, 10.5% in Kondha and 9.5% in Juanga primitive tribes. The Pf% was 93.5% in Bondo, 91.6% in Didayi, 92.7% in Kondha and 91.2% in Juanga population and the spleen rate in children of 2 to 9 years was 25.8, 35.1, 26.3 and 24.4% in Bondo, Didayi, Kondha and Juanga tribes respectively.

### *Diarrhoeal Disorders*

Water-borne communicable diseases like gastrointestinal disorders including acute diarrhoea are responsible for a higher morbidity and mortality due to poor sanitation, unhygienic conditions and lack of safe drinking water in the tribal areas of the country. In a cross sectional study conducted by RMRC, Bhubaneswar in 4 primitive tribes of Orissa, the diarrhoeal diseases including cholera was found to occur throughout the year attaining its peak during the rainy season (From July to October). During 2002 to 2003, 12.7% of Bondo, 13.2% of Didayi, 10.4% of Kondha and 12.6% of Juanga children (0- 6 years) and 10.9% Bondo, 11.6% Didayi, 10.2% Kondha and 6.9% Juanga adult population presented with acute diarrhoea. Bacteriological study of the rectal swabs revealed Vibrio cholerae in 2.5%, Escherichia coli in 39.2%, Salmonella in 0.23% and Shigella spp in 1.8% of all culture positive cases while 56.3% of rectal swabs were culture negative. Among the V.cholerae isolates V.cholerae O1 Ogawa was the predominant serotype. The acute diarrhoeal problem was basically due to the poor environmental hygiene, lack of safe drinking water, improper disposal of human excreta which was further aggravated by low literacy, low socioeconomic status coupled with blind cultural belief, lack of access to medical facilities leading to serious public health problem encouraging faeco-oral transmission of enteric pathogens. In a similar study conducted by RMRC, Jabalpur in Hill Korwas, it was observed that 0.1% population suffered from acute diarrhoea.

### *Intestinal Parasitism*

Intestinal protozoan and helminthic infestations are the major public health problems and were observed in 44.6% Bondo, 44.9% Didayi, 31.9% Juanga and 41.1% Kondha primitive tribes of Orissa. Amongst helminthic infestation hookworm was most common (21% in Bondo, 18.7% in Didayi, 14% in Juanga and 18.2% in Kondha). Children (aged 0-14 years) were more affected than the adults. A repeat stool examination after 4 months of antihelminthic and antiprotozoal treatment revealed significant reduction in the worm burden (from 38.9 to 18.9%). Most of these infections are due to indiscriminate defecation in the open field, bare foot walking and lack of health awareness and hygiene. These are preventable with repeated administration of antihelminthic and protozoal treatment at 4 months interval which can be used effectively in national parasitic infection control programme. Studies conducted by RMRC, Jabalpur also revealed that intestinal parasitic infection is widely prevalent in 75% of Abhujmaria, 57.8% of Baiga and 6.7% Kamar primitive tribes of Madhya Pradesh.

### *Micronutrient Deficiency*

Micronutrient deficiency is closely linked with nutritional disorders and diarrhoea. Deficiency of essential dietary components leads to malnutrition, protein calorie deficiency and micronutrient deficiencies (like vit A, iron and iodine deficiency). Vitamin A deficiency in the form of Bitot's spot, conjunctival xerosis and night blindness was observed in 8.9, 25.9 and 11.4% Bondo; 13.7, 24.2 and 27.6% Didayi; 14.9, 17.9 and 7.4% Juanga; and 3.4, 12.6 and 6.9% Kondha tribes, respectively. However, other micronutrient deficiencies like iodine deficiency (goiter), vitamin B complex deficiency (in the form of angular stomatitis) were not encountered. Similarly a high percentage of vitamin A deficiency was observed in 24.4% of Birhor tribes and 53.3% of Sahariya tribes of Madhya Pradesh. Goitre was also observed in 3.4% of these tribes.

### Skin Infection

Skin problems like scabies is a major health problem amongst the primitive tribes because of overcrowding and unhygienic living conditions as also close contacts and lack of health awareness. In a study conducted by the RMRC, Bhubaneswar, 20.6% of Bondo, 6.9% of Didayi, 10.7% of Juanga and 15% of Kutia Kondha tribes were affected with scabies (both infective and noninfective), which is comparable with the findings in Birhor primitive tribe (7%) of Madhya Pradesh.

Other communicable diseases such as tuberculosis, leprosy, yaws and venereal diseases, though have been described as significant health problems in several major tribal populations of the country, very few published reports are available concerning these diseases in the primitive tribes. In a prospective study undertaken in Orissa, the incidence of tuberculosis and leprosy was found to be 1.4% in Bondo, 3.9% in Didayi, 0.7% in Kondha and 1.6% in Juanga tribes. Yaws was reported only in 0.2% Bondo population of Malkangiri district compared to high incidence of 7% in Abhujmarias of Madhya Pradesh.

### Hereditary Haematological Disorders

Hereditary haematological disorders especially sickle cell disease, G6PD deficiency, haemoglobinopathies and allied haemolytic disorders are important public health problems and occur in high frequencies among different tribal groups and scheduled caste population. These result in a high degree of morbidity and mortality due to haemolysis in vulnerable population.

Sickle cell gene is widely prevalent among the tribal population in India. These have been investigated in over 100 tribal population spread over different parts of the country. The prevalence rate varies widely (0.5 to 45%) among different tribes. Interestingly this gene is restricted amongst the tribes of central, western, southern and eastern

India and is conspicuously totally absent in north-east India. There are many primitive tribes who have been identified to be in high-risk group. Majority of the tribals of Orissa have a common gene pool that is relatively unmixed with other nontribal population. High degree of inbreeding among some of the primitive tribes results in relatively high prevalence of genetically inherited diseases like sickle cell anaemia, G6PD deficiency and thalassaemia.

The incidence of sickle cell haemoglobin was found to be 22.3% in Baiga and 14% in Bharias of Madhya Pradesh and 3% in Kondha, 7.4% in Kharia, 3% in Munda, 14.2% in Gonda and1% each in Santal, Bhatudi, Bhuyan and Kolha tribes of Orissa. Contrary to the expectations the frequency of sickle cell gene was observed to be low (0.6% in Bondo, 3.2% in Didayi, 1.3% in Juanga and 1.5% in Kondha) among primitive tribes of Orissa similar to that of Hill Korwas of Madhya Pradesh. The intriguing feature of sickle cell disease in Orissa is the presence of high fetal Hb, and less sequestrational crisis.

The frequency of G6PD deficiency gene in various primitive tribal population of Orissa was very high (Munda 15.9%, Kharia 14.2%, Bhuyan 12.9%, Kolha 9.8%, Bhaturi 9.5%, Santal 9.0% and Saura 7.7%). In a study conducted by the RMRC, Bhubaneswar, the prevalence of G6PD deficiency was found to be 0.36% in Bondo, 1.6% in Didayi, 7.3% in Juanga and 4.8% in Kutia Kondha primitive tribes. An indepth molecular analysis amongst the G6PD deficient tribal subjects including Juanga primitive tribes of Keonjhar district of Orissa revealed the presence of a new variant of G6PD known as G6PD Orissa. This particular enzyme is responsible for protecting red cell membrane from oxidative stress, preventing haemolysis from offending agents and providing selective advantage against falciparum malaria.

Thalassaemia also contributes significantly for the anaemia cases in tribal population of Orissa. Studies have shown that the frequency of thalassaemia gene varies from 1.9% in Kharias to 8% in Santala, 1.7% in Bhumija, 2% in

Kolha, 5.2% in Munda, 6.2% in Saura and 7% in Lodha primitive tribes. The prevalence of thalassaemia was 0.5% in Bondo, 3% in Didayi, 2.6% in Juanga and 2.3% in Kutia Kondha primitive tribes.

The primitive tribes of Orissa and their health scenario presents a kaleidoscopic mosaic of various communicable and non-communicable disease profile keeping in pace with their socio-economic development. Among these there are communities who still depend primarily on hunting and food gathering as primary source of livelihood. The wide spread poverty, illiteracy, malnutrition, absence of safe drinking water and sanitary conditions, poor maternal and child health services, ineffective coverage of national health and nutritional services, etc. have been found, as possible contributing factors of dismal health condition prevailing amongst the primitive tribal communities of the country. Many of the infectious and parasitic diseases can be prevented with timely intervention, health awareness and IEC activities. Some of the intervention programmes can be included in the national programme also.

## Customs and Practices

The tribes of Orissa are at various stages of socio-economic development. At one extreme are the group which lead a relatively secluded and archaic mode of life keeping their core culture intact, while at the other extreme there are communities which are indistinguishable from the general agricultural communities. Any society—tribal or otherwise, comprises of organised groups of people who have learnt to live and work together interacting in the pursuit of common goals. Each society has its own rules of business and tricks of trade which helps its people to define their relationship with one another and live and work together. Therefore a society is a going concern and functions and perpetuates itself on the basis of the rules for living together.

The tribal people express their cultural identity and distinctiveness in their social organisation, language, rituals and festivals and also in their dress, ornament, art and craft. They have retained their own way of managing internal affairs of the village mainly through two institutions namely, the village council and the youth dormitory. The dormitory is the core of tribal culture and it reinforces the age-old traditions.

In Orissa this institution occurs among many tribal communities in some form or other. The Juangs call it Majang and Darbar, the Kondhs call it Dindaghar, the Bhuyans call it Dhangarabasa and among the Bondos it goes by the name Ingersin. Of all the tribes the dormitory system is well organized among the Juang. Conspicuous in the village, the Mandaghar is the largest hut. It has wall on three sides and is open in front. The wooden parts and side walls are carried with decorative symbols depicting animals. The boys hang their changu, a flat tambourine like drum which is used at the time of dancing. In front of the Mandaghar is the small open space where dance takes place almost every night after the day's work is over. The dormitory is so to say a school of dancing and expression of the communal art of the people. The elders of the village assemble at the dormitory house every day for every important event in their corporate life. Here they discuss matters concerning the welfare of the village, settle the distribution of swidden and fix date and time for celebration of the village festivals, etc. In these respects the dormitory may be considered as the centre of social, economic and religious life of the village.

The amazing conglomeration of traditions, beliefs, sorrows and philosophies that together constitute and vitalise the rituals and festivals of the tribes, has descended from antiquity and has been preserved unimpaired to the present day. Every facet of their life covering round-the-year activities is intimately connected with religious beliefs and ritual practices. It is these aspects of their culture that give meaning and depth to their lives, and solidarity to their social structure.

### Belief in the Supernatural Powers

The tribes believe that their life and work are controlled by supernatural beings whose abode is around them in hills, forests, rivers and houses. It is very difficult to standardize the Gods and spirits as their composition continually changes when old ones are forgotten with the introduction of new ones. Their Gods differ from one another in composition, function, character and nature. Some are benevolent; some are neutral and some are malevolent. The malevolent spirits and Gods are cared more than their benevolent counter parts as they can bring misery.

Manipulation of environment being the main concern of the tribals, all the ritual acts are directed towards stimulating natural processes. Illness or misfortune is attributed to displeasure and malicious act of the Gods or ancestors. The sacrifice of different kinds of livestock accompanied by all the rites and ceremonials of fetishism is considered appropriate appeasement. Moreover, their extremely superstitious nature prohibits the undertaking of any enterprise unless the Gods are first appeased and the omens, after being carefully considered, are adjudged to be propitious.

Among the tribes there are religious functionaries who cater to their spiritual needs. For example, the hierarchy of priests among the Saoras may be divided into three categories. The Buyya is a priest who presides at agricultural festivals and offers sacrifices that especially characterize these occasions. The Kudan is a shaman who combines the functions of priest, prophet and medicine-man. The sacerdotal head among the Juang is called Nagam or Buita, Pujari or Sisa among the Bondos and Jani among the Kondhs. The post of these officials are mostly ascribed but not achieved.

### Crisis Rites

As most of the tribes of Orissa, practise agriculture in some form or the other, and as rest others have a vital stake in agriculture, sowing, planting, first-fruit eating and harvest rites are common amongst them. Their common cyclic rites revolve round the pragmatic problems of ensuring a stable economic condition, recuperation of the declining fertility of soil, protection of crops from damage, human and live-stock welfare, safety against predatory animals and venomous reptiles and to insure a good yield of annual and perennial crops.

The annual cycle of rituals commence right from the initiation of agricultural operation, for instance, among the Juang, Bhuyan, Kondh, Saora, Gadaba, Jharia, Didayee, Koya and Bondo, who practise shifting cultivation. The annual cycle begins with the first clearing of hill slopes during the Hindu month of Chaitra (March-April) and among others it starts with the first-fruit eating ceremony of mango in the month of Baisakh (April-May). All the rituals centering agricultural operation, first-fruit eating, human, live-stock and crop welfare are observed by the members of a village on a common date which is fixed by the village head-man in consultation with the village priest.

Thus the ideological system of all the tribes surrounds supernaturalism. The pantheon in most cases consists of the Sun God, the Mother Earth and a lower hierarchy of Gods. Besides there are village tutelaries, nature spirits, presiding deities and ancestor-spirits, who are also propitiated and offered sacrifices. Gods and spirits are classified into benevolent and malevolent categories. A peculiarity of the tribal mode of worship is the offering of blood of an animal or a bird, because such propitiations and observance of rites are explicitly directed towards happiness and security in this world, abundance of crops, live-stock, plants and progenies. Sickness is not natural to a tribal, it is considered as an outcome of the machination of some evil spirits or indignation of ancestor spirits or gods. Sometimes, sickness is also considered as the consequence of certain lapses on the part of an individual or group. Therefore, riddance must be sought through propitiation and observance of rituals.

Among all the tribes conformity to customs and norms and social integration continue to be achieved through their traditional political organizations. The tributary institutions of social control, such as family, kinship and public opinion continue to fulfill central social control functions. The relevance of tribal political organization in the context of economic development and social change continues to be there undiminished. Modern elites in tribal societies elicit scant respect and have very little followings. And as the traditional leaders continue to wield influence over their fellow tribesmen, it is worth-while to take them into confidence in the context of economic development and social change.

### *Marriage*

Marriage as an institution is recognised by all the tribes and castes of Orissa. Marriage is not an occasion for happiness in Orissa. When the bride takes leave of her parents and elders and companions, sorrowful verses are recited dolefully by the bride and sometimes by others of whom she takes leave. These verses, recited while weeping are known as 'Kandana'. Many folk tales and folk songs take as their theme the day-to-day family scene in a typical joint house hold. The newly-wed young bride must not only cater to the varying tastes and humour the changing moods of the various in-laws, but also observe the family customs, rituals, fasts and other observances peculiar to her husband's family and village.

Some of the forms of marriage prevalent among the tribes are marriage by capture or institutionalised force (often a mock capture arranged by agreement between the parties), marriage by intrusion when a partner intrudes into the family of the unwilling partner or unrelenting parents-in -law, or marriage by elopement when two lovers elope into the forest or to some distant place because their marriage was opposed by their relatives, marriage by agreeing to serve in the bride's parents house either on a trial basis or under a custom of bondage. In most of the tribal groups the very fact of living together of a man and woman through any of the traditionally recognised manners constitutes a marriage for all social and economic purposes. Before marriage, in some tribal communities such as the Juang, the Bhuniyan, the Ho, the Kond, the Oraon, the Bondo and the Gadaba, youth dormitories offered opportunities for a lot of sex-play and experimentation in companionship. Pre-marital sex relationship is also known to be common among the Santhals, the Saora and certain other tribal groups. Even then this pre-marital sex is disciplined and institutionalised through observance of certain social taboos on sexual contact between girls and boys belonging to the same clan. But faithfulness in marriage at least on part of the wife is insisted upon and rigidly enforced. All over tribal India, divorce is granted on persistent cases of adultery and the wronged husband, often also the wronged wife, has the right to claim compensation or restoration of the money and goods given to the other party at the time of marriage.

In the former princely states, as also in the zamindaries till their abolition soon after independence, concubinage was a recognised custom. The concubine or 'poili' or 'rakhni' was given a social status much lower than that of the married wife, but placed higher above the prostitutes. The children of the concubine were customarily given some share in the property of the father and the concubine had the right of maintains from her man and her sons and step-sons. The custom was so widespread that it was often institutionalised.

In tribal societies or among the Hindu peasants in Orissa, to remain unmarried is a curse, not only for the boy or the girl, but also for the parents and the other relatives. Similarly widowhood is considered as a punishment for some serious sin committed either in this life or in the previous life. For, among the higher castes in Orissa, widows were not given in marriage and had to undergo a number of fasts and penances and a veritable self-denial, closing their eyes to all the pleasures of life. They were not treated well either in their father's house or in their husband's, as they were considered inauspicious persons and hence a burden. The widows among the so called lower castes and among the tribals did not have to face such an ordeal, provided they were of a marriageable age and if they were not considered witches. Widow remarriage was usually practiced apart for the inheritance of the elder brother's widow by one of the younger brothers.

### *Fertiltility and Birth*

A barren woman is considered so inauspicious that it is believed that no other woman should take a bath where she takes her bath. They blame the woman and not the man in almost all cases. A large number of fasts, penances and other observances aimed at the propitiation of several gods and goddesses including Shiva and Parvati and many local deities, devotion to the spiritually powerful Sanyasis, bathing at and visiting some famous centres of pilgrimage-all these are done to remove the evil fate of barrenness.

In tribal society barrenness is also a matter of concern for the relatives and may lead to a divorce or marriage with a second or even a third wife. The preference for having sons is widespread in tribal and non tribal societies in Orissa. The ceremonies connected with child birth are more elaborate and lively in the case of the male child than that of the female one. The Hindu families of higher castes become anxious to have at least one male child, so that he will be ritually qualified to offer the proper oblations to the ancestral spirits. They believe that, unless such oblations are offered by a male descendant, who continues the patrilineal line of descent, the ancestors will be tormented in a special hell.

### *Death and Funeral*

Hindus of Orissa cremate their dead, but they make some exceptions. Young children, adults who die of epidemics or of snake bite, and sanyasi who has forsaken the world are all given a burial and in some cases floated down the river. In tribal society the custom varies from community to community. Those who are Hinduised like Gond, the Bhuiyan and others cremate their dead whereas others bury them. But if a tiger kills a person he or she is not cremated, even if cremation is the usual custom.

When a pregnant woman dies, the foetus is taken out of the womb and is given a separate burial. As the pregnant woman is universally believed to become a dangerous ghost which tries to snatch away babies out of her own frustration, her bones are broken and thrones and other inhibiting materials put in her grave in order to pin her down at the place where she is buried.

Whether Hindu, Christian, Muslim or tribal, all have the common belief of the immortality of the soul. Among the Hindus the soul is reborn in human or in some other form according to the balance of religious merits earned in the previous lives. The disembodied soul may go to heaven or hell in accordance with one's "Karmaphala" or the balance of the fruits of action through a series of former lives. Every year the ancestral spirits are offered "Shraddha" oblations at least once.

The Muslim and Christian souls await the final judgment from God at the end of the world. But among the tribal people the soul usually goes to the underground world but always maintains contact with the living descendants, protecting or punishing them by bringing illness or misfortune if they morally or spiritually go astray.

Funeral ceremonies in almost all communities are so expensive that many tribal families get themselves literally bound to richer brethren or to neighbours for generations because of the debts they incur to meet these expenses. On the completion of the funeral ceremony the close relatives, and among the tribal group, the whole village, indulge in merriment.

***Law and Criminality***

Almost all the castes have the caste panchayat at various levels, at the village in whole or in a small group of villages, in a region and in a few cases for the caste group as a whole. This panchayat of sub-castes elders had the right to supervise the social interactions especially in taking of food and drink from member of other castes and avoiding sexual contact with members of the so called lower castes. Besides this, the panchayat used to sit in judgment on cases of choice of transgression of marriage regulations, divorce, and adultery cases or in cases of partition in a family and in cases of choice of occupation and client etc. Further, the panchayat was competent to ostracise members of the sub castes when they contravened its regulations and injunctions and it could also prescribe ritual expiations in case of some specific sins committed.

Though the Hindu Raja was the highest court of appeal in social and caste, matters, and he had to rely up on his family Brahman Purohit or the other learned Brahman Pandits, the caste panchayats were left much to themselves and led a semi-autonomous and self-regulatory existence. Each tribal community had at least a village council looking after the village affairs, rituals social, economic and political. Among the Oraons, the Mundas, the Santhals and the Hos etc., there was an inter-village tribal organisation with a series of officials holding hereditary positions as periodically selected. Among the tribes of Orissa murders are rarely committed for the gain of property. But murder for revenge is rather frequent, as also murder for jealousy in sex.

**Tribal Festivals**

A large number of festivals and fairs are celebrated in Orissa. These differ from tribe to tribe, from caste to caste and also from region to region. Those among the tribes who are Hinduized perform many rituals and observe some festivals of their tribal past, especially those which do not directly conflict with Hindu customs and deities, by eschewing sacrifice of cows, buffaloes or offer of wine or partaking of these oblations. The christianized sections do not usually observe the tribal rituals and festivals, unless these can be harmoniously blended with Christianity.

One example may be given from the Sundargarh Oraon custom of ceremonial sowing of the paddy seeds, sanctified in the tribal way by sprinkling the blood of the sacrificed chicken. Among the catholic oraon, in a similar ceremonial sowing, the paddy seeds were blessed by Mother Mary in a sanctifying ritual at her altar in the local Church.

Among the tribesmen, festivities connected with sowing, harvesting and consumption of first fruits, and among shifting cultivations, the feeling of the jungle and burning it down for reduction to ash manure, are important ones. Interestingly, enough, success in ceremonial collective hunting in April-May often is believed to contribute to the success of their agricultural efforts . The Santhals have a special spring festival of rejoicing with sprinkling of water, special songs and dances.

When the roles of the deities are acted out by men, and thereby many traditional social barriers fall. Usually, the supreme god is not offered any specific worship among tribals. But among the Santhals of Mayurbhanj ,one may perform the worship every fifth year or at least one in a life-time. Bondo festivities have a great relevance for the tribal communities of Orissa. The Bondos spend a great deal of time on their religion, and the feasts and holidays are an important part of Bondo life.

Moreover, the collective festivities foster a sense of solidarity of the village and fortify one's confidence in undertaking major activities in economic and social life as possible. Thus proving herself to be virtuous and devoted. The wife presents a number of delicacies to her husband at the end of her fast. Pusha Punein is celebrated by the tribesmen of north Orissa, specially the Bhuiyan, the Gond and others. They celebrate this festival on a day closet to the actual full moon day of month. The whole village joins in the celebrations of feasting, drinking and dancing.

### *Dandanata and Danda Jatra*

Dandanata is derived from 'Danda' a pole and 'mata' a dance which is performed in a fair called 'Danda Jatra'. This is celebrated in the month of Vaishaka (April-May). This fair is celebrated through dance, song and physical feats and the pole represents of Lord Shiva. The devotees are called 'Bhokta' and there are thirteen in a 'Danda' party. The leader is 'Pata Bhokta' , who leads a life of abstinence for twenty-one days prior to this festival.

The Bhoktas move from village to village and perform at a house only when invited. The Bhoktas roll on the hot sand in the mid-day sun of summer, dance, and sing praying for the welfare of house holder. Whether someone in the family is childless or poor or suffering from some incurable diseases, the householder usually vows to become a 'Bhokta' next time if his miseries are removed.

The austerities and physical sufferings include walking on fire, piercing the back with sharp nails, using poisonous snakes as garlands and making them sting the body, piercing the tongue or walking on a sharp sword edge etc, apart from fasting and abstinence. These are aimed in order to please and secure booms from Lord Shiva. Variations of 'Danda Jatra" are found in almost the whole of Orissa one variation is Jhamu Jatra or Nian Patua consisting of walking on a trench of fire, and the another one is 'Uda Jatra" or Uda Patna in which the devotees are hooked from their back muscles and are swung high round a pole.

### *Chandan Jatra*

This fair is celebrated for twenty-one days in the month of 'Jaishtha' (May-June). When a smaller replica of Lord Jagannath is taken to the sacred tank for boating after being smeared with 'chandan' or sandal wood paste. This is aimed at providing cool comfort and relief from the summer heat. This is celebrated at places where there is a Jagannath temple and a lot of merriment goes with it when pilgrims congregate. The main centre of this fair is at Puri, the celebrated 'shrikhetra'; the original seat of Lord Jagannath.

### *Chandrabhaga Mela*

The fair at Chandrabhaga begins on the seventh day of the bright fortnight in the lunar month of Magha (January-February) and continues for seven days. It is held at the mouth of sacred Chandrabhaga river near the famous temple of Konarka. This sacred site figures in the myth of shamba of the Mahabharata days who was cured of his leprosy by worshipping Lord Surya, the Sun God. The Sun Temple of Konarka and the sacred site refer to the prevalence of a strong solar cult in the coastal Orissa. It is believed that whoever takes a bath in the Chandrabhaga will be cured of leprosy and bareness. Magh Saptami mela is observed at the same time at the Join centre of Khandagiri, near Bhubaneswer, for seven days.

### *Dola Jatra*

Beginning with the Purnima or the full moon day in the lunar month of Phalguna. The Radha and Krishna images from the Vaishnava temples begin the ritual journey to some important centres of congregation or Melana. With Holy or sprinkling of red 'abir' powder and chanting of bhajan and kirtan, the devotees come in a procession with images of Radha and Krishna carried in the Vimanas to the site of the fair. The deities pay a visit to several villages on their outing and receive homage and offerings from devotees. At the site of the fair chanting if spiritual songs and recitation of the Bhagavata and other scriptures are usually organised. In western Orissa this ceremonially inaugurates the just use of green mango, Chaar berries,

Mahul flower and paluash flower-all jungle fruits, flowers offered to deities. This is known as 'Gundithaai Parba' in western Orissa.

### *Patua Jatra and Chandak Puja*

These are allied to the Banda Jatra described for month of Vaishakha and aimed at propitiation of Lord Shiva for boons. The months of Chaitra and Vaishakha are specially sacred for Shiva worshippers or the 'lower castes' presumably derived from Buddhist society. The same physical tortures for spiritual benefit are undergone and they overlap in time and in the rituals with the variations of Dand Jatra.

### *Pana Samkranti*

Pana Samkranti or Chhatua Samkranti is celebrated to mark the first day of the solar month. On this day a small pot with a hole at the bottom filled with 'pana' or sweet drink is hung on a basil (Tulsi) plant. The falling of water from the pot symbolizes the falling of rain and thus this Samkranti marks the commencement of rainy season and of the cultivation cycle. The people of coastal Orissa ceremonially consume the flour of horse gram (chhatua) after offering it to the basil plant.

### *Akshaya Trutiya*

This festival is celebrated on the third day of the bright fortnight of the lunar month of Vaishakha. This important festival is held in every farming household. It is characterised by the ceremonial sowing of paddy in the field. Oblation is offered to the goddess of destiny, 'Shathi'. This is the most auspicious day to start the construction of house buildings, digging of tanks and wells. This is the day on which the construction of the chariots for Ratha Jatra of Lord Jagannath and his brother and sister starts.

### *Rajaparab*

Raja is one of the most popular festivals of Orissa, though it is not observed in western Orissa. The first day of the Raja festival is always celebrated in the last day of the solar month of Jaishtha. The festival continues for three days. It is believed that the Earth goddess had started to menstruate on the first day of the Raja and after the third day she is taken to a ritual bath and returned to normalcy. So this is called as the menstruation period of the earth, so the earth is to be avoided like a woman.

Therefore men and women avoid touching the earth. Practically for three days there is a complete stoppage of work and especially boys and girls take to the swing and sing the typical Raja songs. Singing, merry-making, feasting and display of gymnastic feats and playing games become the most important preoccupations for this three days. On the fourth day, when the earth is ritually clean and is ready for fertilization, the ceremonial ploughing is undertaken in the paddy fields.

### *Chitau Amavasya*

This is celebrated on the new moon day of the lunar month of Shravana. A special type of rice cake called 'chitau' is offered to Lord Jagannath at the temple. This cake is prepared and eaten with relish in almost every household. Gendeisuni, the goddess of snails and oysters is duly worshipped. These creatures are offered cakes and requested not to bruise the feet of farmers when they go to remove weeds from the fields.

### *Nabanna*

A widely practiced custom among the tribal as well as non-tribal population of Orissa is the offering of the first fruits to the deities, especially to the village deities. Paddy is the most important crop which is considered as Goddess Lakshmi. There is a special variety of early paddy which is already ripe by this time. A porridge made of new rice is offered to the ancestral spirits and to the local deities.

### *Gahma Purnami*

This festival is celebrated as a merry festival of 'Gahma Pumei', on the full moon day of the lunar month of Shravana and is especially auspicious to agriculturists. On this day, cattle, especially plough cattle, are colourfully decorated and given special offering and are worshipped as 'Go-Lakshmi'. That is the day of rest for the cattle. This festival has much attraction for some tribal groups like the Hill Bhuiyan of Orissa that in these lean months of semi-starvations.

### *Garbhama Samkranti*

This festival is celebrated on the first day of the solar month of Karthika. This is the time when the paddy plants or the ears of corn are forming. This is compared to pregnancy and hence the name 'Garbhma'. These pregnant rice plants represent Lakshmi the Goddess of wealth and fertility and are worshipped with offerings in the paddy fields. They believe that through supernatural intervention a huge quantity of corn will thus harvested. All the family members eat to their heart's content.

### *Kumar Purnima*

This festival is celebrated on the full moon day of the lunar month of Ashwina bring untold pleasure to the unmarried boys and girls. The worship of moon God is held at home as Janha Mamu (Moon, the maternal uncle.) brings them various delicacies and new clothes.

### *Chhadakhai*

In the sacred month of Karthika many people forego their favourite non-vegetarian dishes till Karthika Purnima as part of sacred ritual. The day after the full moon is the great day of release from this religious taboo and all indulge in non-vegetarian dishes to their heart's content.

### *Prathamashtami*

This festival is celebrated for the well being of the first born in the family, whether boy or girl. The celebration falls on the eighth day of the dark fortnight of the lunar month of Margashira. Oblations are offered to God Ganapathi to protect the child against all hurdles in life. The child is given a new dress, feasted and blessed by the parents and other elders and friends.

### *Dhamu Samkranti*

This festival is celebrated on the first day of Solar pousha month. The month of pousha is considered the month of plenty. After collecting the harvest there is a festival of general rejoicing with special sweets of 'Maun'.

### *Shamba Dashami*

The festival is celebrated on the tenth day in the bright fortnight in pousha lunar month. The myth has it that Lord Krishna's son, Shamba, was cursed by a sage and he could get rid of his leprosy. The dreaded disease only by worshipping the Sun God at Arka tirtha, which is located on the Konark beach in Orissa. Women fast and worship Sun at dawn, midday and dusk and offer a variety of rice cakes and other delicacies. A mixed vegetable soup, known as 'Ghadghada' with leaves, tubers, local beans and pulse is a typical delicacy.

### *Chaiti Ghoda Nata*

It is the most important festival of the fishermen of Orissa. Goddess basuli with a horse shaped head is worshipped from the full moon day of lunar Baishakha. According to the myth in Kaibarta Purana, the supreme god slept on the leaf of a banyan tree which was buffeted in the sea. He created a man out of the dirt of his ear to hold the rudder firmly and thus keep his leaf-bed steady. When he was dozing, the man was swallowed up by a gigantic fish. Again the leaf bed swerved and god angrily captured the fish and brought the man out.

The man and his descendants became the inveterate enemies of fish. They were ordained by god to earn their livelihood by catching fish. A part of the leaf was transformed into a horse. Under god's orders Vishwakarma built a boat and the man and his horse has become the presiding deity of the descendants of the first Kaibarta or fisherman and boatman. The divine horse breathed its last on the eighth day of Baishakha and God consoled the first Kaibarta that this horse was goddess of Basuli and her worship would bring him salvation.

The representation of goddess Basuli is made of well-decorated horse-head made of wood attached to a trunk built of bamboo pieces and is coloured brown and decorated with garlands of red flowers. A man enters through a hole in the trunk and holds his head giving the appearance from a distance as he is riding a horse. Holding the reins he dances and the horse dances backward and forward to the beating of a drum. He sings songs composed by the folk poets.

### *Karma*

The karma is a famous autumn festival which starts from the eleventh day of the bright fortnight of the month of Bhadrab and continues for some days in the month of Ashwina. The festival is celebrated in most of Orissa's villages in Sambalpur and Phulabani districts. The story behind this celebration goes: six sons of a rich merchant set sail in a ship for trade, leaving the youngest brother at home. When they returned they saw to their amazement that their wives danced in the 'Karma' festival, while the youngest brother was playing on the drum. Being enraged, they drove away their wives. At this, 'Karma' (the god of fortune) got angry and all their wealth vanished. They repented for their folly of driving out the goddess of wealth along with their wives. With the counsel of their wives they went in search of the God of fortune and met a milkman on the way. The latter requested them to ascertain from the God why the number of his cows was fast decreasing.

After some time they saw a strange man bearing on his head a piece of broken earthen pot with fire burning in it, and another man carrying a husking peddle on the shoulder. The next man they met was shivering in the suffering of these persons from the God and the means of getting free from them. The God after due worship was kind to them and on return they found that their house was filled with gold and jewels.

## Tribal Arts

Tribal art is entirely folk art; it is the concern of ever common man and woman in the community and does not admit of improvisation by an expert. The traditional architecture of the tiny tribal houses, gable or dome-shaped, has an eye-catching appeal of its own. The houses of the Santal and Ho tribes have their walls decorated in pretty colours and painted with figures of animals, birds and flowers. The doors of the Kondh houses are skillfully carved with traditional figurines. The Saora ikons drawn on their walls are highly appreciated. The joy of free life find expression in tribal art and craft. It is through this endeavour their cultural self-image and aesthetic sensibility are visualized. The artistic skill of the tribal people is not only manifested in their dance and music but also in their dress and ornaments, wall-paintings, wood carvings and decorations, etc.

The beautiful wall-paintings and floral designs of the Santals and the ikons of the Saoras which depict geometric designs and stylistic figures of plants and animals are the best example of tribal art. The multicoloured designs and relief figures of animals and human beings which decorate the walls of Mandaghar in Juang society are indeed works of very high order. Similar wall-paintings and decorations as observed among the Mundari group of tribals are also very attractive.

### Tribal Dances

Some of the famous tribal dances of Orissa are mentioned in the description that follows:

#### *Juang dance*

The Juang dance which goes by the popular name of "Changu dance" is performed by both men and women. Besides, they perform other types of dances such as deer dance, elephant dance, bow dance, pigeon dance, bear dance, koel dance and peacock dance. They dance and sing when they are in happy mood. The dance also forms an integral part of their social and ritual festivals. The Juang do not have any special dress for dancing. While dancing the girls stand in a straight line in front of the boys. While the dance goes on, the line becomes semicircular. The girls hold each other's wrist or hand-in-hand and move forward and backward in bending posture. The boys stand in a straight line which becomes a curve during dance. The musical instruments which are used during their dance are Badakatha (Drum), Dhola (Small drum), Madala and Changu (Tambourine).

#### *Saora dance*

The Saoras do not dance frequently as the Juangs and the Gadabas do. The Saora dance is very simple and lack all the artistic exuberances. Generally the Saoras dance during ceremonies and festivals, marriages, and when some important person visits their village. In their dance, group of men and women jumble up together and while dancing the drummers and the dancers advance towards each other alternatively with the rhythm of the music. Colourful costumes are worn during the dance. Other decorations include feathers of white fowl and peacock plumes. Besides, old coloured cloths of cotton and silk are tied as turbans by men and wrapped around their chest by women. While dancing they carry swords, sticks, umbrellas and other implements and blow whistles and make peculiar sounds. The musical instruments used at the time of dance consist of drums of various sizes, brass cymbals, brass-gongs and hide-gongs.

*Gond dance*

Among the Gonds of Koraput, dance is performed throughout the year. Besides this, dances are performed on special communal occasions like marriage. The boys dress themselves with colourful aprons and turbans during the dance. The turbans are adorned with "cowrie" shells and the apron is adorned with small pieces of mirror. The girls are dressed in hand-woven sarees and silver ornaments. A dancing group is ordinarily formed with 20 to 30 persons of both sexes. Only unmarried boys and girls participate in the dance. The musical instruments are played by boys. Two boys lead the dance with wooden drums. The girls dance in circles with simple steps of one and two, very often bending their bodies forward. The steps of the boys are more varied and subtle.

*Koya dance*

Dance among the Koyas is richly varied and sophisticated. The most important occasion for dancing is the worship of the mother goddess in the month of Chaitra (April-May). Ordinarily both boys and girls participate in dancing but the girls are more conspicuous. However, in the festival only girls participate. During the dance, the girls keep rhythm by beating sticks on the ground which are fitted with small bells. Dance groups are formed by about 30 to 40 persons. The most conspicuous movement about Koya dance is the complicated winding and unwinding of circles formed by girls.

*Gadaba dance*

Gadaba dance is performed by women who wear the famous "Keranga" sarees and have their distinctive hair style. The men play the musical instruments. Chaitra and Pausa are the dancing seasons. The Gadaba women dance in semi-circles with steps of three and four which they gradually change to eight. The body is often bent forward. Very skillful moves are made on the heels.

*Kondh dance*

Kondh dance is mostly confined to unmarried boys and girls and free mixing of the sexes is allowed during dancing. The dances are performed especially when the boys or girls of one village visit another village. The dance forms an item in the daily routine of the Kondh, when the boys and girls in their dormitories meet after the day's toil. No instrument accompanies the dance of the Kondhs of Koraput. The girls dance in lines and the boys dance behind and in front of them. The dance of the Phulbani Kondh is more colourful. The girls wear sarees in two pieces and bangles on their ankles. They dance in rows, facing rows of boys who sing songs and play on hand drums. Songs play a very important part in the dance. Special dances are performed during buffalo sacrifice, called the Kedu festival.

*Oraon dance*

The dance of the Oraons of Sundargarh and Bolangir districts is performed in front of the village dormitories. The boys and girls participate in the dance. The line of dancers go round and round headed by the leading dancers.

### *Paraja dance*

The Parajas dance during the Chaitra parba, the dance often lasting from dusk to dawn. The girls wear colourful handwoven sarees; silver and brass jewellery; and hold a bunch of peacock feathers in their hands. The movements are extremely graceful and the music is provided by the drum, flute and the "Dudunga" - a country-made string instrument.

### *Naga dance*

The dancer has a heroic feature and wears a special dress. He dances with a heavy load of weapons to the sound of the battle drums. He has ten main requirements, Viz. 1) A shield of the hide of the rhinoceros, 2) a sword, 3) a Kukri, 4) a gun, 5) a horn used as a whistle, 6) an iron shield, 7) a toilet box, 8) bow and arrows, 9) tiger skin, and 10) a bell. His bow bears the face of a tiger and looks awesome. He possesses a long crown with a big flower at he end decorated with glittering peacock feathers. He has a string of beads on the neck, feathers of 'ara' ( a bird with brown feathers found in lake Chilka) on his arms, a mirror and a string of beads on his wrist, flags on the arrows, handkerchief tied to the hands, a small bell attached to the thigh. He smears his body with 'rama raja' (a powder of yellow colour) to save himself from the scorching heat of summer. He decorates his forehead with vermilion. He wears an artificial beard and moustache. Dressed up he looks very ferocious. This dance is not accompanied by any song.

### *Ghumra dance*

The 'Ghumra' - a kind of drum of the size of a pitcher - produces a deep musical sound. The drummer ties the rope of the ghumra round his neck, makes it hang and plays on it, sings and dances to its tune at social functions like marriages or any religious festival. Sometimes a competition is held between two parties. Each party consists of twenty to twenty-five men and the dance goes on the whole night. Ghumra is prevalent among the 'Sahara' and other Aborigines and Harijans and songs have love as their main theme. The other forms of folk dance like 'Humo', 'Bauli', 'Jhulki', 'Jamudali', 'Mayalajar', 'Gunjikata', 'Rasarkeli' and 'Puchi' are prevalent among the Oriyas and Aborigines of Orissa.

## Tribal Crafts

Tribal crafts are simple and artistic. The common items of manufacture are baskets, head dresses, textiles, combs, necklaces, bangles, earrings and articles with artistic specialty for use by tribal communities. Tribal art depicts the beauty and simplicity of their life. The continuity of tribal culture through the past, present and future is also maintained through tribal art.

Some of the tribal communities like the Bondo and the Gadaba have their own looms by which they weave clothes for their own use. These hand spun textiles of coloured yarn are examples of best artistic skill of these people. So also among the Dongaria Kondhs the ladies are very much skilled in making beautiful embroidery work in their scarf. The tribal women in general and the Bondo, the Gadaba and the Dongaria Kondh women in particular are very fond of using ornaments. The Bondo women who are considered most primitive, look majestic when they wear headbands made of grass, necklaces of coloured beads and girdles made of brass on their bodies. All these are expressions of their artistic quality and aesthetic sense.

The tribal people turn out excellent handicrafts for their own use. The wood carving of the Kondhs, metal works by lost wax process among the Bathudis, cane and bamboo basketry works among the Juangs and Bhuyans, are all symbolic of artistic creation.

### *Pottery*

Though there are very few potters among the tribals, the tribal people extend their patronage to the other potters. The elemental quality of earth as a substance has long been used by them in the execution of both ritual and utilitarian objects. A variety of roof tiles, utensils such as pots, bowls, plates and jars, and cooking stoves meet specific requirements of daily life. Simultaneously the potter creates votive offerings in strong forms of bulls, elephants and horses as well as terracotta temples and toys.

### *Bamboo and cane*

Bamboo and cane have all the fertile, lively and tactile qualities of nature's raw materials which craftspersons have successfully harnessed. The structural qualities of bamboo, its high-tensile strength and pliability have led to its widespread use for architectural purposes. Besides which, bamboo splits are woven together to make baskets of diverse shapes and sizes depending on the nature of goods they are required to carry or store. Similarly the elasticity and sturdiness of cane has been utilized in the manufacture of a variety of domestic goods, while countless local fibres and reeds are used by people with household skills to make ropes, strings, brooms and the like. These products are largely geared for local consumption. However, the potential of these materials is so great that new applications can be explored for the new customers.

### *Plaster and Papier Mache*

*Papier Mache*: This skill has been creatively practised by craftspersons from all over Orissa. Paper, waste cloth and different kinds of natural fibres are soaked and beaten into a pulp, then mixed with a variety of seeds and gums for strength and as protection from termites. Special clays and bio-wastes are added for body and reinforcement. The entire process results in a malleable that it requires little skill to be moulded into countless forms. However, despite its versatility this craft has remained neglected.

*Plasters*: The application of plasters to her dwellings is often the rural woman's medium of creative expression reflecting both in terms of colours and symbols, the close identification of man with nature. From clay come the colours ochre, geru, charcoal grey and white which are either used naturally or mixed with pigments purchased from the markets. The images created by her are timeless yet ephemeral, with the sun and the rain taking their toll. The predominantly geometric forms - a straight line, a square covered in dots, waves, triangles pointing to the sky and downwards - can have the most disparate of meanings but the symbolism of fertility is implicit in all of them. The tools used for applying the plasters whether on hut walls or floors are basic. They use twigs, fingers, whole hands and rags.

### *Stone Crafts*

Artisans practising the craft of stone carving in Orissa have remained largely tradition-bound while producing objects of ritualistic, decorative and practical use. Turned utensils for both cooking and serving and artefacts of tourist interest are made in Khiching located on the borders of Mayurbhanj and Keonjhar districts, from a semihard, grey stone which takes on a deep, dark polish, while beads and figurines are carved out of soft stones available in many shades of orange in Phulbani district.

### *Santhal and Sarosa Paintings*

Tribal paintings are like prayers that become part of the offerings made to gods, ancestors and spirits. Members of the Saora tribe draw ritualistic pictographs on the inner walls of their mud dwellings called 'Ittlans'. The icons are painted to preserve the abundance of the crops, avert disease, honour the dead, promote fertility, honour the tutelaries and so on.

The spirit is then invoked and invited to occupy the one dimensional painting which actually represents a house made for it. Once captured therein, it is propitiated with appropriate chantings. The icons are a curious amalgamation of an early memory and contemporary impressions. Since they are basically the expressions of an agricultural community there is an emphasis on nature, the great outdoors and also on the cycle of ploughing, sowing and harvesting. But as the outside world increasingly impinges on their lives, cars, chairs, tables and planes have begun to appear innocently in the paintings, and are offered as vehicles for their gods in hierarchical order.

### *Handlooms*

Orissa is a thickly tribal inhabited state, consisting of sixty two tribes living in different parts of the state - in the highlands, forests, valleys and in the foot hills. They make their own traditional ethnic cottage and live in it. In order to proclaim the self identity intra group wise, socially and culturally different tribes live in different places. Each tribal community has separate mode of living and they differ significantly in their dress, ornaments, skill in building houses, and moreover in their way of life. This difference in their life is clearly discernible from their material culture, art objects from the paintings and drawings and also from the size and shapes of different objects that they use. To the tribals, dress is a cultural need and it is also a part of their tradition.

Among the tribals the use of dress is very significant and worthwhile. The tribals do not use dress just merely to hide their nakedness rather it reflects the racial feeling and their cultural identity. The tribals use separate costumes at the time of festivals and ceremonies. In a specific tribe the dresses from birth to old age has immense variety. The costumes of the male members of the tribe and the females are also different. It is a fact that the female community pay more attention in covering their body.

In some tribal communities the women folk want their male partners to be dressed elegantly and impressively. A tribal woman also wears a variety of dresses from her birth to death corresponding to different stages of her life. For instance, a Dhangedi (a maiden) adorns with fine clothes to attract the attention of others while the Gurumai, the priestess wears formal clothes to worship the goddess for the betterment of her community. Dress also helps them in many adversities and also helps to propitiate gods and goddesses who safeguard them against the malevolent atrocities of the ghosts, spirits, etc.

The tribals also use dress according to the position of individual in the society like the clan's head, the priest, and the revenue collector etc. The dress that they use at the time of marriage, birth, death, worship etc. are also different. They use dresses keeping in view the occasion, age, sex and other factors. For example, the priest does not use the normal dress at the time of worship. And again at the time of dancing they dress in a very attractive manner. And the dancing costume has also special significance. They also wear dresses in different styles. While dressing they also keep in their mind the surroundings. They also think of their convenience and inconvenience while dressing themselves for an occasion. Especially they do not like to dress very pompously at the time of any work. But when they go for shopping to the near by market place or to visit any fair or festival they dress themselves quite exuberantly and exquisitely.

Different tribal communities use different kind of dresses, differing in their colour and size. Their dresses are designed keeping in view their necessity and their surrounding. The socio-cultural and the religious views of the tribals slightly contribute for the variety in their dresses. There are several tribes like the Bondo and Gadaba who weave their own clothes. While the other tribes purchase their dress from another community or the neighbouring Damas or Panas.

The tribal dress and ornaments mostly belong to the non-tribal group and there are very few tribal artisans. The non-tribal artisans like the weavers they live adjacent to the tribal villages. These people manufacture the costumes of a specific tribe and sell them in the weekly village market. Sometimes these weavers are being paid in cash or in kind in the form of agricultural products. The tribal costumes are very simple and it provides immense comfort to the wearer. Generally, in the Kandha community the Dongria Kandha, the Kutia Kandha and the Desia Kandha, Lanjia Saora and the Santhals depend on other communities (non-tribal artisans) for their clothes. Lanjia Saora and some other tribal community make threads by themselves and give it to the Damas to weave for them. And again they purchase that cloth from the Damas by cash or kind. While the Bondo and the Didayi, the Gadabas weave their own clothes though the Dangrias purchase the cloth from the neighbouring Damas. They knit fine needle work on it and use it.

There is a little similarity among the tribals in their dress those who live in a specific area. The Koyas, the Halabs and the Gandias are inhabitants of the same districts. Though it seems that they have some kind of similarity in their costume but in reality they differ from each other. The Kandhas live in a specific area, like the Kutia Kandha and the Dongria Kandha both the communities live in two different sides of the same hill. But as far as dress is concerned they differ significantly. Similarly, the Mundas and the Santhals though they live as neighbours they differ in their dress and culture. The Juangs and the Bhuyan high lander live in close proximity but they differ in their dress. The Kisans and the Gonds though live in the same belt they have also difference in their dress. At times there are similarity of the dress in colour, design and pattern but they differ in their cultural and social life as well as in their ritual and rites.

The artistic nature of the tribals is very innate in their heart and mind. To them the artistic and aesthetic essence is to make life more enjoyable and to fulfill the cultural, social and religious needs. Even there are some tribes they envisage a better future with the help of art and craft, for the tribals art objects and the skill of the artist is a fit medium to propitiate their deities, gods and goddesses. The tribal art is not the contemporary one. It has the heraldry of a hoary past. It was the art which once widely acclaimed in the midst of the forest, the mountains, and in the springs. Art is the base and basis of the tribal life. It is the economic, social and cultural reflection of the tribal life. Hence art is the yardstick by which they measure their success.

The material culture is also part of their artistic life. Even their costume and dress materials have the touch of artistic workmanship. It is also reflection of the art which had been passed onto them from generation to generation. That art has the accumulated knowledge of ages, which has assimilated in their social tradition. It is a medium to express their inner quest. Dress has multifarious significance in their social life. At the surface level one can observe that they use dress only to avoid the nakedness, or to protect from cold, rain and sunshine. But in fact, the tribal costume exhibit the uniqueness of the specific community, their self-identity.

The possession of the right kind of dress is a matter of pride and a great source of enthusiasm. The "Ringa" of the Bondos and the embroidered shawl of the Dangarias have a special social and cultural significance. The Dangria shawl has a direct link with the marital relationship and the success of their conjugal life depend upon it. The dance costume of the Lanjia Saoras as well as their general dress is a fine testimony of their rich cultural heritage. At the time of dancing from the dress of the clan's head "Gamango" they get the trace of the regal pride and heroism.

The origin, history and development of tribal textile commensurate with the general history of man's progress from primitive barbarism to civilization. The state of nakedness was disgusting, to avoid that the tribals used leaves as their dress. This was used in a crude form. Then they used bark of the tree as their dress. This gave them much discomfort, so they used some son bark to avoid this inconvenience. It was not also so soothing, hence they started extracting fibres from the barks and subsequently converted it into thread. Gradually they came to know more about fibre, thread etc. and then began the weaving of clothes. Later on, they also dyed the fibres to make it beautiful. They also use turmeric to colour the threads. These are also several trees in the forest that excrete colour in their bark and the tribals use the bark of these trees to dye the thread. Firstly, they boiled the bark and soak fibres in it. By that way they got various coloured threads and wove according to their requirement. Sometimes instead of making the coloured threads themselves, they purchase them from the market and then weave. Some tribes like to wear clothes of a single colour, while some others like to use multi-colour clothes and at times they knit fine embroidery work on it and make it fit for their use. Through the dress they reflected their traditional culture, artistic skilfulness and thoughts, for which their cultural life flourish on the base of dress. It gave a special lustre to their community life and differentiated one tribe from the other.

To weave clothes they use their own indigenous technology. They use bamboo and other trees to get the fibre usually, they install the wooden loom in front of their house or in the backyard and some of them also install it in the narrow path of the village. They weave during their leisure time. Both men and women weave. In some communities only women weave. The women weave various clothes for them as well as for the male members of their family.

In the olden times the tribals wove their clothes from their loom. But now a days, after they came in contact with the civilized world, they purchase their clothes from the market, resulting in the decay of their culture. Now a days they do not have the slightest inclination to wear old fashioned clothes and have even expressed their hesitation to use their traditional cloth. After the advent of the industrial textile culture, they have already forgotten about their looms.

In the changing scenario they no more boast for their tradition and culture. In some of the tribal communities the dress culture is in a complete state of extinction. And in some other communities it is in a dormant state or on the way of decay. In the Kutia Kandha tribe it has almost decayed. In the Didayi community to find a cloth woven in their own fashion has become a difficult affair. Among the Bondo community the alien cultural assimilation is so strong that, forgetting their own traditional dress they have started wearing the dresses of the non-tribals especially the print sarees manufactured by textile industries.

Among the Santhals the condition is the same as in the other communities. Though the elderly members of the community wish to preserve their tradition, the younger generation abhor the idea. The young ones of the community are not at all worried about the depletion of their culture and the disintegration of their social and community life, to which the elder members express their dissatisfaction. The intrusion of the alien cultures shuns them. Neither are they capable of restricting it, nor can they fully assimilate it. They are caught in a dilemma which is unprecedented in their racial history. The industry based textiles and the process of deforestation is also to some extent responsible for the partial annihilation of their cultural life. It is not a simple matter that ponders only the tribal communities rather it is a matter of contemplation and retrospection for the researchers, philosophers and thinkers those who really value their pristine culture. It is a seed time to preserve and revive their culture which is gradually decaying, whole-hearted efforts be made by adopting various measures and techniques to preserve and revive it, or else a great cultural tradition will be buried in the sandy-shores of time.

# 6

# Tribal Development in Orissa

Orissa is regarded as the Homeland of the Tribals having a total tribal population of about 7 million, which is 22.21 per cent of the State's total population according to Census. The State has the third highest tribal population in the entire country, which accounts for roughly 11 per cent of the total tribal population of India. The tribals mostly inhabit the western hilly regions of the State, mainly in or in close proximity to forests. More than 50 percent of Orissa's tribal population is found in the undivided Koraput, Sundargarh and Mayurbhanj districts, while Koraput alone accounts for more than 25 per cent of the tribal population of the state.

There are 62 communities listed as Scheduled Tribes (ST) in Orissa under the provision of the Indian Constitution. More than 80 per cent of them live in designated scheduled areas. There are 13 sections of these tribes in the State of Orissa who have been identified as Primitive Tribes, who are very primitive in nature from the cultural and technological standpoints. The tribal population in Orissa is among the poorest, most vulnerable and exploited groups in the State. Most tribal communities are confined to the more hilly and remote areas of the State. These areas have been the habitat for some tribes for centuries, whereas the others have been slowly driven out of the more fertile plains by the non-tribals in recent times. Historically, tribals have had a life style characterised by close dependency on the forest for shifting cultivation, collection of forest produce and hunting.

Concepts of money management, savings and planning have traditionally not been of major importance, although the highly developed mixed cropping strategies in shifting cultivation witness conscious strategies of risk-aversion and ecological adaptation. The average literacy rate among the tribal is 22.3 per cent (10.2 per cent for tribal women), much lower than the State average of 49.1 per cent accounting to 1991 census. Maternal, Child and Infant Mortality rates are extremely high among tribal communities in the State.

Tribals in Orissa have never lived in isolation from the surrounding society. During feudal times, many tribal communities were integrated as subjects, tenants and in a few cases, even warriors under the smaller rulers and zamindars. The relationship was that of patron and client. Although it contained a good amount of exploitation of tribals through taxation in kind, it did not challenge the social and cultural integrity of the various tribal communities for territorial control, access to forest produce, taxation and defence. With the abolition of zamindary system, and its feudal arrangements, tribals became the immediate subjects and tenants under the State. As such tribal communities lost the feudal patronage and became exposed to non-tribal infringement on their customary rights to land and forests. However, a number of national and state level legislations have been enacted to protect the traditional entitlements of tribals and also to protect them from exploitation by the non-tribals.

## Economic Status of Tribals

The tribal economy in the State of Orissa is primarily subsistence oriented and based upon a combination of agriculture, forestry and wage labour. Although tribals are mainly dependent on agriculture, collection from forest continues to play a major role in household consumption and income generation. But the dependence of tribal on forest resources varies from area to area. In some areas with serious deforestation, such as Koraput district, collection of forest produce is now of declining importance for the tribal economy. In other areas, typically in the interior valleys of dense forests, cash earnings from non-timber forest produce such as sal and tendu leafs (for plates and bidis) is still of great importance for the household economy. The general pattern is that there is more dependence on forests among the shifting cultivators, pastoralists and hunter-gatherers, and least among the settled agriculturists.

With the decline in output from forest produce, as well as shifting cultivation, tribals are increasingly becoming dependent on seasonal wage labour, both as agricultural and unskilled construction workers. Tribals are usually paid the minimum daily wage of Rs.50 (fixed by government), although there is evidence of tribal women being paid much less than that. Although difficult to establish in monetary terms, the income of most tribal households issubstantially lower (Rs.4,000-6,000, Annual income) than the official poverty line of Rs.11,000, accounting to 1992 BPL survey of the Panchayati Raj Department, Government of Orissa.

In Orissa, the livelihood and survival of tribals largely rests on their access to land and forests. The legal status of tribal land is at times complex, and takes many different forms. Tenure may be in the form of individual ownership based on legal rights (patta/ryoti rights) or it may constitute usufructuary rights (i.e. right to collect fruits, leaves, waste wood and timber, etc.) to common property lands, usually set aside for grazing or orchards. In addition to these two categories of tenure, tribals in most parts of Orissa cultivate a considerable amount of socalled encroached land. Encroached land is divided into two categories: government land, which is mainly cultivable waste (Abada Yogya Anabadi). Podu (shifting) cultivation is often carried out on cultivable waste or other category of forest land on hill slopes. However, shifting cultivation is not allowed on reserve forestland, except at the discretion of the Forest Settlement Officer. The law entitles ownership (patta) to tribals who have cultivated nonobjectionable government land continuously for at least 12 years. Another category of encroached land is labelled "objectionable", and includes e.g. land set aside by government for development purposes, gochar (community grazing) land, orchard land, and other land for public use.

Forests are considered common property by tribal communities in Orissa as is elsewhere in India and are shared equally. Tribals have a strong sense of attachment to the forest as their ancestral territory. They maintain de facto usufructuary rights to the forest products and to shifting cultivation in certain designated zones on hill slopes, irrespective of the legal status of the land/forest. However, tribals do not usually practise podu in forests declared as Reserve Forests and their collection of forest produce is restricted. Apart from firewood and wood for house construction, the other major forest products upon which tribals are dependent, are honey, tendu and sal leafs, mahua (madhuca indica), tola (mahua oil seeds). As an example of community forest management, tendu trees are pruned by the entire village and leafs collected by individuals are sold to the Forest Department or in the local markets.Both shifting and settled agriculture are characterised by poor soil quality, traditional technology, crop rotation, and fallow periods. Apart from indigenous systems of terracing and check dams (munda) in the up-hill areas, tribals have little access to government sponsored irrigation schemes in the State of Orissa. Most settled agriculture is carried out on the lower hill slopes, which are usually not included in the larger irrigation schemes. Agricultural practices in most parts of Orissa among the tribals are characterised by rain-fed annual cropping, both on settled and agricultural land and podu land on the higher hill slopes. The common annual food crops are millet, sorghum, maize and pulses.

In Orissa, hill slopes suitable for shifting cultivation are usually defined as common property of a particular village community and the boundaries of the particular area is well defined in relation to neighbouring areas cultivated by other villages. The individual households cultivation on the podu land have usufructuary rights. The area cultivated by a household depends on a mixture of the following factors: (i) available household workforce; (ii) status in the community; and (iii) mutual agreement between household, often governed by the village elders or leader(s). There is a clear, and unequal, gender division of labour in shifting cultivation, with men doing the land clearing and women doing all other agricultural operations. A household typically cultivates more than one small patch of land at a time. When soil fertility is reduced, the cultivator shifts to another area. The idea of regeneration period or period of recuperation for the land was traditionally 10-12 years, but with increasing pressure on land, cultivators now usually return to the same plot after only two to three years of interval. In some cases cultivation even becomes permanent, resulting in soil degradation and very low productivity.

## Social Status

Most tribal villages in the tribal pockets of Orissa consist of compact settlements with close-knit and lineage based communities located near or inside the forest. The habitation pattern itself reflects the strong social organisation in most tribal communities. Village leaders and elders, sometimes formally organised in traditional village councils, are quite powerful in terms of internal cohesion and jurisdiction. This leadership coexists with the statutory Panchayats, but since a Panchayat usually covers more than one village, authority in each tribal village is still vested in the traditional tribal leaders. When a traditional village leader is also Sarpanch andmember of a Panchayat, this usually means mere prestige for the village and the possibility of access to external resources for local development.

Tribal women play an active role in both household affairs and also in providing economic input in some form or the other for survival of families. They contribute the major part of the labour required for agriculture and collection of forest produce. In addition to this, they take up wage labour whenever available. In extreme cases, as is observed in some parts of Orissa, tribal women even work during night shifts in canal and tunnel excavation work for irrigation projects. Women are usually paid less than men for the same labour time. In social and household matters, the status of tribal women is generally higher than that of non-tribals. They are often viewed by outsiders as "strong" and "independent". But their relative "freedom", and visibility far away from villages, is tied to a very heavy work burden, and they usually have little influence on village level decision making.

## Legalisation for the Protection of Tribes

Under the powers vested under the Fifth Schedule, the following regulations have been promulgated in the State of Orissa to protect the interest of the tribals in the State:

### *The Orissa Scheduled Areas Transfer of Immovable Property (by Scheduled Tribes) Regulation, 1956, (as Amended in 1993).*

Under Section 3(1) of the Act alienation of tribal land to other than ST is prohibited, unless permitted in writing by competent authority. Under Sections 3(2) and 3(a), illegal alienation and unauthorised occupied tribal land shall be restored to the tribal owners. The competent authority, now vested with the Tahsildar, has been authorised to initiate proceedings on application by any interested party and to evict unauthorised persons occupying tribal land. In addition, Officers on Special Duty (Land Reforms) have been posted at Sundargarh, Panposh, Baliguda, Parlakhemundi and Koraput exclusively for disposal of such land alienation cases.

***The Orissa Scheduled Areas Money Lender's Regulation 1967***

This Regulation for controlling and regulating money lending operative in Scheduled Areas is also in operation. Besidesthese two Regulations, specifically enacted by the Tribes Advisory Council, the following Acts of Orissa State have been made operative in Scheduled Areas.

***The Orissa Debt Relief Act, 1980***

This Act provides relief to ST debtors, by making the loans contracted by small farmers, rural artisans and agricultural labourers before the commencement of the Act as deemed to have been wholly discharged. The properties pledged by a ST debtor shall be released in favour of the debtor forthwith on commencement of the Act. The Civil Courts have been barred from entertaining any suit or proceedings in debt recovery. For this purpose, Sub-Collectors and Tahsildars have been empowered to dispose of cases as Judicial Magistrates in summary trial.

***The Bonded labour System Abolition Act, 1976***

This Act aims at liberating and rehabilitating bonded labourers among the ST by the Government of Orissa.

***The Orissa Land Reforms Act, 1960***

The Orissa Land Reforms Act, 1960 (section 22 and 23) apply to the ST population living outside the Scheduled Areas and protect them from land alienation. No tribal land can be transferred to a person not belonging to the same community without the written permission of the Revenue Officer. (About 45% of the area of the State is declared as Scheduled Area with 62 different tribal groups.)

***The Orissa Reservation of Vacancies in Posts and Services (for and ST) Act, 1975***

This Act makes provision of reservation of posts for SCs (16.25%) and STs (22.50%) for initial appointments and promotions in State Government and other authorities under their control. The amended Section 4 of the Act reserves one third of posts in Class II, III and IV for women in direct recruitment from these scheduled categories.

## Tribal Development Programmes

The Department of Welfare, headed by a Cabinet Minister, is responsible for the development and welfare of scheduled tribes, scheduled castes and other backward Classes in the State of Orissa. Administratively it is headed by the Commissioner-cum-Secretary of the Department, under whom three Directors-cum-Additional Secretariesare heading the wings of the department for the development of each of the above groups.

As stipulated in the Fifth Schedule of the Constitution, a Tribes Advisory Council has been existing in Orissa since 1950. The Orissa Tribes Advisory Council Rules of 1950 guide the functioning of the Council. The Council has upto 20 members, of whom three fourths are scheduled tribe Members of the State Legislative Assembly. The Chief Minister is the Chairman, the Minister of Tribal Welfare, the Vice-Chairman, and the Secretary of the Department of Welfare is the Secretary. The Tribes Advisory Council advises Government of Orissa in all matters regarding tribal development and welfare. The Council examines the applicability of State and Central laws to the Scheduled Areas, delineate the boundary of the Scheduled Areas, recommend new regulations or propose revisions of the Schedule of the scheduled tribes.

Scheduled Areas constitute more than 44 per cent of the State land area in Orissa. They cover 67 per cent of the tribal population (118 Blocks in 12 Districts). All Blocks with a tribal population of 50 per cent or more are defined as Scheduled Areas, and constitute a Tribal Sub-Plan (TSP) area. A TSP receives funds specially allocated for tribal development from all departments, and is administered by the district level Integrated Tribal Development Agency (ITDA).

Each Integrated Tribal Development Project under the ITDA is headed by a full-time Project Administrator who reports to a Project Level Committee, a sub-project under the District Welfare Committee (with the District Collector as Chairman and the District Welfare Officer as Secretary). The District Welfare Committee reviews the implementation of tribal projects. At the Block level, the Welfare Extension Officer and the Block Development Officer (BDO), execute the various tribal projects within the Block, and are responsible for residential schools for tribals.

In Blocks outside the TSP, where a population pocket is 10,000 or more, and where 50 per cent or more are tribals, the Modified Area Development Approach (MADA) is adopted to ensure the development and welfare of scheduled tribes. 47 Blocks in Orissa are covered by MADA. In still smaller pockets of tribal concentration (population of 5,000) of which minimum 50 per cent are tribals are covered under the clusterapproach. Presently 12 Blocks have identified such clusters. Besides these comprehensive programmes, there are several other projects (e.g. 17 Micro Projects) assisting scheduled tribes in securing rights, maintaining traditions and improve the socio-economic conditions.

## Development Interventions for Tribals

### *Approach and Overall Strategy for Tribal Development in the Five Year Plan Periods:*

Soon after the beginning of the First Five year Plan, when Community Development Approach was evolved, the areas inhabited by the tribals also received special attention. In the year 1954, Community Development approach in the tribal areas were initiated by setting up a small number of Special Multipurpose Tribal Development (SMTD) Projects covering a limited number of blocks of the State as pilot projects. Subsequently, in the year 1956 there was a reorientation in the approach to Tribal Development (TD) and the functioning of the SMTD were reviewed at the end of the Second Five Year Plan and with the beginning of the Third Five Year Plan the concept of Tribal Development Block was introduced and 75 T.D. Blocks were identified for extending special development programmes and this strategy continued until the end of the Fourth Five Year Plan. At the end of the Fourth Five Year Plan, it was revealed that the TD Block approach also did not yield any meaningful result as the problems of the tribals varied from place to place and were area specific in nature. As a matter of fact till the end of the Fourth Five Year Plan period, the approach to the tribal development were basically generic in nature and were tried to be achieved through implementation of various sectoral programmes.

With these backgrounds it was decided to formulate a new strategy for the development of the tribal areas through area specific approach right from the beginning of the Fifth Five Year Plan. The tribal development problems during the Fifth Plan were visualised as two distinct categories such as (a) areas inhabited by more than 50 per cent tribal population and (b) tribals located in dispersed manner. During this Plan period it was decided by the government to formulate an area development approach with focus on the tribals in case of the former categories of the tribals taking into consideration the local problems and felt needs of the tribals and for the dispersed tribals, family oriented programmes were decided to be extended.This is how the Tribal Sub-Plan approach came into force with the beginning of the Fifth Five- Year Plan in the State of Orissa. During this period for the implementation of the tribal development programmes, identification of development blocks in the State where tribal population was in majority and such places were covered under one ITDPs with a motive to adopt an integrated and area specific approach of development. For such projects, special funds provisions were made from State Government as well as from the Government of India under special Central assistance.

But during the Sixth Five Year Plan, the effort shifted to beneficiary oriented development schemes and during this phase the scope of the Tribal Sub-Plan approach became more focussed and Government adopted the Modified Area Development Approach (MADA) for smaller contiguous areas with a total population of 10,000 where tribal concentration is 50 per cent or more. The same development approach continued during the Seventh Five Year Plan and only the dispersed tribals were brought within the purview of the Tribal Sub-Plan during this Plan period.

It is observed that during the above plan periods, until the end of the Seventh Plan period, the basic approach of development followed was Socio-Economic development of tribals through a number of income generating schemes and through Infrastructure Development Programmes. Despite all these efforts, it was revealed that the pace of development of the tribals was far from satisfactory and therefore during the Eighth Five Year Plan period the State started adopting the Maharashtra Model of Tribal Development through a single line demand through the Tribal Development Department. Under the changed system, instead of the past practice of planning from top to bottom, the exercise got reversed and the approach became from bottom to top. Thus the decentralised system of planning was made for each tribal area with the ITDA as the base. Under such a changed arrangement, the tribal development department could be able to decide the priorities of the schemes to be implemented in the tribal areas on the basis of eliciting their felt needs. This approach adopted during the Eighth Five Year Plan proved to be relatively more beneficial as compared to the earlier plan periods.

During the Ninth Five Year Plan spanning from 1997-2002, the major thrust of tribal development has been shifted to accelerate growth in employment, provision of basicminimum services to the people, eradication of poverty, provision of food security. In order to guarantee that the above objectives are achieved and the quality of life of the tribals is increased, the

Government of Orissa has given high priority to as many as seven basic services in the tribal inhabited areas. Along with these emphasis has been laid on the Agriculture and Rural Development Sectors for the tribals with a view to bringing them to the mainstream.

## *Specific Strategies and Programmes*

Orissa has the largest tribal concentration after Madhya Pradesh and Maharashtra in the entire country. The following are some of the major strategies and programmes, which are under promulgation in the State for the welfare of the tribals.

### *Land alienation*

In order to prevent exploitation of scheduled tribes by members of other communities relating to landed property and to check and regulate land alienation in the Scheduled Areas, necessary protective regulations have been made through the enactment of the Orissa Scheduled Areas Transfer of Immovable Property (by Scheduled Tribes) Regulation, 1956 (Regulation 2 of 1956) which came into force with effect from 4th October, 1956. Since then a number of cases of alienation has been prevented. The achievements made after promulgation of the regulation since inception and upto the end of March 2000 is as follows:

I Total No. cases instituted 86999

II Total No. cases disposed of 84721

III Total No. scheduled tribes benefited 46439

IV Total areas restored (in acres) 42497.16

*The Orissa (Scheduled Areas) Money Lenders Regulation, 1967:* According to the Regulation, prevention of money lending operations in Scheduled Areas are entrusted with Panchayats in conformity with the Central Act which is in force with effect from 24th day of December 1996.

*Liquidation of rural indebtedness*

The State Government have enacted the Orissa Debt Relief Act, 1980 which was given operational effect from 13th March 1981 with a view to providing relief from indebtedness to small farmers, rural artisans and agricultural labourers. Any debt incurred by a scheduled tribe debtor before the commencement of the Act including the amount of interest if any, payable on such debt shall be deemed to have been wholly discharged. No such debt due from a scheduled debtor shall be recoverable from him or from his property either movable or immovable through attachment or sale in execution of any decree or order relating to such debt. No civil court will entertain any suit or proceeding against a scheduled debtor for recovery of debt or interest.

*Bonded labour*

With the enactment of the Bonded Labour System (Abolition) Act, 1976 a Centrally Sponsored Scheme the bonded labour system has been abolished since 1976. As per the provisions of the Act, liberated bonded labourers are socio-economically rehabilitated with employment opportunities including self-employment so that they do not relapse into bondage. By the end of February 2001; 19167 numbers of STs have been released out of which 18411 have been rehabilitated.

*Labour welfare*

With a view to protect the interests of the tribal labourers regarding payment of proper wages for their services rendered, the State Government have posted Rural Labour Inspectors under Centrally sponsored scheme for effective implementation of minimum wages. These officers work in addition to the Assistant Labour Officers and Labour Officers functioning under the Labour and Employment Department in the said areas. These measures adopted in the Scheduled Areas have gone a long way in preventing exploitation of tribals.

*Forest policy*

The tribal people usually depend upon various forest produce like timber, fodder and saleable Minor Forest Produce (MFP) items like tendu leaves, sal seeds, mohua flower, resins etc. for their sustenance resulting in a symbiotic relationship with the forests. However, due to their simplicity, they are sometimes subjected to exploitation at the hands of certain unscrupulous middlemen and forest contractors dealing with MFP items. With a view to preventingexploitation of tribals, a number of measures have been taken, such as abolition of private contractors, purchase of minor forest produce by Tribal Development Co-operative Corporation, etc.

*The Orissa Reservation of Vacancies in Posts and Services (For SCs and STs) Act, 1975 (ORV)*

The Orissa Reservation of Vacancies in Posts and Services (for SCs & STs) Act, 1975 has been in force since 1st July, 1976 for ensuring adequate representation of scheduled castes and scheduled tribes in posts and services. The percentage of reservation for SCs and STs in initial appointment and promotions for all categories of posts subject to a few exceptions is 22.50 per cent and 16.25 per cent respectively.

*Micro project for development of primitive tribal groups*

At the time of formulation of Tribal Sub-Plan during the Fifth Plan, it was felt that among the tribal groups there are a number of tribes which still continue to be in pre-agricultural state of practising shifting cultivation and are at subsistence level of economy, either dependent on forests or on poor lands. It was further recognized that these tribal communities would need special attention. Many of these tribes are scattered all over the country and their socioeconomic conditions differ. In most cases they are adversely affected by changes taking place around their habitat. The primitive tribes residing in the Micro Projects get hundred percent subsidies in individual family beneficiary oriented schemes funded out of special Central Assistance provided by Ministry of Tribal Affairs. These also aim at developing the core sectors like Agriculture, Horticulture, Soil Conservation, and Animal Husbandry besides facilitating drinking water, education, and health. At present 17 Micro Projects covering parts of 20 blocks in 12 districts are functioning in the State for the all-round development of 13 Primitive Tribal Groups with a population 59,710.

### Monitoring and Evaluation

Monitoring and evaluation are the tools to assess the proper implementation of plans and programmes. Further, monitoring assumes important role when different agencies/departments are involved in the process. At present, arrangements have been made at different levels to monitor and review tribal development programmes regularly, Project Level committees forITDA/MADA/ Cluster, Governing Body for Micro Projects with officials and Non-Officials as Members have been constituted and functioning. These Committees/Bodies review the programmes periodically.

#### *Integrated Tribal Development Agencies (ITDAs)*

Since the beginning of the Fifth Five Year Plan, the concept of Tribal Sub -Plan for tribal development is being formulated and implemented in the State. The Subdivisions having 50 per cent or more tribal population were brought under the Tribal Sub-Plan approach. Under this approach, 21 ITDAs covering 118 blocks of 12 districts have been functioning in the State.

#### *Modified Area Development Approach (MADA)*

The concept of MADA was evolved towards the end of the Fifth Five Year Plan. Contiguous smaller areas having a population of 10,000 or more with 50 per cent tribal concentration were identified and included under the MADA Scheme. By the end of the year 1990-2000, 46 MADA pockets covering 5,67,071 tribal population have been operating in the State. For their welfare, individual benefit oriented and community benefit oriented schemes are implemented in the ratio of 75% and 25% outlay respectively under Special Central Assistance provided by Government of India.

*Cluster approach*

During the Seventh Plan period, the Cluster approach was adopted for contiguous areas having population of 5000, of which 50 per cent or more are tribals. By the end of 1999-2000, 14 Cluster pockets covering parts of 13 blocks of 10 districts were functioning in the State covering 52,793 tribal population. Funds were provided by Government of India under Special Central Assistance for implementation of community benefit oriented and individual benefit oriented schemes.

*Dispersed Tribal Development Programme (DTDP)*

The tribal families living outside the above project areas like ITDA, Micro Project, MADA, Cluster are covered under the DTDP implemented through the Scheduled Caste and Scheduled Tribe Development Finance Cooperative Corporation Limited.The Orissa Reservation of Vacancies in Posts and Services Act, 1975

In order to fulfil the obligation embodied in Article 14(4), 46 and 335 of the Constitution of India, Government of Orissa enacted the Orissa Reservation of Vacancies (for Scheduled Castes & Scheduled Tribes) Act, 1975 in posts and services and the Rules made there under. The main intention is to give adequate representation to SCs and STs in the posts and services through reservation. In making Act and Rules as provided under the Constitution of India to safeguard the interest of SCs and STs in posts and services, Orissa has become a pioneer State in India. Section-19 of this Act has got overriding effect on all other Acts and Rules and Regulations of the State.

*Academy of Tribal Dialect and Culture (ATDC)*

The Academy has been functioning at Bhubaneswar since 1979 with the following objectives:

(a) Preserving and promoting tribal dialect, art and culture,

(b) Organising tribal dialect training centres,

(c) Promoting study, dissemination and compilation of tribal literature,

(d) Preparation of grammar books and primers in tribal languages,

(e) Conducting cultural programmes like seminars, conferences and tribal exhibitions to depict tribal art, culture and heritage,

f) Publication of works on tribal art, crafts, culture and heritage, social customs, language and dialect,

(g) To encourage and organise adult literacy programmes in tribal areas.

*Scheduled Caste & Scheduled Tribe Research and Training Institute (S.C. & S.T.R & T.I.)*

The Institute is functioning since 1952 at Bhubaneswar primarily with the following broad objectives:

(a) Research activities for diagnostic and monographic studies of the scheduled tribes and scheduled castes,

(b) Determination of ethnic status of different communities, STs or SCs,

(c) Identification of primitive tribes and pockets to be covered under ITDP.

*Tribal Development Cooperative Corporation Of Orissa Limited (TDCCOL)*

The TDCCOL was registered under the Orissa Cooperative Societies Act, 1962 and has been functioning with effect from 4th October 1967 as an apex cooperative organisation. The main objectives of this Corporation are as follows:

i) To procure Minor Forest Produce (MFP) and Surplus Agriculture Produce (SAP) collected by the tribals at fair and remunerative prices and to arrange their marketing.

ii) To supply essential commodities and other consumer goods to tribals at fair price.

iii) To arrange for the processing of procured commodities with a view to adding value and creating employment opportunities.

iv) To advance consumption-cum-production loans to the tribals in order to protect them from moneylenders.

The achievements of the corporation during the year 1999-2000 were the following:

A Turnover in respect of MFP Rs. 143.33 Lakhs

B Turnover in respect of SAP Rs. 126.86 lakhs

C Turnover in respect of Consumer Business Rs. 333.95 Lakhs

D Turnover in respect of Consumer System Rs. 68.19 Lakhs

E Forest Royalty paid Rs. 20.14 lakhs

F Purchase and Sales Tax paid Rs. 8.62 Lakhs.

*Orissa Scheduled Castes and Scheduled Tribes Development Finance Cooperative Corporation Limited*

The Orissa Scheduled Caste and Scheduled Tribe Development Finance Cooperative Corporation Limited is functioning as catalytic, promoter and guarantor for implementation of various economic development programmes for the benefit of scheduled castes and scheduled tribes. This Corporation is also the sole channelising agency for utilisation of SCA under SCP for scheduled castes and tribes on the sectoral programmes through line organisations / agencies of the State.Educational Programmes The Department of SC & ST Development has the following programmes to promote primary and secondary education in the State for the tribals:

(a) Scholarship for both Pre-Matric and Post-Matric SC and ST students.

(b) Hostel facilities for both Pre-Matric and Post-Matric SC and ST students.

(c) Supply of N.T. Books to Pre-Matric SC and ST students.

(d) Supply of uniforms, cots beds and utensils etc. to Pre-Matric SC and ST students.

(e) Special pre-examination and pre-recruitment coaching facilities to SC and ST students.

*Distribution of NT Books to Scheduled Tribe & Scheduled Caste Students*

The ST & SC Development Department is supplying NT Books to ST and SC students from Class I to Class V, while the School and Mass Education Department is providing books to students from Class I to Class VII free of cost. The Director Text Book Production and Marketing usually supplies those books at the block level.

| Year | Distribution of NT Books to Scheduled Tribe & Scheduled Caste Students | |
|---|---|---|
| | No. of Books | No. of Students |
| 1998-99 | 60,57,000 | 1514353 |
| 1999-2000 | 5194611 | 1316932 |

Construction of Hostel Buildings for scheduled tribe and scheduled caste students in schools and colleges also have been done in the State, the details of which is given below:

| Year | Name of The Programme | No. of Hostels | No. of Seats |
|---|---|---|---|
| 1998-99 | CSP | 23 | 690 |
| 1998-99 | KBK Programme | 200 | 8000 |
| 1999-2000 | KBK Programme | 200 | 8000 |

*Construction and operationalisation of hostels for ST girls*

In the years 1998-99 and 1999-2000 the Department has received funds to construct 501 hostels (489 for ST Girls and 12 for ST/SC Boys). The Chief Minister had made a public announcement on the eve of Utkal Divas 2000 to operationalise 200 hostels by July 2000. The Department have operationalised most of the hostels by June 2000. For operationalising these hostels fixed costs to the tune of Rs.77.85 lakh and recurring expenses to the tune of Rs.351.25 lakh have also been made.

*Reconstruction and repair of school buildings and hostels*

Government of India, Ministry of Tribal Affairs have provided funds to the tune of Rs.296.05 lakh for repair and reconstruction of the Departmental School/hostel buildings. The department has since taken up the reconstruction of 252 school buildings/hostels in the 14 cyclone affected districts. This exercise of repair and reconstruction have been completed by 30th June 2000.

*YOGA*

It has been proposed to impart yoga training to the ST/SC students in the residential high Schools and Ashram Schools of the State. Three Yoga training camps imparting yoga training to PETs of High Schools and Asst. Teachers of Ashram Schools have already been completed.

*Functioning of ITC Khariar Road*

Although a sum of Rs.197.08 lakh was spent for construction

of buildings, development of infrastructure and purchase of tools and equipment since 1992-93 on the said ITC Khariar Road could not be made functional till 2001. From 2001-2002, the ITC has been made functional.

*Procurement of minor forest produce*

There was no collection of Mohua seed by any State Agency during 1998-99. But from 1999- 2000 the T.D.C.C. have been procuring about 2000 MTs of Mohua seeds every year, which is involving transfer of funds to the tribals. The procurement of Sal seed for the crop years 1998 and 1999 were 5892 MT and 5568 MT respectively. This year a revised target of 30,000 MThas been fixed which will involve transfer of funds to the extent of Rs.9 crore to primary gatherers, mostly the tribals.

Non-Timber Forest Produce (NTFP) is an important source of livelihood of tribals who constitute majority of the primary gatherers of NTFP. Most of the primary gatherers are women and have limited access to the market. Therefore they were becoming an easy prey to unscrupulous traders who exploited them. As a result these primary tribal gatherers were deprived of getting fair prices for the produces gathered by them. Against this background, the State Government have formulated a new policy on NTFP, which has come into force with effect from 31.3.2000. With the coming into force of this policy, the ownership rights on 60 NTFP items in forests within the concerned Grama Panchayat area are vested with the Gram Panchayats. Government in Forest Department have formulated a policy relating to oilseeds in pursuance of the announcement made by Hon'ble Chief Minister on the eve of State Level Seminar organised by TRIFED on 23.6.2000.

*Construction of museum for tribal arts and crafts*

This Museum was conceived in the year 1987 under the Centrally Sponsored Plan wherein the funding pattern was 50 per cent of Government of India Share and 50 per cent of State

Government share. But due to various constraints the work had not progressed. Department in the mean time has taken steps and completed the construction of the museum and the museum has been in operation since 2001.

*Village grain bank scheme*

The Village Grain Bank scheme was launched in 1996 for the villages in the areas identified by the Central Planning Committee (C.P.C) as vulnerable from the point of view of starvation/malnutrition among the tribals. The C.P.C has identified 69 blocks in undivided KBK districts, i.e., Koraput, Bolangir and Kalahandi. However, there are many other blocks besides the identified area outside KBK districts where food insecurity is palpable and requires urgent State intervention.

***Maharashtra Model of Single Line Demand***

22.21per cent of the entire population in the State of Orissa are tribals. Therefore, 22.50 per cent of the plan allocation should be earmarked for tribal development in the Tribal Sub-Planarea. The Maharashtra Model of Single Line Demand envisages demarcation of equi-ST population proportionate funds out of total State Plan Outlay for tribal Sub-Plan by Planning and Coordination Department, at the disposal of Scheduled Tribe and Schedule Caste Development Department, which in turn shall allocate such funds among the line departments after deciding inter-sectoral priorities and schemes tailored to the basic felt needs of the tribals. This Maharashtra Model of Single Line Demand has been followed by Government of Orissa and early results indicate that it is becoming beneficial for the tribals.

*Atrocities on scheduled castes and scheduled tribes*

All cases registered under P.C.R Act, 1955 and Scheduled Caste and Scheduled Tribe (POA) Act, 1989 and related sections of the I.P.C are treated as Special Report Cases. The investigation of these cases is supervised by an officer in the rank of DSP (Deputy Superintendent of Police) or above and the progress is monitored by the SP through the protection of Civil Rights Cell. At the State Headquarters, the Human rights Protection Cell monitors the progress of investigation of these cases. The allegations of atrocities received from the members of the scheduled caste and scheduled tribe are inquired into promptly by the Police Officers of the district and also by the offices of Human Rights Protection Cell. Besides Goverment in Home Department are reviewing the atrocity cases against ST and SC on quarterly basis to monitor the progress of investigation, completion of joint inquiries and other allied problems of scheduled caste and scheduled tribes.

## Development Status of the Scheduled Tribes in Orissa

Although the Development Status of the scheduled tribe population in the State of Orissa is far from satisfactory, yet some improvement has been marked in different spheres. An attempt has been made below to analyse some development indicators to assess the development status of the ST people of Orissa indicating the major areas where significant attempt for tribal development has been made.

### *Development of Tribal Women*

Scheduled Tribe women constitute about 50 per cent of the total tribal population. The sex ratio amongst scheduled tribe population is 1062 females for 1000 males according to 1991 census. Although the females outnumber males, they are the most neglectedsection of the society. They confront specific problems which need to be addressed properly.

In tribal societies, women are burdened with multifarious responsibilities. Apart from being engaged in domestic activities, like rearing of children, cooking etc. they play a major role in economic activities. They are mostly engaged in different agricultural activities, collection of forest produce including firewood and in marketing their surplus agricultural and forest produces. They work more than men in all the socio-economic spheres and are far more concerned than men about the maintenance and the economic well being of the family.

With this background in view, it is proposed to formulate suitable schemes for socioeconomic development of tribal women in Sub-Plan area with active participation of Orissa Khadi and Village Industries Board (O.K.V.I) and newly constituted Mahila Bikash Samabaya Nigam. In tune with the recommendations of the Working Group set up during the Seventh, Eighth and Ninth Plan periods women beneficiary oriented income generating programmes will be taken up in crafts such as bamboo and cane work, rope making, tailoring, weaving, leaf cup and plate making, honey extraction, preservation of food and dairy products, etc. by providing financial assistance, technical knowledge and necessary tools and raw materials.

Since the tribal women traditionally do the work of marketing and enter into transactions in respect of their surplus agricultural and forest produces, it is contemplated to organise women cooperative societies in the Sub-Plan area by providing working capital, Membership fees etc. These societies will be responsible for procuring MFP and SAP and other finished products of different traditional crafts and cottage industry for which financial assistance will be provided. Each women cooperative society will have at least 50 tribal women as its members and in each of the 118 tribal Sub-Plan Blocks four such societies will be organised. Besides, in each of the 17 Micro projects one women cooperative society will be formed. For each cooperative society Rs.25,000/- will be provided towards the Membership fees and working capital.The task of child rearing belongs solely to women. Due to lack of knowledge in health care practices, they are not able to take proper care of their children. As a result, the infants suffer from various types of diseases which could have easily been avoided. Therefore, it is proposed to organise basic training programmes on health and hygiene for tribal women in all the 118 tribal Sub -Plan blocks and 17 Micro Project areas.

### Agriculture

Tribals constitute about 26 per cent of the total number of land -holders in the State and operate over an area of 29 per cent of the total operational area. They are, by and large, marginal and small farmers or landless agricultural and non-agricultural labourers. The tribal areas have an undulating topography interspersed with forests. Therefore agriculture in such areas is mostly rain-fed and subject to vagaries of monsoon. The tribal farmers suffer frequently from drought and the crops fail in most of the years. Due to undulating surface of land, the facilities of assured water supply could not be extended to most of the uplands.

The Departmental seed sale centres have been increased from one per each block headquarters to two for easy availability of the seeds. Attempts have been made to increase the sale outlet of fertilizers and pesticides through cooperative and private sector. Soil Testing Laboratories have been established in each district except the District of Kendujhar. The farmers could use chemical fertilizers judiciously on the basis of the soil analysis report of their soil from the soil-testing laboratory.

Incentives have been provided to farmers for free distribution of minikits seed of improved high yielding varieties, for raising high value crops in dug-well ayacuts and for demonstrations on crop substitution and mixed cropping in rain-fed areas. Funds have been provided for purchase of debentures from Orissa State Cooperative, Land Development Bank with a view to giving lands to the agriculturists for land shaping, land development, horticultural plantation, minor irrigation including dug wells and purchase of agricultural implements for agricultural purposes are taken up.Soil Conservation Soil erosion is an acute problem in the hilly terrain of Orissa the inhabitants of which are mostly tribals. The sloppy uplands mostly suffer from topsoil erosion due to want of appropriate conservation measures. Wastelands devoid of vegetation are subjected to severe erosion. As a result, productive lands are sand cast down below. Shifting cultivation is also pre-dominant in hilly slopes causing devastation of valuable forest growth.

To tackle the problem, Soil Conservation Department is implementing different measures on watershed basis with a view to developing watershed for development of natural resources like soil and water and to increase productivity and production and side by side maintain the eco-balance. It has been accepted that watershed based integrated development is the key for overall development of the area. There is a thrust to make the tribals participate right from planning to the execution stage.

### *Horticulture*

The thrust Area for horticulture development in the Tribal Sub-Plan area during the Ninth Plan include production of planting materials in fruit orchards, establishment of mixed orchards etc.

### *Forest Development*

Forests constitute about 36.70 per cent of the geographical area of the State and the tribal population is concentrated close to the forest areas. Forest plays an important role for fodder, timber, medicinal plants and saleable Minor Forest Produce. The life and culture of the tribals are closely linked with the forests.

The policy of the Government is to protect the customary rights of the tribals to collect the NTFP items including fuel wood for bonafide use and consumption. No forest royalty is levied from those primary gatherers. Long -term leases for collection of the Non-Timber Forest Produce (NTFP) items have been given to the Tribal Development Cooperative Corporation to protect the interest of tribals in the trade of these commodities.The World Food Programme is implemented in the predominantly tribal districts and is aimed at income transfer and providing food security to the forest labourers who are mostly tribals. The generated fund under this programme is utilised for welfare measures in tribal areas, such as digging of wells and tube wells, providing medical aid, etc.

Participation of local village community in regeneration and management of degraded forest areas is the cornerstone of Government Policy on forestry. Since tribals reside mostly in forest areas, institutional arrangement have been made to get adequate representation of tribal members of the community in the village level forest committees.

### *Fishery*

The main objectives of development of fisheries in Sub-Plan areas where the concentration of the tribal population is the most are as follows:

(i) Making tribals fully aware of the modern capture and culture technologies, which would give higher yields in terms of money.

(ii) Helping them to supplement their earnings through self-employment.

(iii) Improve the nutrition standard of the tribals through intake of cheap animal protein like fish and to increase the natural stamina to fight diseases.

### *Animal Resources and Dairy Development*

In order to boost up the occupation of Animal Husbandry and Dairying in the tribal areas, the following programmes have been taken up during Ninth Plan period (1997-2002).

(i) Increase in the livestock productivity through cross breeding programme relating to cattle herds in the tribal areas.

(ii) Boosting up milk production through induction of cross breed cows by means of the Frozen Semen Technology artificial insemination.

(iii) Training of tribal farmers on live stock management including fodder cultivations.

(iv) Efforts for upgrading the local breeds of pig, sheep and goats for higher meat production.

(v) Provision of income generation through small animal rearing.

(vi) Introduction of the package programme for mobile animal health care units in the tribal areas to reach the remote places in the interest of treatment of livestock.

(vii) The selection of tribal villages for introduction of cluster programme on fodder cultivation and poultry breeding activities.

### *Land Reforms (Survey & Settlement Operation & Implementation of Land Ceiling Law)*

The necessity for preparation of correct Record of Rights and also updating them need not be emphasized. Since it is a pre-requisite for giving benefits to the confer title and possession, the tribals face difficulties in availing credit facilities from the Commercial/Cooperative Banks as a result the moneylenders of vested interest very often usurp their land. Revenue Courts and Civil Courts also find it difficult to uphold the rights of the tribals in the absence of up-to-date records. It is for these reasons that preparation of land records in the tribal area is considered to be very important.

### *Health Care Facilities*

The primary objective of the Health Policy of the Nation as

well as of the State is to provide preventive and curative health care to all sections of the society including the tribals in remote and inaccessible areas. During Seventh and Eighth Five Year Plan periods attempts have been made to provide health care at the door steps of the tribals, who are mostly inhabitants of hilly tracts by establishing more numbers of Sub-Centres, P.H.Cs/S.H.Cs and Community Health Centres/Upgraded P.H.Cs, Ayurvedic Dispensaries and Homeopathic Dispensaries under the Minimum Needs Programme in Sub-Plan areas.

In pursuance to the National Health Policy greater attention has been focused on tribal areas for development of rural health infrastructures.Under the policy, it was decided to establish one P.H.C. for 20000 populations and one Sub-Centre for 3000 populations in tribal areas. The norm for opening of C.H.C. in tribal area is common for both tribal and non-tribal areas i.e. one C.H.C. for every 80,000 to 1.20 lakh population serving as a referral Institution for four P.H.Cs.

To attain the goal of 'Health for all by 2000 A.D.' emphasis was given on wide application of Indian system of medicine for treatment. A number of projects have been sanctioned in the Ninth Plan to provide health facilities in TSP areas.

### *Communication*

Villages in tribal areas are widely dispersed and do not have proper road communication system. Unless a proper network of roads in the widespread tribal areas is developed the tribal areas will remain isolated from the mainstream of economic and social development.

The working group for Development of STs during Ninth Plan, taking into account the special needs of the Tribal areas for accessibility, recommended the following: i. Database for coverage of tribal villages and habitations by all weather roads should be generated and maintained by the State Government. ii. The present object of covering 50 per cent of villages with population for 200 to 500 in hilly areas and 50 per cent tribal villages with population 500-1000 within a definite time frame of 10 years should be revised to cent per cent coverage of tribal habitations having a population of 100 and above within the next 10 years. iii. Backlog of coverage of villages having various densities of population should be made up during the Ninth Plan. iv. All the ongoing programmes e.g. Minimum Needs Programme as well J.R.Y. and EAS etc. should be taken advantage of in a coordinated and planned manner to meet the above mentioned objectives. v. Culverts on seasonal Nalas and Bridges and others to be provided on priority to be taken up and completed before road construction.Water Resources Development A lot of emphasis has been given to water resources development in tribal areas. During the Ninth Plan period it has been programmed to create an additional irrigation potential of 5196 hectares Kharif and 1641 hectares Rabi in the Tribal Sub Plan Area with an investment of Rs.1941.69 lakh. During 2000-01 a sum of Rs.1266.49 lakh has been proposed for the purpose.

### *Cooperative Institutions*

Cooperative institutions have been playing a very significant role in the socio-economic development of trials. Their exploitation in the field of credit as well as marketing can be checked to a great extent by strengthening the cooperative institutions in the tribal areas. The cooperative institutions have the following three basic objectives.

(a) To provide timely and adequate credit to the tribal members for improving their economic conditions.

(b) To procure surplus agricultural and minor forest produce from the members at reasonable prices and provide necessary marketing facilities.

(c) To supply essential and other consumer articles of daily necessity at fair prices.

*Working of Tribal Development Cooperative Corporation*

The TDCCOL was registered under the Orissa Cooperative Societies Act 1992 and has been functioning with effect from 4th October 1976 as an apex cooperative organisation. The main objectives of this Corporation are as follows:

(i) To procure Minor Forest Produce (MFP) and Surplus Agriculture Produce (SAP) collected by the tribals at fair and remunerative prices and to arrange their marketing.

(ii) To supply essential commodities and other consumer goods to tribals at fair price.

(iii) To arrange for the processing of procured commodities with a view to adding value and creating employment opportunities.

(iv) To advance consumption-cum-production loans to the tribals in order to protect them from moneylenders.

(v) TDCC was set up with a specific objective to purchase Surplus Agricultural Produce from the tribals and the Minor Forest Produce collected by them at reasonable price, arranging for their marketing in a best possible manner and supplying of essential commodities. Thus TDCCOL is not an ordinary Corporation (business entity). It has a vital role in the growth of employment generation in tribal areas. This uniqueness has to be preserved for the benefit of the poor tribals for whom TDCC symbolized economic and in many cases social emancipation. This is especially so in the typical free framework of tribal economy. The Corporation continues its market intervention operations in spite of loss sustained.

***Panchyati Raj Programmes***

Various Income Generating and employment-oriented development schemes are being implemented in the State though Panchayati Raj Department with a view to alleviate poverty of the people including the scheduled tribes. For the purpose of implementation of different developmental programmes the tribal area has been identified as Sub-Plan area.

While preparing The Annual Plan of the Department due weightage have been given for earmarking funds for the Sub-Plan area under different schemes which are executed by the Department. The important Poverty alleviation schemes are as follows: (I) Swarnajayanti Gramswarozogar Yojana, (ii) Jawahar Gram Samridhi Yojana, (iii) Indira Awaas Yojana, (IV) Employment Assurance Scheme.

### *Educational Development Programme of ST and SC Development Department*

Education of tribals is one of the cardinal basic inputs, the importance of which cannot be over emphasized. Educational Development will create awareness and rapid economic development among the tribals. Besides, advancement of education will also ensure bringing a sizable section of the population i.e. the tribals to the mainstream of national consciousness.Due to historical reasons education in the tribal belt of State has been looked after by both the Departments. Education and ST and SC Development. ST and SC Development Department is playing most vital and leading role by providing of special type of schools for education development of the scheduled castes and scheduled tribes. Special types of educational institutions were started in the tribal areas in accordance with the recommendations of the Partially Excluded Area Enquiry Committee.

The ST and SC Development Department have so far established 218 High Schools, 149 Ashram Schools, 143 Residential Sevashrams, 919 Sevashrams, besides 1548 Primary School Hostels with capacity to accommodate 40 students each.

### *Rural Safe Drinking Water Supply*

The problem of providing safe drinking water in the Tribal Sub Plan Area is very acute mainly because the sub-soil water table is very low. All the tribal villages and hamlets that are situated scattered have not been provided with safe drinking water facilities yet. As a result of which tribal women and girls used to cover long distances daily for potable water.

A massive survey of all rural habitations in the State identifying the status of drinking water supply and quality was carried out during 1991-92. Certain fundamental changes were made for the collection of information by the survey. The salient changes were :

(i) For the first time the unit of coverage was taken as a habitation/basti instead of a Census Village to get a micro-level picture.

(ii) The concept of partial coverage was introduced to assess the availability of drinking water. The norm fixed for full coverage was the availability of 40 liters of safe drinking water per capita per day from a public source within a distance of 1.6 k.m. or an elevation differential of 100 meters.

Accordingly, 33.941 habitations/ Bastis have been identified in T.S.P. Area out of the total 80,387 habitations/Bastis in the State. By the end of Eighth Plan 1992-97, 26,560 habitations/ Bastis have been fully covered, 1817 habitations/Bastis have been partiallycovered and 3304 habitations/Bastis are uninhabited. Nevertheless, 2260 habitations/Bastis were still left as drinking water problem village in Tribal Sub-Plan Area at the beginning of the Ninth Plan.

## Problems of Triabls of Orissa

The tribals of Orissa in recent times are confronted with a number of serious problems, which are thwarting their survival and lowering down their quality of living. Some of the major problems which this vulnerable section of population is facing in the State of Orissa are the following:

### *Land Alienation*

The biggest problem of the tribals of India in general and Orissa in particular is Land Alienation. According to the latest statistics, nearly 88 per cent of the scheduled tribes are engaged in agriculture and a large section of the non-tribals are grabbing the land of the tribals, which they have been cultivating for ages. In addition to this, by manipulation, the non-tribals are also taking huge chunk of land on lease in the tribal areas. It is surprising to note that there are large number of instances in the State of Orissa where the land encroached by the tribals are also getting alienated in fervour of the non-tribals. Thus, truely speaking the problem of land alienation among the tribals is very critical and is becoming more critical day by day. Although the State of Orissa have promulgated a legislation titled "Orissa Scheduled Areas Transfer of Immovable Property (Scheduled Tribes) Regulation 1956", land alienation is taking place in the tribal areas in very great numbers by violating the rules and by manipulation of the nontribals. Since the tribals are thereby getting dispossessed from the land and getting further impoverished, Government of Orissa will have to enforce the regulation in a very meticulous manner in order to protect their interest.

### *Shifting Cultivation*

The second biggest problem the tribals of Orissa are confronted with is the Shifting Cultivation. In fact, Shifting Cultivation or the Slash and Burn Cultivation is an age-old practice among the tribals of Orissa. This in principle means cultivating a plot of land for a temporary period and then leaving it fallow. It consists of clearing the forest slopes, burning the fallen trees and bushes and broadcasting the seeds in the ash covered soil.Usually after a couple of years of cultivation, the place is deserted and the tribals traditionally used to come back to the same place after a gap of 6 to 10 years. But with the increase in tribal population and consequent pressure on land, this gap has almost reduced to zero and the tribals have started doing cultivation on a very regular basis on such land. This is causing adverse effects on the neighbouring forest and causing largescale damage to the forest growth. Secondly, with the promulgation of the stringent forest law, Shifting Cultivation as well as the entry of the tribals to the forest have been restricted. This has caused serious problem for continuing the age-old practice of shifting cultivation and the tribals who were largely depending on this type of cultivation are confronted with acute livelihood and food insecurity crisis. Keeping this in view, it is highly desirable for Government to provide viable alternative economic opportunities in place of shifting cultivation for these tribals to ensure them a sustainable livelihood.

***Indebtedness***

One of the major problems faced by most of the tribals in the State of Orissa is the problem of indebtedness. As a matter of fact, since most of the tribals do not have access to financial institutions in their area and even if it is there in some places, they do not have the working knowledge about the same to take advantage of this. The unscrupulous local moneylenders lend them money with exorbitant rate of interest and exploit them. Thus, once the tribals take loan from these moneylenders they get into the debt trap and become impoverished and submerge in debt. Although there is legislation in the State of Orissa entitled The Orissa Debt Relief Act, 1980, tribals are still plagued with the same problem in many areas. In order to give respite to the tribals from this, the existing legislation should be very strictly enforced.

***Unemployment and Poverty***

Unemployment and Poverty looms large among the tribals of Orissa despite large number of development interventions and poverty alleviation programmes launched for their economic upliftment. It has been estimated that more than 90 per cent of the tribal families are below the official poverty line and the number is ever increasing. The unemployment incidence is also growing thick and fast with the passage of time. Due to this stark poverty marked by acute lack of employment opportunities, large numbers of tribals are migrating out to distant places in search of employment to eke out their living.Large Scale Migration As has been indicated above, due to lack of employment opportunities and stark poverty large number of tribals are migrating out to far off places in search of livelihood. In the process many of them are ending up as bonded labourers and majority of them are getting into the impoverishment trap. The migration rates are increasing every year and there has to be some dent made into it, so as to stop the exploitation of this vulnerable group of population from the clutches of the unscrupulous people.

### *Education*

Education is the key to development, but the education scenario among the scheduled tribes of Orissa is in a very bad shape. It has been observed that the literacy level among the tribal people in general and the tribal female in particular is abysmally low. There has been very high rate of school dropouts and the enrolment rate is also equally low among the tribals. It has also been observed that the teachers are very irregular in the schools located in the tribal areas as compared to the general schools. Empirical studies indicate that one of the major reasons contributing to the low literacy level of the tribals is the unsuitable scheduling of the school timing, which clashes with the work schedule of the economic activities of the tribal families in which even the potential school going children participate. Hence, for ensuring more enrolment of children in the school in the tribal areas and also to ensure higher rate retention of children in the school, the time schedule of the schools need to be adjusted in the tribal areas according to their suitability and also to guarantee the regularity of the teachers in schools located in the tribal areas.

### *Housing*

Housing is one sector, which is in very deplorable state in the tribal areas of Orissa. Majority of the houses of the tribals are unfortunately located on Government or Forest land, which are unauthorised and on which the tribals have no legal right. More over, the houses are constructed in such a manner that there is no scope for ventilation and the hygienic condition is at its worst. Along with the human beings the domesticated animals are also housed together. In addition to this, the houses are always swampy and the per person floor space use is so less that it adversely affects the health condition of the members of the family. Thus, housing is a very important sector, whichmust be taken care of for the tribals. In fact, each tribal family should be targeted for a well ventilated and hygienic house on authorised land and guaranting this will go a long way in improving the quality of life of the tribals in the State.

### *Communication*

Poor communication to most of the tribal areas is also another important factor, which hinders the development of the tribals in the State of Orissa. In fact, there are number of tribal villages in the State which are not accessible throughout the year and there are some villages which are approachable only for four months a year. This inaccessibility is slowing down the pace of development of the tribals and because of this many development interventions are not reaching out to them. Hence, care must be made to improve the communication to the tribal villages, which are having poor communication. One of the first steps that should be taken in this regard is to make investment in improving the physical infrastructure - the road for improving accessibility to the inaccessible tribal areas.

### *Displacement*

In recent times, a large number of development projects are coming up in the State of Orissa. Ironically, these development projects are coming up mainly in such areas where there is predominance of tribal population. Statistical figure indicates that more than 40 per cent of the displaced families in development projects in Orissa are the tribals. There are a large number of such Development Projects, which are in the pipeline and are likely to further displace many more tribals. It also has been revealed from a number of researchers that the tribal displaced families have by and large failed to restore their pre-displaced living standards in the post-displacement stage and they have become further impoverished as compared to their former standards of living. This is precisely because the tribal families are not getting compensated for the land which they were possessing for ages, as they are encroached and have not been settled in their favour. Secondly the tribals are not getting successfully adapted to the non-forest based economy in the new place as they are getting dispossessed from the forest on which their life and living centres around. Therefore, some special provisions and package should be evolved for the sustainable and meaningful rehabilitation of the tribal displaced families of development projects.Health The tribals of Orissa are found to be suffering from many chronic diseases but the most prevalent among these taking heavy tolls of them are water borne diseases. This is mainly due to the unsafe and contaminated drinking water. Because of the unsafe drinking water, skin diseases, diarrhoea, dysentery, cholera, guinea worm, tapeworms and many other serious consequences, which often becomes fatal occur to the tribals.

Due to lack of water drainage system, the water accumulates in the tribal areas and this becomes the breeding place of the mosquitoes. In fact, very fatal type of malaria takes away large number of lives in the tribal Orissa. Coming to the health services, it has been observed that in a large number of tribal pockets there are dispensaries without a doctor. Besides, even if there are doctors and there are health care facilities, in a number of tribal areas the tribals because of their adherence to traditional cultural practices believe more in the traditional healing practices and they do not prefer the modern health care systems. This is precisely due to lack of health education among the tribal people. One of the main indicators of poor health status of the tribals of Orissa is the alarmingly high rate of infant mortality. It has been estimated that there are some tribal pockets where the IMR is as high as 200 per 1000 live births. Keeping all the aforementioned facts in view, to ensure better health status of the tribals, there is an urgency to impart health education to the tribals, provide safe drinking water in the habitations where the tribals stay and also to ensure that the doctors are in place in the tribal areas.

## Reasons of Failure in Tribal Development

Although a lot of efforts have been made by Government for the welfare of the tribals in the State of Orissa from the First Five Year Plan period onwards and a lot of innovative programmes have been drawn up in the tribal areas with a huge budgetary provision, yet most of the programmes have not met with the desired result and the pace of tribal development in the State has been rather very slow. On the basis of close examination, it is observed that the following are some of the key reasons of failure of tribal development in the State of Orissa which needs to be carefully looked into by the administrators and planners at the helm of affairs for taking corrective measures for registering sustainable tribal development in Orissa and for meaningful implementation of different tribal development programmes:

— Top down approach in planning

— Lack of participatory approach in plan formulation and implementation

— Generic and not area specific approach

— Indebtedness of the tribals d ue to the local moneylenders
— Inaccessibility to the habitations/villages where the tribals reside and where the programmes are meant for implementation
— Illiteracy and lack of awareness among the tribals about the programmes getting implemented
— Lack of employment opportunities
— Lack of proper monitoring and evaluation by an independent external agency of the programmes in operation
— Lack of a perspective plan for a particular tribe or a tribal inhabited cluster/village
— Lack of an integrated approach
— Lack of a culture friendly development approach
— Non involvement of NGOs for the implementation of the development programme
— Land changing hands from the scheduled tribe people to the non scheduled tribe people
— Liquor addiction
— Restriction of entry to the forest (by promulgation of the forest policy) on which the life and living of the tribals depended for ages without providing any viable economic/income alternatives/ opportunities
— Setting up of Development Projects and Consequent Displacement of Tribals without compensating them for the customary land they possess for generations and without resettling and rehabilitating them properly.

The above identified factors stand as barriers for the success of the tribal development programmes in general and the development of the tribals in particular in the State of Orissa.

It is a fact that the development of the tribals is taking place in Orissa, but the pace of development has been rather slow. Unless the pace of development of the tribals are speededup, the all-round development of the tribals can not be achieved to the desired level within a reasonable time frame. Looking at the factors responsible for the poor and slow development of the tribals and the critical areas that concerns development of this vulnerable section of Orissa's population, the following strategies are suggested which may be adopted by the planners and policy makers for effective implementation of programmes and for sustainable development of the tribals of the State, who are languishing in poverty amidst plenty:

— A perspective plan of 5 years duration to be prepared for each tribal village/group during the 10th Five Year Plan on the basis of the identified felt needs to be elicited from the tribals in a consultative manner.

— Usually any development plan, especially in the State of Orissa is annual in nature, but it will be more meaningful if an integrated annual action plan is drawn up involving all the relevant line departments incorporating quarterly targets/mile stones to be achieved.

— Before making an action plan/perspective plan for a tribal village, Social Mapping of each tribal village indicating detailed interventions needed (village wise) needs to be done.

— One NGO to be associated for each village or a cluster of villages consisting of 500 households for implementing the integrated tribal development perspective action plan.

— An independent external Monitoring & Evaluation Agency (one for each block) to be in place for ensuring timely completion/execution of the perspective action plan.

— Roles and responsibilities of each stakeholder associated in the implementation of the perspective plan will be specified and incentives as well as disincentives should be introduced for the key stakeholders to ensure accountability.

— Before the start of the implementation of the action plan or for that matter any tribal development programme in a given area, orientation training to the key stakeholders should be a prerequisite.

— Before the implementation of a programme in a tribal village, Focussed Group Discussions should be done by the executing agency to explain the people the details of the programme.

— Tribals throughout the State are confronted with the single largest problem, that is they occupy land and cultivate land on which they do not have any recorded rights. The first and foremost step in the direction of tribal development in Orissa is to survey the land in all the tribal areas of the State and the unobjectionable encroached land occupied by them to be settled in their favour

— Micro credit provision should be introduced in all the tribal villages through the NGOs and it should be managed by the community, which can effectively drive away the private money lenders from the tribal areas.

— To avoid distress sale of land, in case of the tribals which is a regular feature in Orissa, a land bank may be created in each Tahasil and the intending tribals who want to sell their land can sell the land to the Land Bank with market value. Establishment of such a Bank will have two fold benefit for the tribals: firstly, they can get the fair price and secondly, they will not have to go to the middlemen and can be saved from being cheated by them.

— A large number of Development Projects are coming up in the tribal pockets of the State and a very sizable number of tribal families are getting physically displaced on account of these projects. Since the tribals have got only customary rights on the land they cultivate and stay, they are deprived of getting compensation for such land. Secondly, the tribals whose life and living centres round the forest, when physically get displaced and relocated at a new place away from the forest, they lose their life support system and get further impoverished. In order to overcome this trauma and restore the livelihood, it must be made mandatory for any private sector companies setting up a project in tribal areas to give a share of the benefit of the project to the displaced tribals. They should also be paid compensation for the land they have been occupying for ages and on whom they have got customary rights. This will go a long way in redressing the adverse effects of the project on the tribals.

— It has been found that for the spread of a programme such as family planning, immunisation, promoting education of the girl child and programme of the like in tribal areas, posters and photo features are exhibited by Government, UNICEF and many other agencies. In these posters, usually photograph of an urban child or a child belonging to western culture and photograph of a place quite alien to the tribals appear. But if the photo features of the tribals will figure in these posters, it will have more acceptability and the programme will have a considerable degree of impact on the tribals.

— In the tribal areas, during the Princely States, the tribals were irrigating their agricultural land through traditional indigenous irrigation systems. But most of such irrigation systems have become defunct now. One of the priorities that should be envisaged in the tribal development programme in Orissa is to identify such defunct indigenous irrigation systems and renovate/rehabilitate them. Once this is done, about 5000 hectares of land can be brought under irrigation in the tribal areas of the State.

— One of the biggest and effective intervention to overcome poverty in the tribal areas of the State is to have more and more Rain Water Harvesting Structures so that more land can be brought under cultivation and cropping intensity can be enhanced, which will have telling impact on the economy of the tribals. That is why one of the first task in the direction of tribal development should be to identify feasible places for setting up Water Harvesting Structures (WHSs) and to build them in phased manner wherever feasible. One way of grounding these WHSs is to make a tie up with the Water Shed Mission which is operating in the State.

— Usually what is happening in most of the tribal areas of the State is that although a lot of works are taken up, they are being executed by the contractors. The contractors are engaging labourers from outside the area. As a result of which the tribals of the area are not getting employment opportunities. In view of this, there should be some executive decision to get all the developmental work (except the hitech works) executed through the VLCs or VDCs in the tribal areas, which will ensure employment opportunities for the tribals.

— Education is the key to tribal development. Unless the educational level of the tribals in Orissa increase, development will bound to be slow. It is observed that enrolment of children in school is very low and dropouts in the school among tribal children in Orissa is alarmingly high. The main reason of this is that the school timing and the working hour of the tribals normally clash and since the tribal children help support their parents in earning, they either do not enroll in the school or dropout if enrolled. Hence, one of the first requirements to ensure better rate of enrolment and higher retention of school children among the tribals is to change the school timing looking at the work schedule of the tribals.

Although Government is making all efforts to ensure tribal development in the State of Orissa, if the above indicated strategies are followed better results can be achieved in respect of the development of the tribals of the State.

# 7

# Tribes of West Bengal

West Bengal contains about 40 recognized communities of tribes—the better known among them being the Santals, Oraons, Mundas, Lepchas, and Bhutias—that make up less than one-tenth of the total population. Bengali is the language of most of the people, with Hindi, Urdu, Nepali, and English as minority languages. English, however, is the language of administration and a lingua franca for business purposes.

## Tribal Communities

About 38 tribal communities are living in the land of West Bengal. They are:

1. Asur
2. Baiga
3. Badia,Bediya
4. Bhumij
5. Bhutia,Sherpa, Toto, Dukpa, Kagatay, Tibetan, Yolmo.
6. Birhor
7. Birjia
8. Chakma
9. Chero
10. Chik Baraik

11. Garo
12. Gond
13. Gorait
14. Hajang
15. Ho
16. Karmali
17. Kharwar
18. Khond
19. Kisan
20. Kora
21. Korwa
22. Lepcha
23. Lodha, Kheria, Kharia
24. Lohara, Lohra.
25. Magh
26. Mahali
27. Mahli
28. Mal Pahariya
29. Mech
30. Mru
31. Munda
32. Nagesia
33. Oraon
34. Parhaiya
35. Rabha
36. Santal
37. Sauria Paharia
38. Savar.

### *Santals*

Santals has wonderful socio-cultural mosaic, which often we round of it in the present caste rifted Indian society. SOme reserachrers argues that Santal and as whole tribals are the original habitants of India. An international study led by Michale J. Bamshad of the Eccles Institute of Human Genetics of the University of Utah of caste origins has found (the findings have been reported in a recent issue of the journal Genome Research) that members of the upper castes are genetically more similar to Europeans, Western Eurasians to be specific, whereas the lower castes are more similar to Asians. This finding is in tune with the expectations based on historical reasoning and the prevalent views of many social historians. In exercising their superiority over native proto-Asian populations, the Aryans would have appointed themselves to higher rank castes.

The following are the main socio-religious characteristics of the Santals:

— Santals have separate religion and it is called "Sarna". Even Indian Constitution does treat Santals religion as separate one.

— Offering during worship is made within the pictorial boundary known as khond as a mark of the mundane relationship of the supernatural power.

— Image or idol worship is absent and there is no as such traditional temple that exists in Santal society.

— Both burial and cremation are practiced. A chicken is dedicated to the dead body.

— The society is devoid of caste hierarchy and therefore, the Santal's is a casteless society. By birth no person, family, clan group is superior or inferior. Santal women enjoys much more freedom than their counterparts in Indian Society.

— Blood offering is prevalent in the community. Earlier practice of cow sacrifice is now restricted.

— Priesthood is not appropriated by a particular clan group or a sect but is owned by the family members of the first settlers of the village. Occasionally selection of a successor of the old priest is held if he leaves no issue (male child). Mainly a divinated person makes such a selection and it is undisputed.

*Livelihood*

Mainly living in the Himalayan sub-mountain region in different districts of Rajshahi division. Their principal home is in radha (in West Bengal), the forests of adjacent Bihar (Jhadkhand) and Orissa, and Chhota Nagpur. The British government assigned a special territory for their living and named it Santal Pargana. It is difficult to definitely say when and why they settled in the East Bengal region. But the census of 1881 shows that there were Santal settlements in the districts of pabna, jessore, khulna and even in chittagong. A survey of the Santal population of present Bangladesh area conducted in 1941 recorded their number as 829,025. The censuses organised after the Partition of Bengal (1947) did not count Santals as a separate group of people, and consequently, their exact number in East Pakistan could not be determined. According to an estimate made by Christian missionaries in the 1980s, the Santal population in northern Bangladesh was over one hundred thousand. According to the 1991 census, the Santal population was over two hundred thousand.

Santals are the descendants of Austric-speaking Proto-Australoid race. Their complexion is dark, height medium, hair black and curled, and lips heavy. mundas, oraons, paharias and some other ethnic groups have a good deal of similarity with the long-headed, broad-nosed Santals in physical features, language and culture. Similarity is also there in their village panchayet administration, in social values, and their characteristic love for dance, singing and music. Santals and related aborigines are among the earliest settlers of the subcontinent and are acknowledged as the progenitors and maintainers of agricultural production system and agro-based culture.

Although the chief god of Santals is the god of the sun (Sing Bonga, in their language), the god of mountain Marang Budu is also dignified enough to have become a village-god. Santals believe that soul is immortal and that supernatural soul (Bonga) determines worldly good and evil. Bonga occupies an important place in their daily worship. Probably that is why house-deity Abe-Bonga is quite a mighty god. Influence of folk Hindu deities is also visible in their religious ceremonies. In fact, Santal men and women are animistic nature-worshippers, but again they acknowledge Thakurjiu as Creator. Idol-worship is not a part of their religious practices.

Santals are fond of festivities. Like Bangalis, they also have 'thirteen festivals in twelve months' ie, many festive occasions around the year. Their year starts with the month of Falgun (roughly, 15 February-15 March). Almost each month or season has a festival or fiesta celebrated with the pomp of dances, songs and music. The Shialsei festival of Santals takes place in the New Year month of Falgun, Bongabongi occurs in Chaitra, Home in Baishakh, Dibi in Ashwin, and Sohrai at the end of Paush. Sohrai is a kind of national festival for Santals celebrated with great pomp on the last day of Paush (around 16 January). To express gratitude to the god of crops is also a part of this festival. It turns splendid with dance, songs, music and pleasant beauty of flowers along with food and drinks. Probably its greatest attraction is the chorus dance of Santal girls. Another important ceremony of Santals is called Baha or the festival of blossoms. The purpose of this festival at the beginning of spring is to welcome and offer greetings to the beautiful blossoming of colourful flowers. It is also characterised with an overflow of dancing, singing and music.

Santals live a poor life. They are compelled to sell their labour at a very low price in tea gardens or elsewhere. Besides, they dig soil, carry loads, or engage themselves in similar works of day labourers. They are accustomed to hard work. Like their simple, plain and candid way of life, their dress is also very simple. Women wear short, coarse but colourful sari, fix flowers on their heads and hair-buns, and make themselves graceful with simple ornaments. Men wear dhutis or gamchhas (indigenous towels). Well-to-do and educated Santals wear modern dress. Skilful workers as they are, Santal women, especially young girls are by nature very beauty-conscious. Santal men and women wear tattoos on their bodies.

Principal food items of Santals are rice, fish and vegetables. They eat crabs, pork, chicken, beef and the meet of squirrels. Jute spinach (nalita) is one of their favourite food items. Eggs of ducks, chicken, birds, and turtles are delicacy in their menu. Liquor distilled from putrefied rice called hadia (or pachai) is their favourite drink. They are also accustomed to distill liquor at home from mahua or palmyra syrup. These drinks are indispensable in their festive ceremonies. Santal women are skilled in making different kinds of cakes.

The Spring Festival of Santals provide young men and women an opportunity to exchange hearts. The hub of such exchange of hearts or choosing one's partner is the akhra (sort of club) just as the dhumkadia of Oraons. In the Santal society, there is no bar against young couples' premarital free-mixing. But in their married life, breach of faith is indeed rare. Divorce is allowed in their community. Paying the bride a dowry is still in vogue but the amount is usually very small. Both widows and divorced women have the right to remarry.

Domination of the male is more prominent in the Santal society although, the role of women in the family is by no means insignificant. Santal women rather take a leading role in earning livelihood or in farming work. The houses of Santals are small but their yards are very clean. Artwork on earthen walls of the house is an evidence of Santal women's liking for beauty and of their artistic mind. Furniture in the house is very simple reflecting their plain lifestyle.

The Santal society is still ruled by traditional Panchayet system and the village headman enjoys special dignity in the society. The community's division into twelve gotras (clans) is still found among Santals. In common practice, marriage between a man and a woman of the same gotra is prohibited. But these regulations are not so effective today.

The Santal language (Santali) belongs to the family of Austric languages. Santali has profound similarity with Kole and Mundari languages. Today most Santals of Bangladesh speak both Bangla and Santali. Also many Bangla words are now adopted in Santali. There is no written Santali literature, but the rich heritage of folk songs and folk tales of Santals is acknowledged by all. Just like the fact that Santals have a language but no alphabet, they have a religion but no canonical scripture.

In the terribly poverty-stricken life of Santals, Christian missionary work of social welfare and, along with that, preaching of the message of spiritual peace accelerated their conversion to christianity. On the other hand, as a result of financial aid from NGOs, desire for receiving modern education is growing among Santals, but poverty is a great obstacle. The Santal community has not been able to free themselves from the rule and exploitation of landowners and moneylenders. Santals took active part in the tebhaga Movement that took place during the period between 1946 and 1950.

Santals cremate their dead bodies. But today, many of them bury the dead in graves. When an inhabitant of a village dies, the village headman's duty is to present himself at the place of the departed and arrange for the last rites with due respect. The custom of holding a sraddha (obsequies) ceremony later at a convenient time is also in practice in the Santal community.

### *Social life*

Santal social organization has very interesting characteristics. It contains flexibility in rigidity. Marriage is one of the important components in the dynamics of Santal society. It, indeed, have wonderful and interesting feature. Therefore, more details description is given here for Santal marriage to have understanding of Santal life, and their feeling and sentiments. It, to some extend, depicts the Santal way of life.

### *Santal marriage*

The Santali name for marriage is called /Bapla/. In Santal society, marriage is one of sacred event of life and marriage adds up considerable respect in society. However, there are some traditions and customs need to be strictly followed in doing so. It is strictly forbidden for any Santal to marry within his or her own sept (Parish). He can marry into any other septs or sub-septs to which his/her mother belonged. There are some septs, which never intermarry with another in consequence of some ancient feuds between them. For example, A Hansdak' male or a female never marries a Murmu female or male respectively. Similarly, a Tudu male never marries a Besra female and vice versa. These customs are no longer in effective prevalent in day-to-day life of Santals. However, myths and tales associated with feud are still told among the Santals.

Girls are married as adults mostly to men of their own choice. In Santal marriage, there is no restriction of age. The bride may be younger, older or of equal age with bridegroom. There are two types of marriage practiced by Santals- the marriage arranged by Raibar is the regular form of marriage. Couple themselves arranges the other forms of marriages.

*Raibar bapla:* This form of marriage is most commonly practiced in Santal society, where parents of both side select the bride and groom. Once they liked each other, then Raibar (match maker ) is appointed to negotiate between them.

Generally, bride's father asks for bride price, which is generally divided among the bride's father, bride's mother, Mother's mother and father's mother. The brother of bride will get bull from groom. It is customs that not fix the marriage date in the month of birth.

*Sanga bapla:* In this form of marriage the divorced women or widow is married with a widower. Here, bridegroom and bride settle the negotiation and mostly male takes the initiatives. In this marriage, bride price is very nominal. The binding ceremony of the Santal marriage is the Sindurdan; Which is here done by not applying the Sidur directly on the parting of the hair of bride by bridegroom, but instead he smears a dimbu flower with vermilion and fix it in the bride's coiffure.

*Kudam bapla:* If a girl becomes pregnant, the young man by whom she becomes so is bound to marry her. Generally young man informs the Jog Majhi (Assistant to head man) of his offence and the girl confesses it to wife of Jog Majhi. Then they inform to parents of bride and bridegroom. As usual, bridegroom pays bride price and bull. Bridegroom at the time of applying vermilion stands facing west and bride facing east

*Kiring Jawae:* If the couple belongs to the same sept, the headman calls for councils of village, and the decision would be always negative. Here boy's father has to bear the expenses of the marriage of the girl to another man. Then headman arranges the marriage for girl far away from village and name of boy is always secret.

*Ghardi jawae:* When a man has minor sons and grown up daughter, he procures Ghardi-Jawae to get in his agricultural work. All expenses of marriage is borne by bride's father. At ordinary situation marriage the bridegroom 's friends are called Bariat; but in this it is the friends of bride that are called so. In this kind of marriage the bridegroom pays nothing for his bride but lives with father in-laws and work for him without wages for five years. When man procure a Ghardi Jawae to get help his agricultural works, in such cases, the girl's father sets aside a bit of land for this Ghardi Jawae and help him to get additional land Once five years of service is over, the Ghardi jawae is free to depart.

*Tunki dipil bapla:* Poor men perform this type of marriage. As they have not sufficient money to bear the expenses of the regular marriage (Raibar Bapla), they resort this type of marriage. The bride is brought to the house of the bridegroom with small basket on her head; a few friends and relatives accompany her to her house. The bridegroom in the presence of these persons applies vermilion on her head and couple then lives as husband and wife.

*Itut bapla:* Forward young men who are not quite sure whether the girl fancy will accept them and take this means of compelling her to marry adopt this. This type of marriage is looked down up and rarely occurs. Generally double bride price is paid and the marriage is still legal. But if girl declines to live, then she must take divorced in full moon and cannot marry as spinster.

*Nirbolok bapla:* This form of marriage can said to be female variety of 'Itut" Bapla. A girl who cannot get a man whom she likes in the regular way, takes pot of rice beer and enters his house and insist upon staying there. They do not adopt any physical force to expel her from house. It is said to quite fair and usually effective to throw red peper on the fire, as by inhaling smoke she will be compelled to run away. If she passes this endurance test without leaving house, she is held to have own her husband and family is bound to recognize her as husband. This type of marriage also rarely occurs in Santal society.

### *Divorce*

Divorce is a common sequel to Santal marriage and is granted at the wish of either husband or wife. The following are the grounds for which the Santal men and women demand the divorce. The husband can demand the divorce if his wife is proved to a witch, or is sexually immortal ad she does not obey him or she lives always in her father's house. The wife can claim divorce, if husband cannot supply sufficient foods, clothing, ornaments etc. Sterility is another ground for divorce. In case husband seeks the divorce, he cannot claim the bride price and he has to pay certain amount of money as fine. If wife demands the divorce then her father has to refund the bride price. The divorce is effected in the presence of the assembled villagers in the following way; The husband is made to stand facing the sun on one leg. He has a cloth rounded his neck each end which is held in the hand along with three Sal leaves. Then taking the name of Sin -Bonga he tears the Sal leaves in the token separation and upset a brass pot full of water. Wife repeats this too. There is belief that if the Sal leaves are not fully torn or the lotta (Brass pot) are not wholly emptied then the couple must again come together.

*Birth and naming ceremony*

When Santal women get pregnant, she and her husband observe certain taboos. The husband during his wife's pregnancy never kills any animal nor participates in any funeral ceremony and does not come in contact with any dead body. The pregnant woman during the evening very rarely comes out of the house. She does not weep when the death occurs of her relative. On the day of moon eclipse, she will not come out of room. She should not sit on courtyard with her hair or cloth hanging downward. After the birth of a child, the house is considered polluted. So the Santals performs the Janam Chatiar ceremony. Until it is done, no other activities can be undertaken like hinting etc. The usual day for the ceremony is fifth day for male and third day for female child. After ceremony, the men and women and children of the village who have assembled at the house each a leaf cup full of rice water with the leaves of Neem (Neem dak' Mandi).

Generally it tastes sour. On the fifth day, the children are given the name. Should it happen to be son and then he takes the name of grandfather. Should it be second son born, he takes the name of maternal grandfather and thus third from paternal grandfather's brother and fourth from maternal grandfather's brother and so on. The same procedure is followed for girls the female relations being in the same order.

*Chacho chatiar*

It is very important ceremony of the Santals that enables the individual to take his place in Santal society and participate in its rights, rules and ceremonies. Without this no Santal can be married or cremated.

***Bitlaha***

It means outcasting Santal from society. This outcast takes place by the order of assembly of villagers. It is resorted when a Santal women indulges in any physical relationships with either Diku (non-Santals) or with a person of name sept. It is worth noting that relatively free sex is prevalent among the Santal society. If it is proved, then the assembly gives the order of outcast and they proceed to carry out the day after annual hunting. A man in the market who carries a branch of sal tree with leaves announces the date of Bitlaha. The person in the market on seeing him understands the matter and counts the leaves that indicate the no of days.

The day of Bitlaha, all female members of village kept themselves away from village. In the early morning bachelors and other male members of the neighboring villages with flutes and drums, bows and arrows meet at the end of Village Street where culprit lives. Drumming is kept terribly high so that it can be heard from long distance. When crowd reaches the house of the offender they tie a short charred bit of firewood, worn out broom ad some used leaf plates on the pole of bamboo and fixed at the entrance of courtyard. Bachelors in undress do desecrate the rooms. The person who outcasted are not allowed to take food with others, and they cannot give their children marriage within the Santal community.

*Jam jati*

By performing this ceremony, an outcasted Santal can be taken back in the society. The outcasted man and women go to the village street with twisted cloth rounded their necks and water in a lota. Before the headman and his assistance, the offenders acknowledge the offence and agreed to pay the fine for it. After taking water from lota and wash their mouth and pass it to all leading man who will repeat the same. After this they entered the village and the courtyard of the outcast who personally wash the feet of the leader of he people.

*Village administration*

The cultural analysis of the Santal village administration would pave the way for a clear understanding of the economic and political stratification and their history and evolution in ancient India. This indeed, will give an idea about the contribution of Santals towards modern social system. The Santal society is characterized by democratic equality. Wealth matters little in the day-to-day life. The clans are regarded as equal to another clans and there is no class distinction either in status or occupation. The village is generally multi clans and each clan has sub number.

The Santal villages are social and political entities with great cohesion and continuity. Each village has well established political organization with a secular headman called Majhi who is a man of great prestige. The village council controls the entire social system of the Santals. The village council or Atu Mone Hor is consisted of Majhi (village headman), Jog Majhi (Deputy village Headman), Paranik (Assistant to village Headman), Goddet (secretary to village Headman), Jog Paranik(deputy Paranik), Naeke (head village priest) and Kudam Naeke (Assitant to village priest). All the villagers are member of the village council. Village council is the institution that settles all the disputes of the villages. Santal community as a whole maintains certain uniform customs and laws with relation to marriage, divorce, birth etc.

Majhi presides over the village council meetings when they are held to discuss the matters related to village. In event of disputes arises with different village, he acts as representative of village. Paranik is the principal assistant to Majhi and representative of Majhi. If Majhi dies without any male issues or brothers, then paranik will get the office. and Goddet. No public sacrifice, no festival, no ceremony such as marriage can be done without Majhi taking initiative. Jog Majhi serves as the supernatant of the youth of the village and he is one the link between younger generation to older generation and he generally passing all the secrets to younger ones. In the absent of Jog Majhi, the Jog Paranik officiates. Equally important is the religious headman called Naeke and his assistant Kudam Naeke.

*Arts & culture*

Arts and culture is integral part of Santal society. It reserves vast & rich cultural heritage. Infact Santals are most remembered by their arts and culture. Here we will give some links towards by some of the scholarly works and also some description of it.

*Santal musical Instruments*

*Tirio*: The instrument most favoured by Santals, is bamboo flute with seven holes. It is viewed as a symbols of love and seduction.

*Dhodro banam*: is a bowed instrument carved out of a single log of wood of a tree which according to Santal story, grew out of the flesh of a human being. It consits of a belly(lac) covered with an animal skin on which rests the bridge(sadam, lit, horse), an open chest( korom), a short neck(hotok)and a head( bohok) which is often beautifully carved in the shape of a human head, a couple or whole groups of humans or of animals. If the is a head, the tuning peg is inserted in the ear(lutur), and the gut string comes out the mouth.

*Phet banam*: is a fretless stringed instrument with three or four strings. The waisted belly is completely covered by animal skin.

Tumdak,is also known as madol, is a two faced drum with a body brunt clay. Both heads the left one broader than the right are covered by bullock hide and are beaten by the left and right hand.

*Tamak*: is a bowl shaped kettle drum. Its body is made of thin metal sheets, covered by bullock hide and beaten by a pair of sticks.

*Junko*: is an onomatopoeic description of sounds of the ankle bells, which are cast in metal in the shape of buds and tied to the feet of dancers from where they produce rhythmical sounds.

*Singa*: is a S-shaped wind instrument played in pairs in weddings. Made of brass of copper, it is usually constructed in the three pierces with mouthpiece at the blowing end and a conic opening at the other.

### ***Oraons***

Oraon, The a tribe of the Proto-Australian origin. The Oraon people are short and black in complexion. Their noses are flat and their hair black and curled. In the subcontinent, they live mostly in Orissa, Chotonagpur, Rajmahal and the adjoining areas of Bihar. According to anthropologists, Oraons, mundas, Malpaharis and santals belong to the same group of aborigine people. From the point of view of language too, they belong to the same Austric family. Many specialists consider that the word Oraon is a distorted form of a totem in the ancient Kurukh language.

Like many other ethnic groups, Oraons worship nature. They however, believe that there is a creator of the universe, Dharmesh, who exists in the sun. Most of their religious ceremonies centre around the sun. Oraons believe in different gods having symbolic representation in villages, agricultural assets, forests, epidemics etc. They satisfy these gods through religious festivals similar to those of the Hindu community. For example, the Bhadu festival of Hindus and the Karam of Oraons are almost identical. This is a worship of trees performed symbolically with the kadam (anthocephalus chinensis) tree or its branches. In fact, bhadu and karam are the name of the same kadam tree in different languages. Religious festivals like the Hariari and Sarhul are associated with praying for the fertility of land and a good paddy harvest.

Oraons worship trees, flowers and fruits for increased crop production and protection of the tribe. Fertility of land and women is the same in their religious prayers. Their vows are closely associated with their lifestyle, the struggle for existence and the pleasures of life. Religious ceremonies and seasonal festivals reflect their way of living and their social needs. They also believe in the power of magic. All religious ceremonies and seasonal festivals of Oraons such as the Basundhara in the month of Baishakh, Bhadri in Bhadra, Jejuti in Agrahayan, Itu in Falgun and Sarhul in Chaitra reflect the tribe's link to agriculture.

Like other tribes, Oraons like to dance, sing and play musical instruments. Their dances and songs are deeply rooted in their social and cultural life. Jhumur songs of Oraons reflect their lifestyle and their religious philosophy. Dhumkuria is as important an aspect of their social life as the Dekachang is to garos, Akhra to Santals and Ghatul to Murias.

Oraons reside in dormitory type of houses that provide the young boys and girls an opportunity to mix with one another and to choose their partners in life. Marriage rituals in the Oraon community are similar to those of Santals and Mundas. Marriages are arranged by the guardians in the family, but the opinions of the brides and bridegrooms are also respected. Child marriage is not recognised. Divorce is allowed. Divorcees, as well as widows, can remarry. Both men and women can marry more than once but men are not allowed a second marriage unless they are widowed or are divorcees.

Oraon men and women wear simple dresses. Women wear coarse sari and men wear the dhuti and the lungi. Poor men wear the gamchha. Oraon women like to wear ornaments and use flowers in their make-up. A recognised social custom is to have tattoos on the body of both men and women. The better off and educated Oraons wear shirts, trousers and panjabi.

Rice is the staple food of Oraons. They take vegetables, fish, or meat with rice. They drink a homemade wine called pachai, which is generally made from rice. Farming is the main occupation of Oraons. Men plough the land and women take part in other types of work. Women work harder than men. They sell fish and vegetables or fruits. Landless Oraon men and women work as coolie-kamin (land labourers). Oraons burn the bodies of the dead. As a mark of respect to the deceased they offer flowers and leaves of sacred trees to the dead on the pyres. The Oraon people also express formal condolence.

Oraons practise the age-old panchayet system in local administration. They did not get much modern education. Poverty is the main cause of their illiteracy. Added to this is their strong adherence to conservative norms and values. Christian missionaries tried to spread education among them. Many Oraons are now adopting christianity. At present, some non-government organisations work among them and implement programmes for their socio-economic development.

### *Oraon culture*

An important aspect of Oraon culture that is intimately related to environmental features is food habits. The Oraons are primarily agriculturists. Their usual diet consists of rice, dal and vegetables. Fish and meat are occasionally consumed. What is striking, however, is that leaves, flowers, seeds, roots and fruits are an integral part of the Oraon diet. These are procured from the forest. Only a few are grown by the people themselves. A study has shown that there are about 21 kinds of common native plants whose leaves are eaten by the Oraons. The number of common native plants whose flowers, roots, seeds, fruits and whole plants that are eaten stand at 10, 10, 15, 25 and 6 respectively. In all, there are 87 kinds of common native plants which are related to the food of the Oraons.

The construction of houses, household items and other artifacts too show a linkage with the environment. Chotanagpur is a land of forests. Many products are obtained from the forest. Some of these are major products and others are minor ones. The Oraon house is usually made of mud walls and tile roofs. All the same, house construction requires the use of timber and bamboo.

It is for minor products that we find greater concern among the Oroans. The Oraon household includes such items as mats, cots, wooden stools, baskets, cups, plates, cushions, rope, mortar and pestle and oil presses. All of these are made from forest products. Hunting implements such as bows and arrows, slings, spears and swords are made from forest products. Similarly, fishing tools such as baskets and traps of various kinds are made of bamboo. Fishing nets are made of twine. Umbrellas are made with the handle and ribs of bamboo covered with gungu leaves. Even the hooded waterproof coat is made of the gungu leaves.

Knowledge of the treatment of diseases is another sphere where we find a close relation between the Oraon community and its environment. Treatment of diseases is invariably based on the use of medicinal herbs found in the region. There are about 34 kinds of disease which are treated with such medicines. These include pain (headache, toothache, stomachache, eye pain, ear pain, migraine), fever (high, ordinary, malaria), wounds, constipation, diarrhoea, dysentery, epilepsy, rheumatism, insomnia, tetanus, eczema, etc. These are treated with medicines based on leaves, roots, the bark of trees, and with plants which grow wild in the jungle. Some of them are grown in their fields by the people themselves.

The major customs among the Oraons, as with any other community, are connected with birth, marriage and death. The linkage of customs with the ecology is best reflected in customs connected with marriage and death. There are many customs preceding marriage with which the environment is very closely connected. There is the custom of men going to the forest to fetch firewood and women to fetch sal leaves for preparing cups and plates. The preparation of the marriage mat and marriage baskets of various sizes are other customs. Setting up a marwa is, however, the most significant. Nine sal saplings with leaves on top are planted in the courtyard in three rows. The middle one of the second row differs in its height. Also planted are branches of bamboo, sidha, bhelwa, mango and mahua. The mango suggests perpetuity of descendants, the bamboo symbolises progeny, the sidha fidelity of husband and wife, the bhelwa protection from the evil eye and the mahua, love between the couple. The marriage ritual would be incomplete without this invocation of trees and plants.

During funerals the Oraons practise burial and cremation. Bodies are buried when crops stand in the field. In this custom, various shapes of branches cover the bottom of the grave, lengthwise and crosswise.

Important festivals of the Oraons pertain to the forest, hunting, agriculture and cattle. Besides these, there are socio-religious gatherings known as jatras, which take place at the commencement of different seasons. It is not possible to discuss all their festivals. I shall confine myself to a few for the purpose of illustration.

The spring festival, known as sarhul, is celebrated when the sal tree is in full blossom. In this festival the Oraons perform the symbolic marriage of the sky with the earth. This is done to ensure the fertility of mother earth. On this day a propitiatory sacrifice is offered to the old lady (the village goddess) who is believed to abide in the sacred grove of the village. Phaggu is a festival which is observed towards the end of February or the beginning of March. On the evening previous to the feast, a young castor (Palma christi) plant and a semar (Bombax malabaricum) branch are planted in an open place. Around these some hay, firewood and dry leaves are heaped. The village priest sets fire to the hay. When fire burns at its brightest the young castor shrub is cut into pieces with an axe. Immediately the young boys of the village light torches from the bonfire and throw the burning torches at fruit trees, saying, 'Be loaded with good fruit'.

*The community and its Environment*

What these selected illustrations show is the scale of interaction that prevails between the community and its environment. Whereas the community's dependence on nature is overwhelming, it is far from being passive. The community acts on nature and transforms it into forms that are of use to it. However, the use of environmental resources is limited to the extent necessary for the community. It is this which leads to harmony between community and environment. Such harmony is, however, possible because of the overriding social values that guide Oraon society. These are the values of equality in society, collectivity in economy, accommodation in history, ethical living in philosophy, folkism in literature and group participation in art and music. On account of these, the attitude the Oraons have towards nature is one of rational adaptation and not of mastery over the world.

Crises in this harmony result from a number of sources. The opening up of the economy to the market and therefore profit is an important factor but is not the only one. Societies guided not by profit but by their assessed needs have been equally instrumental in the destruction of environmental wealth. What seems to be at the back of disharmony is the attitude of rational mastery over the world rather than rational adaptation to it. What has led to this shift seems to be a spirit of competition and domination rather than cooperation, the hallmark of traditional societies.

After having tentatively explained what makes possible harmony between community and environment, we shall explore the ways in which the Oraons contribute to sustaining the existing order. We have seen how nature enters into the very fabric of Oraon society — their food, houses, domestic goods, artifacts, rites, rituals, customs, festivals, etc. This shows how the natural order enters into the social order of the Oraons. The two orders are not separate, discrete, autonomous. Rather, they are integral to each other. At the same time, the social order is also a moral order to the Oraons. Hence there are ways through which the moral order is maintained. In Oraon society, these orders are maintained either through prohibition or propitiation. Taboos surrounding the use of environmental features are varied. These are observed on different occasions and by different sets of people. Restrictions surrounding hunting or the commencement of a season or totemic institutions may be taken as illustrations. Propitiation of village deities in charge of different environmental features is another way by which the moral order is thought to be maintained in Oraon society.

*Education*

The Oraons, a tribal community, are among the poorest sections of the landless or daily wage labourers in West Bengal. The infant mortality rate among tribals in the state is high at 85 deaths for every 1000 live birth as compared to 51 deaths for infants belonging to non-tribal communities. "We were blind," explains Kamini Oraon, a neighbour. "Just because we never learnt to read and write does not mean our children should not grow up to be human beings, SSK has changed our lives."

Today more than 80% of the children belonging to the Oraon village go to the village school. The Panchayat (local governance) plans to upgrade the school to cover class eight and bring more and more children under its fold. The Shishu Shiksha Karmasuchi programme (SSK) reaches out to thousands of such excluded children living in far flung areas of the state.

Initiated in West Bengal in the year 1999 against the backdrop of about 2.7 million children being out of school, the programme today reaches out to more than 1.4 million children. While there has been overall improvement in literacy in the state during the last decade, there were clear significant differences across socio-economic groups, which persisted and suggested a need for targeted interventions for universal coverage. To address the problems of access and community involvement the Department of Panchayats and Rural Development, Government of West Bengal (P&RD) initiated an alternate form of education system owned by the community - the Shishu Shiksha Karmasuchi (SSK) programme. Starting in 1999 with 715 centers, the SSK has grown to 16,397 centers running presently. SSK targets the difficult to reach children catering to their specific needs through flexibility in terms of school timings, management by the community, and engaging community teachers who belong to the same community as the children.

SSK is a fully recognized elementary education system in the sense that a child graduating from an SSK center gets the same status as the child who graduates out of a formal primary school. The curriculum and text books followed in these centers are the same as followed in the formal schools. SSK is thus academically equivalent to the formal school system. However, it differs from a formal government school in the sense that it targets the difficult to reach children catering to their specific needs through flexibility in terms of school timings, management by the community, and engaging community teachers who belong to the same community as the children.

The SSK programme adopts a three pronged strategy to reach its objective. This includes

— Mobilizing the community by setting up a center based managing committee to establish and monitor child education centers for the out of school children.

— Providing academic support to the Sahayikas (para teachers) and the community to enable them to create a positive learning environment and by establishing efficient monitoring and information system at the center, village, block and district level to plug loop holes.

### *Mundas*

Munda a very small group of aboriginal people living in different parts of Bengal. According to some estimates based on information gathered by some non-government organisations, there are 212 Munda families in the country. As counted locally, 1,163 Mundas live in scattered villages of koyra and dumuria upazilas of khulna district and shyamnagar, debhata and tala upazilas of satkhira district - all falling within the sundarbans. The ecosystem of the Sundarbans seems to suit the indigenous ways of living and cultural traits of Mundas.

Until recently, Mundas (and Mahatos, another tribe bearing close affinity to them) were known as bunos or jungle clearers. They came to this country about two hundred years ago from Ranchi and Chota Nagpur of the Bihar State of India to help reclaim land for agriculture for zamindars and dig lakes and ponds for them. They also came to work as wage labourers in the Duars tea plantations in Jalpaiguri district, close to the tea gardens in Bengal. According to a 1921 census, as many as 34,601 Mundas were working in the Duars tea estates as against 115,350 oraons and 23,488 santals, who too came from the same region. They had a deep attachment for their homes and lands back in Bihar.

British settlement officers of the time reported from Ranchi that "large numbers of those who emigrate to Assam and the Duars return, if they are able to save a little money, and buy back the farms they had lost, or acquire some land in the vicinity". According to some accounts, Mundas along with other tribes akin to them came from the Rajmahal Hills of India and settled in the northern part of Rajshahi district. Some of them, like the Oraons, Mahatos and Santals, settled in this country permanently and were employed in agriculture, at indigo factories and at tea plantations. These days most Mundas and Mahatos depend mainly on agriculture.

Ethnically, Mundas are described as a large Dravidian tribe of Chota Nagpur closely akin to the Hos and Santals and on linguistic grounds classified as Kolarian. The name Munda is said to be of Sanskrit origin meaning headman of a village. This titular designation is used by the members of the tribe. Mundas and Oraons are also known by the general name of Kol. The languages of the Munda subfamily are spoken in parts of northern and central India and comprise more than 20 tongues, the important of which is Santali written in Roman, Devanagari, Bengali and Oriya scripts. These languages belong to an Austroasiatic family of languages spoken by about 65 million people. The Munda languages, spoken by about 4 million tribals, are closely related and are referred to by the single name of Kherwari.

Mundas are divided into 13 sub-tribes and some such sub-tribes are Kharia-Munda, Mahili-Munda, Oraon-Munda, Bhuihar-Munda, and Manki-Munda. The sub-tribes are again divided into numerous sects or kilis along totemistic lines. Mundas are of medium stature, stocky in build and black in skin and are known for their hard work as labourers especially in removing forests and cutting earth. Initially, they came as seasonal labourers but as demand for their services increased, more of them flocked in. Many of these workers settled in different parts of Bengal. But as jungles and forests dwindled under pressure of population and consequent clearing and settlements, they found their traditional occupation not economically viable any more. To survive, they resorted to alternative occupations such as agriculture, fishing, van driving, small businesses and jobs.

A Munda may not marry a woman of his own sect. Adult marriage is in fashion and sexual intercourse before marriage is tacitly recognised but as a common practice, the matches are made by the parents. A bride-price is a custom and in a late 19th century study, it was found to be Rs 4 to 20. sindur dan, or the smearing of vermilion on the forehead of each other by the pair is the essential and binding part of a marriage ceremony. Munda widows may marry again by the ritual known as sagai. Divorce is allowed at the instance of either party but in case of adultery the seducer is required to pay to the husband the full amount of the bride-price. After marriage, a Munda son with his wife remains part of the joint family. In the past, Mundas used to burn the body of their dead but wood being expensive, they put fire to the face symbolically and then bury it.

At the head of Munda religion stands Sing-Bonga, the sun. There are other gods to take care of different aspects of human and natural life and they require constant propitiation by way of sacrificing of animals or fowls to keep the diseases off and save crops. The Munda festivals are mostly related to seasons and crops. Some of these are: Sarhul or Sarjun-Baba, the spring festival in Chaitra (March-April); Kadleta or Batauli in Asad (June-July) at the commencement of the rainy season; Nana or Jom-Nana, the festival of new rice in Aswin (October-November); and Kharia Puja or Magh Parab, the festival of harvesting the winter rice.

Mundas and Mahatos in Bangal claim to be Hindus. They perform Shyama puja and Kali puja sometime in November, Ashadi puja in July and Bhadu puja in September. They also observe poush-parbon as harvesting ceremony. They are not, however, caste bound like the Hindus. They are very simple people and do not associate themselves with criminal activities. It is rare to see them even engage in quarrels or fighting with neighbours. They live in thatch houses. They are quite hospitable and it is their tradition to entertain guests with jawa or country liquor. They love to drink jawa and sing at weddings and other festivals. Special dishes include crabs, mice and snails.

Mundas have a montri or minister for all villages of a given area. He resolves conflicts among the tribals with the help of modols (village leaders). Continuous inflow of Bangalis from other regions creates ecological stresses for the dwindling forest, animal and aquatic resources of the Sundarbans. Only very recently, Mundas started sending their children to schools and with the help of some NGOs, they are taking to income generating activities to mitigate their poverty. This may be one reason why the number of the aboriginals in the area including the Mundas has been falling.

## Tribal Arts

### *Dances*

In ancient Bengal, dancing was popular entertainment. Courtesans and temple girls (devadasis) were required to be proficient in the art of dance prescribed by Bharata in his 'Natysastra'. Popular forms of dancing were rendered at mundane celebrations and on other occasions by low-caste tribes Nats and Domnis (women of the Dom caste) who practiced dancing and singing as hereditary professions.

In the Middle ages, probably the institution of temple girls become obsolescent and class dancing was limited to courtesans. As a result dancing came to be looked down up on in respectable society.

Rabindranath Tagore has the credit of rehabilitating dancing as a fine art to be learnt by young as a part of their education. In his school at Santiniketan and later in his university Viswabharati, he provided ample facilities for training in these acquirements. He had profound admiration for the rich treasure of the classical dances of India but he thought these required too rigid a discipline and too elaborate a training to be feasible for the general public.

He therefore introduced a simple course of instruction in dancing to his songs of the seasons. By 1926 this developed into a flexible system compounding elements of Bharatnatyam, Manipuri, Kathak, Kathakali and folk styles. This creative system was very well received by the Bengali public and has since grown into a major cultural activity. A large number of institutions teaching the elements of classical dances and presenting ballet compositions have come into existence in Calcutta and the towns.

Evolution of an Indian ballet tradition has been the quest of institution presided over by Udayashankar, who well versed in European ballet made his debut in this field in 1929 and has made Calcutta his headquarters since over a decades ago. During the last twenty five years the new dance movement has made considerable progress not only in West Bengal but also other parts of India and Bangladesh.

The Santals inhabiting the plateau Fringe have their own system of group dancing to the accompaniment of song, the flute and Madal (a minor drum) to express their joy of life. It is full-blooded and exuberant but notably free from vulgarity or obscenity.

### *Chhau Dance*

The Chhau dance of Purulia district is a sophisticated dance system in Bengal. The Chhau dance is a mask dance. There is no Chhau without mask. This dance is usually performed by male dancers. Chhau dance of Purulia has some characteristics of primitive ritualistic dance in its vigour, style and musical accompaniment mainly the drum. The symbols were once used as facial painting or body painting by dancers who were thus recognized as personifying the characters they stimulated and the masks appeared later. The best Chhau dance groups or parties are located within Baghmundi P.S. They are the best because of their traditional vigorous and heroic style of performance. The other groups (Domordi-group, Birgram-group, Madla-group etc ) are more sophisticated and refined both in their themes and dance-styles. The Chorda-group of dancers are not only best performs of heroic Pauranic themes, but also are very much selective about such themes for their performance. Chhau mask dance is predominantly a Bhumij art. All the majority of dancer are Bhumji.

### *Tusu Parab*

Makara Sankranti is an important festival in all parts of Bengal. The *Tusu Parab* is held in Birbhum on this occasion. Groups of young girls gather every evening throughout the month of Pousa (December-January) and sing songs which have been termed by the generic term Tusu. On the day of Makara Sankranti the groups go out of the village to a nearby tank or river with the goddess Tusu symbolized in small clay figurines or sometimes merely as cow-dung balls.

After a sacred bath they return to worship and make offerings of rice to the deity. Different groups meet, sing songs near the river-bank or the pond and compete with each other. The songs are accompanied by simple group movements: there is no other accompaniment. The men also have their particular songs and dances for the occasion and these are known as the Bhaduriya Saila. The dance content is more predominant here: men dance in circles clock-wise and anti-clockwise.

### *Jhumar*

In Chaitra, another type of composition known as the *Jhumar* is sung and danced. Jhumar can be sung and danced by only one men and women or both depending upon the particular occasion. The Jhumar at Chaitra is a typical men's dance which is accompanied by drum and cymbals. At time of the transplanting of the paddy only women sing and dance the Jhumar. This is then known as the Ashariya Jhumar. Into the agricultural songs of transplanting paddy was impregnated the theme of the love of Radha and Krishna and other stories of mystical union. The basic tune of the Jhumars remained more or less the same. The development of the Jhumar provides an interesting instance of an old form absorbing a new content.

### *Agricultural Dances*

The agricultural dances have gradually given place to dances which are purely devotional or religious in character. Practically each different sect has its own music and dances. The worshippers of Shakti, dance in the Chandi mandir of Siva, in the dance hall called Gambhira and those of Vishnu in the Natmandir. All these pavilions are specially constructed for the dance in front of the shrine. The Gambhira festival is held on this day. So also is the Kesvar where Siva is worshipped. Gazan dance is performed by men dressed in saffron robes who carry a Dhanuchi (incensed burners). This is exclusively performed by men; the musical accompaniment is provided by decorated drums and brass gongs (Kanshi).

The ballad singers, the boatmen, the fishermen and the professional musician dancers, actors, acrobats and even jugglers have their distinctive songs and dances. A characteristic feature of these is the musical accompaniment which consists of a one stringed instrument called the ektara. The dance movements are by and large, restricted to short sequences which intersperse the singing. The footwork is elementary, but the movement of the pelvic griddle is difficult and characteristic. It is freely used by men singing the songs to indicate a dramatic moment.

### *Raibense Dance*

The *Raibense dance* of Birbhium district is a traditional system with a martial motif. The dancers rhythmically flourish staves as they execute vigorous steps. These dances have their strict codes and disciplines unlike the crude and vulgar exhibitionism of the Domnis whose vogue has dimnished greatly. The dances of the Raibenshes of Burdwan and Birbhum seem to be the last surviving vestiges of war-like traditions. The technique of the dances is so vigorous that there has been a new interest in teaching these dances to educated boys and girls of urban centres specially by the Bratachari organisation.

Dance is a series of vigorous physical exercises, in which the erect torso has an important part to play. The dancers begin in a single file and then make a circle. Hops, jumps and circles are characteristic. Skills with the shield and the spear and the trishul are common. A percussion instrument accompanies the dance.

### *Theatre*

*Jatra,* is the traditional theatre form of Bengal. The Jatra is performed by travelling troupes under the management of a man called Adhikari. Although, originally the Jatra had only the themes of Radha and Krishna, today Jatras are written and performed by writers and dramatists of rural and urban centres.

### *Music*

Music is a passion with the Bengalis who express their feelings, emotions and spiritual experience in songs. The open spaces, the winding rivers and the beautiful villages have from the long past have inspired rural bards to compose and sing songs of their joys and sorrows to the tune of the bamboo flute and the ektara (one-stringed lyre) or the dotara (two stringed lyre) and the dhal and khol (percussion instruments). Some raga forms native to Bengal were admitted into the corpus of North Indian or Hindustani music. Elements of the Karnatic school of music are also found in these songs. There are different styles in classical ragas.

### *Kirtan style*

Kirtan is a sophisticated style of vocal music deriving from Dhrupad. The lyrics of the Vaishnava poets are classified into episodes in the early life of Sri Krishna. Couplets of the lyrics are sung in a chaste raga in slow dhrupadic measure by the leader of a group of singers and their significance is elaborated in recitation or song.

The refrain is taken up by the group in quicker and quicker tempo until the chorus finishes in a crescendo and then the next couplet is taken up by the leader. The process goes on until a particular episode is completed. Tampura and khol, are used for accompaniment. In recent times the box, harmonium and the violin are also used.

The Kirtan style is distinguished by its elements of group singing and its use of complicated time-measures (talas) belonging to the pre-Mughal school of Dhrupad. Four sub styles of Kirtan style have developed in course of time. These are Manoharshahi, Garanhati, Mandarini and Reneti schools, each with its distinctive manner of presentation and incorporating some features of the different classical styles. There is in Kirtan a harmonious combination of the mode and the lyrical message.

### *Gharana style*

The Charyapadas, the collection of Bengali devotional songs, were sung to the classical ragas, whose tonal formulation is different from the standardized formulation developed in the time of the great Mughals by musical masters of northern India. The court at Delhi patronised classical music. The tradition was set by Mian Tansen, court musician of Emperor Akbar, an exponent of dhrupad style, who ruled the musical world of northern India. As the Mughal authority declined, the disciples and descendants of Tansen started leaving Delhi. A number of them found warm reception with Bengali feudatory chiefs.

A descendant of Tansen, a 'dhrupadiya' named Bahadur Khan, settled himself in the court of the feudatory chief of Vishnupur and started a school of music which came to be known as the Vishnupur school or Gharana which produced a line of eminent musicians, many of whom were retained by wealthy landlords interested in Indian classical music.

Prominent among such patrons in the mid-nineteenth century were the members of the Tagore family, Saurindramohan Tagore and his brother Jatindhramohan Tagore whose efforts made Calcutta a main centre of Hindustani classical music in Bengal. Some other masters of this school were retained by Devendrnath Tagore for coaching the members of his family and also for setting the music of Brahmo devotional songs in the solemn and dignified style of Dhrupad.

A lighter style of song which had great vogue in nineteenth century Bengal is Tappa, originally introduced during the first half of the century by Ramnidhi Gupta or Nidhu Babu who composed a number of memorable songs of secular love in Bengali which became quite a fashion among the gentry in a short time. By and by its features were assimilated in popular music of diverse kinds-in songs of devotion, in Jatra songs and other compositions by later composers.

Thumri was a later arrival, having been introduced by Nawab Wazid Ali Shah of Oudh. Thumri was the lightest of all classical styles. It took a considerable time to earn popular appreciation which came only after Kazi Nazural Islam and Atulprasad Sen composed scintillating love lyrics in this style during the early years of the present century.

### Folk Songs

The main varieties of folk songs may be classified into three groups-Baul, Bhatiali, and Sari. Baul songs are compositions of the Bauls - wandering minstrels of the Sahajiya sect who seek by their own special way of spiritual quest to discover

God. They are usually un lettered but deeply wise in their mystic philosophy and compose songs in their moments of inspiration and dance as they sing, oblivious of their surroundings in their ecstasy.

The melodic structure of the songs are simple and shows the basic models in the major and minor scales and the tempo is quick and tripping. Bhatiali is a song of the river side and broad fields, drawing out in long, slow measure and with a melancholy content generally a contemplative yearning for a beloved. Sari is essentially the boatmen's song, rendered with verve to the accompaniment of vigorous rhythmic strokes of the oar as the boat glides on the river and is usually sung in chorus. The melodic structure of both types are simple.

*Musical instruments*

In instrumental music Bengal has produced great masters in the Sitar, the Sarod and the Esray. The great teacher, late Ustad Alauddin Khan has developed the art of the flute into the first rank for the exposition of classical music. The' modern' style has pressed into service the guitar, the violin cello and other musical gadgets of western origin. The portable box harmonium, which evolved in Calcutta about eight decades back is ubiquitous despite the frowns of orthodox classicists. For concert music the violin, the clarinets and the cornet are extensively used.

Some itinerant rural singers also use the fiddle for accompaniment. The Bauls use the ektara and the dotara, bayan (percussion) and ankle-bells. The wealthy traditionally call for naabat consisting of the sehnai and nakkara (percussion) for auspicious ceremonies. In major public celebration like the Durga Puja the instruments of choice are the Jaidhak (major Indian drum) and the Kansi (brass gong) played in a variety of rhythmus and time measures. The khol and cymbals are the invariable accompaniment for Kirtan music.

## Tribal Crafts

### *Pottery*

Hand-made pottery is predominantly a woman's art in West Bengal. Women of Kumbhakar (potter) caste and of Patua caste generally make variety of dolls and toys. These hand made figures, small dolls and toys are done by pressing and moulding methods. In Bishnupur (Bankura), Chaurigacha - Katalia (Kandi - Murshidabad) and some other places in Midnapore and Bankura the most primitive method of hand-modeled pottery is still pursued almost exclusively by women.

In West Bengal big jars are usually prepared by men and comparatively small pots are made by women. Clay modeling by hand is widely practised by the women of Patidar Chitrakar (Painters) castes. In Bankura Midnapore, Birbhum and some areas of Howrah, Hooghly and Murshidabad districts, women of Kumbhakar and Patidar-Chitrakar are engaged in making hand - modeled pottery as part time occupation. The women of Sankhari (conchshell carvers) families in Bishnupur (Bankura) make clay figurines of mother-dolls at a particular time of the year, especially for ritual purposes. Two principle variants of West Bengal Pottery are Bankura-style and Krishnanagar-style. Some important and interesting items are:

*Mangal ghat*

Mangalghat is a kind of small vase which is commonly used all over Bengal in all kinds of rituals. In birth initiation and marriage ceremonies, in the festivals and rituals of all Gods and Goddesses these auspicious vases of various shapes and sizes are counted as essential requisites. These are mostly painted.

*Lakshmi ghat*

These are auspicious vase of the Goddess of wealth. There is fairly a large variety of Lakshmi-ghat in West Bengal, mostly done in pairs, one for Lakshmi and another for Ganesh. Of these, Tamluk Lakshmi - ghats are most decorative and beautiful. Lakshmi's face is shaped on the upper fringe of the vase, with sharply drawn eyes and crest and the trunk of Ganesh in the other vase is also fine. In Raghunathbari, the vases are placed like bowls on an earthen stand which looks like a wine-cup. The Jhargram type, is the simplest one with a little long neck marked with two dots for eyes. It has a look of tribal simplicity.

*Manasa ghat*

The most conspicuous type of Manasa ghat is found in Bankura and Garbeta area of Midnapur. Based on earthen jars turned upside down, the face of the serpant-Goddess, along with the attached snake-hoods, give the vase a peculiar shape and form. The number of snake-hoods varies from one, three, five, seven, to more than hundred arranged in ascending tiers according to the size of the vase.

*Tulsimancha*

One of the finest unique specimens of potter's craft is the Tulsimancha of Midnapore. Tulsimancha is generally a raised pedestal, either brick-built or earthen. The terracotta tub - like Tulsimancha with decorative motifs (mainly of Gods and Goddesses) are hardly found outside Midnapore.

The terracotta Tulsimanchas are rectangular, hexagonal or octagonal in shape and the average size varies from 3feet to 4feet in height and 1.5 to 2 feet in diameter. In each side of the pot, the images of Radha-Krishna and other Gods and Goddesses are separately fixed in medium relief. The curved borders of all sides are beautifully decorated. Both the upper and lower sides of the Mancha are obviously open and the lower side which is placed on the ground, is much wider that the upper side. It may be placed on the ground anywhere and filled with earth. Then a tulsi plant or any other small plant may be planted on it.

*Dakshin roy's head*

Another interesting piece of pottery which is basically a Ghat or vase, shaped into the figure of a local village deity is Bara - murti. This is also a vase upside down. The upper part is elongated into the form of a leaf with painted leaves and flowers on it and below it on the round surface the face of Barathakur is drawn. It is commonly worshiped in pair and also sold by potters in pair, of which one is God Bara and the other, his consort Narayani. In the Narayani ghat the moustache is absent. Eyes, eyebrows, moustache and beard are all sharply painted by brush.

The worship of this Bara - murti is widely prevalent in the south of 24 Parganas district, where almost in every village the rituals are observed on a mass scale during the last day of Bengali month Pous and the first of Magh, corresponding to 14-15 January. The painted terracotta heads of Bara is placed under trees in pairs. Locally Bara is popularly known as the severed head of 'Dakshin Roy' who is a tiger-god. It is one of the most popular people's God in south 24 Parganas, associated with an environment of forest, which is likely to be the Sunderbans.

*Ritual vessels*

In marriage ceremonies, vessels of different shapes and sizes are necessary for sending gifts to bride's and bridegroom's houses, especially varieties of sweets. Earthen vessels were used in the past because it were considered more sacred and auspicious than glass-pots or metal-pots. Of these earthen vessels some interesting varieties are found in Bankura, Midnapore and Murshidabad, which are painted and decorated.

Harhis are not painted in all places and even where these are painted, the painting is not done by the professional potters of Kumbhakar caste, but by Patuas or scroll-painters, as in Midnapore (Narajol). In Bankura, the vessels are not painted by brush, but etched and engraved with pointed needles by potters (generally women). The designs are geometric and symbolic. Fish is a common subject in all drawings on these auspicious vessels. The Patuas paint flowers and leaves with fish. The other designs are of trees and flowers, symbolically executed.

Formerly in some areas these vessels were painted with different scenes of marriage ceremony like palanquin with bride and bridegroom, reception of the bride after marriage at her father-in-law's house etc. The composition of the scenes was done with colour. Such painted vessels are not found now. The potters and also their patrons have vanished from the social scene. Some fragments and survivals of this unique piece of pottery can be traced in the store rooms of the old, landed aristocracy in Murshidabad mainly for whom, the potters produced these painted terracotta vessels.

*Putul*

The dolls are usually made by pressing and moulding methods. Now-a-days these are mostly prepared in mould. The mould may be prepared in parts and on each mould - piece the required quantity of clay is firmly pressed to get the intended shape and look. Clay paste is used for joining together the moulded parts. Then the object is dried, burnt and painted by brush.

Mica - coated Red Dolls are made by moulding method. It is found in Howrah district : Puilya, Tantiberai, Tulsiberai and Sariyala - Balipota and in Midnapore.

*Pressed - nose Dolls:* The size of this doll is 1-2 inches to 4 -5 inches. It is found in Tulsi - berai, Tantiberai, Sariyala - Balipota, Antila and Kalikapur, Patihal and Jagatballavpur in Howrah district, in Midnapore town and in Berachampa - Debalaya. The dolls of Jagathballavpur and Midnapore town have blue and red stripes on white coating.

*Mother - Dolls:* Of all the mother - dolls the most interesting and unique types are made by Bankura potters.

The types vary in different centres. Panchmura, Rajagram and Sonamukhi which are the three principal centres of Bankura pottery produce different type of mother - dolls. The dolls of Sonamukhi have red colour but the Panchmura dolls are generally black. Dolls of Sonamukhi and Rajagram have 'bonnets' also.

*Dolls with Hip Jars*: These are popularly known as '*Kalasi Kankhe Putul' or dolls with hip - jars.*' Housewives on the village roads with water filled earthen jars on their hips in pleasant relaxing mood 'has been captured by the women potters and shaped perfectly into the hip-jar dolls.

There are numerous representations of village life in dolls. The different types of these dolls are hair - caring, milk - maid (Goalini), wheat-crusher, horse - rider and elephant - rider. All these dolls are done by pressing method and by women potters. Of these, hair-caring is a peculiar type of doll which depicts a woman sitting in front with her child sucking her breast and another woman from behind is caring her hair. The size of the doll is about 5" x 6"x3". It has all the qualities of sculpture and looks like a piece of wood-carving or stone-carving.

*Patua-made dolls*: Patuas or Chitrakars are scroll-painters. Some types of clay dolls, figures of deities and animals are made by women of Patua-caste in West Bengal in Midnapore, Bankura, Howrah and 24 Parganas. Silate (slate-like) dolls: These are like plaques with holes for fixing on walls. These are coloured dolls and the favourite colours are green, red and blue.

### *Bankura pottery*

The principal centres where the terracotta horses and elephants are produced are Panchmura, Rajagarm, Sonamukhi and Hamirpur. Each of these four centres has its local style. Bankura horse is very popular. The Bankura pottery is mainly used for ritualistic purposes. The rituals are almost all exclusively associated with local village gods and folk-festivals in the worship of various kinds of tribal, semi-tribal and folk deities. The Panchmura-style of pottery is the best and the finest of all the four types.

The symmetry of shape, the rhythm of the rounded curves of the body, especially of the horse, have lent a dignity and charm to it's form which is incomparable. Simplicity and dynamism are the chief components of Panchmura-style. It is more sophisticated than the other three types-Rajagram, Sonamukhi and Kamirpur types are a little less sophisticated and more massive. In Jhargram and Gopiballavpur areas in Midnapore district, within the tribal belt, the terracotta horses assume a crude near-primitive form and are fully hand modeled.

The tools used for making Bankura Pottery are Ucha which is a semi circular piece pf bamboo used for surface finishing, Balya which is a stone tool of about 3.5 " (inches) by 3 " used as a beater of the inner surface of a pot, Pitna which is a wooden beater of about 10 " by 4 " used for beating and shaping the outer surface of the pot or Chiari made of bamboo of about 4.5 " by .5 " used for decorating clay figures. Other than these tools, there are potters wheels and kilns for firing. The kilns are generally of circular or parabolic (Kula-type or bamboo fan shaped) with enclosures on all sides with a permanent stoke-hole. It is locally known as Sheuna Poan and the circular type is known as Berasal Poan.

### *Dokra metal craft*

The metal smiths using the lost wax process of metal casting or hollow casting method in West Bengal, are known as Dokra Kamars. The ironsmiths are known in Bengal as Kamars or Karmakar and other metal smiths as Sekras. The word Dokra in Bengali is used with contempt for those who are socially low and despised. Of all craftsmen in West Bengal, these metal smiths are socially most persecuted and are being treated as social outcasts. Hence they are called Dokras.

The Dokras are now dispersed over the western part of West Bengal in four districts namely Bankura, Purulia, Midnapore and Burdwan and are mainly concentrated in Bankura and partly in Purulia. The Dokras who lived in a small suburb called Rampur on the fringe of Bankura town have shifted to Bikna. These Dokras make various kinds of images and figures of gods and goddesses, birds and animals, like Lakshmi, Lakshmi-Narayan, Siva-Parvati flanked by Ganesh and Kartik, elephants, horses, owls, peacocks etc.

The Dokras of Netkamla and Bindhyajan do not make ritual objects, like images of deities and animal figures. Their main items of production are measuring bowls or paikona of different sizes and mal or anklets and ghunghru or tinkling dancing bells for the Santhals. The Dokras of Lakshmisagar make images of deities and figures of animals and sell their products in local markets and fairs.

In Purulia the Dokras are widely known as Mals or Malhars to common people, although the Dokra artisans are considered lower in social rank. In Purulia, there are some semi-nomadic Malhars, who move about from village to village, take shelter in community houses, outhouses or temporary camps under trees and make various kinds of metal products by the lost wax process. They make paikona, dhunuchi, pancha pradeep, anklets, ghunghrus with mixed aluminium by the lost wax process but do not make any images or figures.

### *The patuas*

A scroll-painter is known in West Bengal as Patua, Chitrakar, Patikar and Patidar. In North-West Bankura and Purulia the Patidar name is more popular, in Birbhum and certain areas of Midnapore the Chitrakar name is more current and in south-west Bengal the Patua name is more widely known. Birbhum and Midnapore districts have the majority of Patuas in West Bengal, distributed over a large number of villages. The Patuas are generally very poor and socially outcast. The Patuas in West Bengal may be divided into three groups, according to the theme or subject they represent on their scrolls.

1. The Patuas who represent mainly Hindu mythological themes.
2. The Patuas who represent the conception of Heaven and various kinds of tortures inflicted by Yama the Lord of Death, on the sinners.
3. The Patuas who represent the theme of the origin of a tribe (which is mainly the Santhals in Western Bengal) and the passage of the Dead from this mortal world to life beyond death.

The first group of scroll-painters who deal mainly with Hindu mythological themes, constitute the most advanced' Hinduized' group. The terms 'Hinduized ' here does not mean their actual Hinduization, but their more frequent contact with and economic dependence upon the surrounding Caste-Hindus who dominate their social environment.

The second group of scroll-painters are Yama-Patuas. The Yama-Pat is an adaptation of the Chakshu-dan pat for the consumption of the Hindu. In the Yama-Pat popular Hindu morality tales are included and 'magic' is totally excluded.

The third group of Patuas are largely found in Jhalda, Barabazar, Manbazar, Jaipur, Raghunathbari and other areas of Purulia district, in some villages in north-western part of Bankura, such as Bharatpur near Susunia Hills, in Kalipahari and Geramdi and Salberia. This is predominantly a tribal zone and among the tribes the Santhals are in majority. In the past, they used to paint scrolls on the theme of the origin of the Santhals. The story of the origin of the Santhals was pictorially depicted through stages on the scroll. The Patidars of this region also demonstrate a kind of scroll, known as Chakshudan Pat (eye giving scroll), after the death of a person, before the members of the deceased's family. The Patidar here performs the role of a tribal magician-priest.In the traditional style of the Patuas, a fresh spontaneity of conception and execution can always be discerned. They are never drawn with the meticulous perfection. It seems there is some influence of Muslim Calligraphy on the bold and vigorous brush lines of the traditional Patuas. Pat-Painting can be traced back to the Buddhist and the Jain tradition. It the richer among the Jains than among the Buddhists.

The Patuas are dying group of folk artists. Those who are still clinging to the traditional profession are not painters and do not know the art of painting. They are simply wandering minstrels, roaming and begging from village to village by entertaining the poor illiterate villagers with Hindu mythological songs, illustrated on scrolls. These illustrations or paintings were done by their fathers and grandfathers.

The traditional myths of Krishna Radha, Kamalay Kamini, Manasa etc, represented in the scrolls were being replaced by newly created myths of British rule generated by the babus and babu-culture. There are also studies of birds, animals, snakes and fishes. A large number of Patuas from the western districts of Bengal started migrating to the city of Calcutta from the beginning of the 19th century and small settlements of Patuas (like Patuatola of central Calcutta, Patuapara of Kalighat) sprang up in the neighbourhoods of important centres of pilgrimage. In these new centers of pilgrimage in Calcutta a new hybrid style of Patua-painting originated and developed, mainly under the influence of European artists and their art-works. One of such notable centres was Kalighat, the most important centre of pilgrimage in Calcutta.

*The mask-makers*

The masks made of clay, paper and cloth are found only in the Purulia district of West Bengal. The mask-makers who are Sutradhars or wood-carvers by caste, are located in two or three centres in Purulia and practically originated from one centre. They were also known as Dutta and Seal. This art depend fully on the local Chhau dance of Purulia found only in west Bengal. Chhau dance is a mask-dance. There is no chhau without mask. The dance and the mask are inseparable. Chhau-dance of Purulia has some characteristics of primitive ritualistic dance in its vigour, style and musical accompaniment. And the Chhau-masks also, even in their representation of Hindu Puranic characters reveal some characteristics of primitive ritualistic masks in their stylization and symbolization.

Chorda is the principal centres of Chhau-mask makers. Chorda is a village in Baghmuni P.S, not very far from the Dak Bunglow and the Ajodhya Hills. The Sutradhars occupy a distinct rank in the caste-hierarchy of the Hindus. Making clay-images of idols is an important occupation of Chorda Sutradhars, along with mask-making. The masks were first made of Simul wood and considering the poverty of local dancers, the cheap materials were introduced later.

The technical stages of production are:

1. Preparation of clay-models.
2. Drying the models partly in sun.
3. Pasting of wet paper twice on these partly dried models.
4. Pasting of paper with glue, six to ten times. The glue is made of gum.
5. Pasting of clay-soaked pieces of cloth twice for parts of the face like eyes, ears, nose etc.
6. Trimming up the whole thing with a small wooden, 'Kurni'
7. Full sun-drying.
8. Detaching the mask from the clay-model, dyeing, painting and finishing.

Various types of Puranic characters, gods and goddesses, birds, animals and demons etc. are made, such as- Ram,

Ravan, Jambubab, Jatayu, Mahisasur, Kirat, Bhim, Arjun, Ganesh, Lakshman, Sita, Abhimanyu, Surpanaka, Kumbhkarna, Siva, Durga, Kali, Saraswati, Krishna, Radha, Balaram and Peacock, Dog, Beer, Deer, Horse, tiger, Lion etc.

There is a mask-making season. It starts from Falgun (January-February) after Saraswati Puja, aiming at Chaitra-Baisakh Gajan festival, which is the peak season of Chhau-dance in Purulia. There were mask-dancers and mask makers in Domordi village. They are Bhatta Brahmins. These dancers has a liking for refined Puranic and Vaishnava themes. The Sutradhars used to carve doors, house-posts or temple-terracotta's. The entire temple-architecture of Bengal is a terracotta art-work done by the Sutradhars or wood-carvers. These declined by the last quarter of the 19th century. After that wood-carvers of Bengal mainly thrived on making Ratha, carving images of Vaishnava deities and saints and wooden figures of Puranic characters for exhibiting at Vaishnava and other festivals. In Calcutta, the Sutradhars of Bengal are now either making clay-images of deities and furniture or turning to other trades.

# Bibliography


Agarwal, L.B., *The Harijans in Rebellion*, Bombay: Taraporewala 1934

Agarwal, P.C., *Equality through Privilege: a Study of Special Privileges Granted to Scheduled Castes in Haryana*, New Delhi : ICSSR,1977

Baboo, B., "Cognition and structure: explaining the 'exploitation' of an untouchable caste in Orissa", *Eastern Anthropologist* 39, 1986: 187-93

Bhai, N., *Harijan Women in Independent India*, Delhi: BR Publishing 1986

Bharadwaj, A.N., *Problems of Scheduled Castes and Scheduled Tribes in India.* [From Jammu: general review from experience by journalist and social worker of distinction] New Delhi: Light & Life,1979

Bhattacharya, B., A "short note on the Sceduled Tribes and Scheduled Castes population of West Bengal", *Bulletin of the Cultural Research Institute* 3, 2, 1964.

Bhowmik, K.L., (ed.) "Development of Scheduled Communities" [1985 Conference papers on tribals], *Current Anthropological and Archaeological Perspectives*, Vol. 6. New Delhi: Inter-India Publications 1988

Burman, B.K. Roy, *Social Mobility Movements among Scheduled Castes and Scheduled Tribes of India*, Delhi: Government of India Press 1970

Chandel, M.P.S., *A Social Force in Politics: Study of Scheduled Castes of UP*, New Delhi: Mittal,1990

Chandna, R.C., Distributional pattern of Scheduled Caste population in India, *Population Geography* 2, 1980.

Chandra, V., *Handbook on Scheduled Castes and Scheduled Tribes*, New Delhi: Office of the Commissioner for SC&ST,1968

Chitnis, S., "Education for equality: case of Scheduled Castes in higher education", *EPW* 7 (31-33), August 1972

Cohn, B.S., "Changing traditions of a low caste", *Journal of American Folklore* 71, 1958: 413-21. And in his *An Anthropologist among the Historians and Other Essays*. Delhi: OUP 1990.

Das, Bhakta, *A Glimpse of Scheduled Castes in Assam*, New Delhi: Omson 1968

Das, B., Untouchability, Scheduled Castes and nation building, *Social Action* 32, 1982: 269-82

Galanter, M., *Competing Equalities: Law and the Backward Classes in India*. Berkeley: University of California Press 1984

Gandhi, M.K., *The Removal of Untouchability*, Ahmedabad: Navajivan 1954

Mahar, J.M., (ed.) *The Untouchables in Contemporary India*, Tucson: University of Arizona Press 1972.

Mahar, P., "Changing religious practices of an Untouchable caste", *Economic Development and Cultural Change*, 1960

Oommen, T.K., "Scheduled castes and scheduled tribes". In S.C. Dube (ed.) *Indian Since Independence - Social Report on India - 1947-72*. New Delhi: Vikas 1977

Parui, S.S., "Untouchability in the early Indian society", *Journal of the Early Indian Society* 39, 1961.

Pundir, J.K., *Changing Patterns of Scheduled Castes*, Jaipur: Rawat 1997.

Saggar, M. & Pan, I., "SCs and STs in Eastern India", Inequality and poverty estimates, *EPW* March 5, 1994.

Santhakumari, R., *Scheduled Castes and Welfare Measures*, New Delhi: Classical, 1994.

Sharma, B.D., "Scheduled Castes and Tribes: a status report", *Lokayan Bulletin* 8/6 1990.

Tripathi, R.S. & Tiwari, P.D. (eds), *Dimensions of Scheduled Caste Development in India*, New Delhi: Uppal 1991.

# Index